The Great Diversity Debate

Embracing Pluralism in School and Society

The Great Diversity Debate

Embracing Pluralism in School and Society

KENT KOPPELMAN

TEACHERS
COLLEGE
PRESS

Teachers College, Columbia University
New York and London

KH

Published by Teachers College Press, 1234 Amsterdam Avenue, New York, NY
10027

Library of Congress Cataloging-in-Publication Data

Koppelman, Kent L.
    The great diversity debate : embracing pluralism in school and society / Kent
Koppelman.
      p. cm.
    Includes bibliographical references and index.
    ISBN 978-0-8077-5221-0 (pbk. : alk. paper)
    ISBN 978-0-8077-5222-7 (hardcover)
      1. Multicultural education–United States. 2. Education–Social aspects–United
States. 3. Cultural pluralism–United States. 4. Racism–United States. 5. United
States–Race relations. 6. Social classes–United States. 7. Sex differences in
education–United States. I. Title.
    LC1099.3.K65 2011
    370.1170973–dc22   2011000485

ISBN 978-0-8077-5221-0 (paper)
ISBN 978-0-8077-5222-7 (hardcover)

Printed on acid-free paper
Manufactured in the United States of America

18 17 16 15 14 13 12 11   8 7 6 5 4 3 2 1

5/1/13

To **Christine Sleeter** and **Donna Gollnick**

Your scholarship and leadership
in the field of multicultural education
have always been an inspiration to me.

Contents

Contents

Acknowledgments

I want to thank Dr. Jon Davies for helping me think about what was necessary for the content and structure of this book, and Dr. Greg Wegner and Dr. Marguerite Parks for reading parts of the book and offering helpful suggestions. I want to thank Brian Ellerbeck at Teachers College Press for his suggestions for revisions and for his assistance throughout the publication process. I am deeply grateful to copyeditor Myra D. Cleary, Production Editor Ericka McIntyre, and Senior Production Editor Karl Nyberg for their assistance on this book. My wife has earned my special thanks for all of her support and encouragement as I worked on the book. Finally, I want to express great appreciation to all the scholars whose work informs this book. I was exploring areas outside my expertise, and I appreciated the thoughtful insights and the clarity of the writing of the various scholars named in this book. If this book is well-received by readers, they deserve much of the credit, but if the book includes any misinterpretation or misrepresentation of their research, the responsibility for those inadvertent errors is mine.

The First Americans

There were no Indians when the Vikings landed in North America. There were no Indians when Columbus landed on the island he christened Hispaniola. There were no Indians greeting Pilgrims at Plymouth Rock or fighting the English settlers at Jamestown. There were no "Indians" there, but there were many indigenous peoples from diverse nations and cultures in those places and across the continent.

There were Micmac, Passamaquoddy, and Abenaki in the northeastern portion of this new land, along with Pequot, Massachuset, Wampanoag, Narraganset, and Mohegan. Going south and west along the east coast, there were Shawnee, Lumbee, Cherokee, Chickasaw, Catawba, Choctaw, and Seminole. Traveling westward there were people calling themselves Huron, Iroquois, Potawatomi, Sauk, Kickapoo, Ojibwe, Illinois, Ho Chunk, and Iowa. Going further west there lived Ponca, Pawnee, Crow, Sioux, Cheyenne, and Blackfoot, and in the southwest were Arapaho, Kiowa, Apache, Pueblo, and Navajo. If Columbus had sailed the Pacific Ocean to the west coast of America, he would have "discovered" any of a number of people, including Yakima, Spokane, Cayuse, Shasta, Yurok, Pomo, Hupa, and Yana. And there were more, many more. Not all of them are named here, but all of them were indigenous peoples and none of them were Indians (Josephy, 1994). To speak of an Indian implies uniformity and ignores cultural diversity among these groups.

Then, as now, America consisted of lands sustaining an incredible mix of diverse peoples. Then, as now, the people had common human needs that were addressed in a variety of cultural contexts. Then, as now, this diversity provided a richness of human experience and yet also could lead to conflicts between groups.

When Europeans came to the continent, they created an image of "Indians" out of ignorance, and because of their lack of interest in the indigenous peoples, they failed to understand the others' unique histories, cultural diversity, and profound wisdom. Europeans took the land and a few cultural fragments from the indigenous peoples and dispensed with the rest. Ironically, these Europeans consisted of diverse cultural groups, but as they engaged in the elimination of Indians from the new lands they planned to colonize, they also began to create a single image to subsume all of their diverse cultures—an image they eventually would call an "American." But the diversity within America persisted, and it continues to persist.

Introduction

As a college professor, I began teaching about diversity issues in 1979, and as I read newspapers and newsmagazines, I looked for stories relating to human differences. Often they were brief reports, usually buried in the back pages. One of the most compelling stories was a local one, but it requires some background information. The Hmong people were living in the Laotian highlands when they became American allies during the Vietnam War. After the United States withdrew from Vietnam, the communist rulers persecuted the Hmong, and many fled to refugee camps in Thailand. By the early 1980s, many were immigrating to the United States and some chose to settle in La Crosse, Wisconsin. As the Hmong community grew, so did the prejudice against it.

The article in the local paper described an incident that had occurred after midnight when a young White male left a bar and saw a young Asian man. Assuming that the Asian man was Hmong, the White male provoked a fight and inflicted severe injuries on his victim. The Asian man was not Hmong, but a Japanese exchange student from my campus. After sharing this article with my students, we discussed the power of prejudice to cause violent behavior, and how such violence can even spread beyond the target group. One student recalled an incident where a heterosexual man was assaulted because his attacker thought he was gay.

Later, another article described the trial of the White male attacker and specifically noted the testimony of the Japanese exchange student. Instead of asking for a severe punishment, he asked the court to show clemency to his assailant. He felt sorry for his White attacker because he believed that the young man was a victim of his own ignorance. Sharing this report of the Japanese student's extraordinary act of forgiveness provoked even more discussion in class as students debated appropriate responses to prejudice and discussed strategies for reducing ignorance among Americans about the value of diversity in our society.

By the time I entered my second decade of teaching diversity classes, I no longer had to search the back pages for diversity stories: They were now often the cover story, the headline, or at least near the front of newspapers and newsmagazines. The decade of the 1990s began with President George H. W. Bush signing the Americans with Disabilities Act to prohibit discrimination against people with disabilities. Later Bush's nomination of Clarence Thomas for the Supreme Court brought gender and race into conflict during the Senate's confirmation hearings as Anita Hill testified about Thomas engaging in sexual harassment toward her when she worked for him (ironically) at the Equal Employment Opportunity Commission.

In the 1990s, Americans also watched a scene of police brutality over and over as the news media showed the videotape that caught White Los Angeles police officers using batons to beat an African American man as he was lying on the ground. Blacks in many urban areas had been complaining of police brutality for years, but now they finally had videotaped evidence. Yet a year later, a jury of ten White people and two people of color (but no Blacks) acquitted three of the four officers charged with the beating, and Los Angeles erupted into the most violent urban riot in our history.

The following year, a new President tried to keep his campaign promise to eliminate discrimination against gay men and lesbians in the military. Ultimately Bill Clinton encountered so much resistance, especially from military leaders, that he had to compromise by implementing the "Don't Ask, Don't Tell" policy, a policy that is back in the news today as activists have continued to demand the right of lesbian and gay soldiers to serve openly in the military. Often this debate is framed as conservative vs. liberal, but I have always reminded my students that conservatives historically have argued that one's private life should be off limits to employers, and that the only issue should be whether or not a person can do the job. As the noted conservative Barry Goldwater once said: "You don't have to be straight to shoot straight."

In the first decade of the 21st century, Americans have seen the nation's courts, including the U.S. Supreme Court, make several rulings curbing affirmative action plans, and yet also ruling in favor of affirming the civil rights of gay men and lesbians. The 9/11 terrorist attacks have fueled the fires of Islamophobia, most recently producing a contentious debate over building an Islamic Cultural Center two blocks from the site of the attack on the World Trade Center. Gender issues have accompanied the growth of women in the workforce, as almost half of workers are now female, as are half of all middle managers. Yet, the glass ceiling remains in place, as only a limited number of women are found in top management jobs.

The ongoing controversy over immigration has included legitimate concerns about protecting the nation's borders from easy access by terrorists, but also irrational fears against Latinos—the largest immigrant group—which have persisted even as immigration has declined during the current recession.

And of course, in the 2008 Presidential primaries, the two top Democratic candidates were a White woman and an African American man, leading to Barack Obama's emergence as the Democratic nominee and eventually his history-making victory as the first person of color to be elected President of the United States.

Yet, even though diversity now is consistently at the forefront of the American consciousness and there has been significant progress on various diversity issues, there is still much debate about diversity. For that reason I have included opposing viewpoints on issues such as the support for pluralism, the need for affirmative action, the value of identity groups, the perception that globalization is reducing cultural diversity, and more. I have provided some historical context regarding the development of the concept of pluralism, the impact of immigration not only on diversity but also on American views and behaviors toward diversity, the evolution of affirmative action programs, and the development of multicultural education in response to the increasingly diverse students in American schools. Although a detailed historical account is beyond the scope of this book, my goal was to offer a historical context sufficient to enhance one's understanding of the current debates over diversity issues.

While I have tried to be inclusive of all diverse groups in the United States, it was not possible to maintain a balance of content between them. In examining the historical record and in reviewing scholarly writing, I found that authors were more likely to focus on diversity stemming from race, religion, ethnicity, and immigration, but I acknowledge that diversity today extends far beyond a few categories to encompass a wide range of groups that have been incorporated into the much more inclusive contemporary concept of pluralism. Finally, this book required me to examine scholarly research from several disciplines. My goal was to describe accurately what these scholars were saying, with minimal personal comment.

The first chapter discusses the identification of similarities as one of the initial responses to human differences. Eventually the recognition among philosophers of legitimate alternative perspectives provided the basis for the concept of cultural pluralism, as expressed in the writings of William James, Horace Kallen, John Dewey, and Alain Locke. As the concept evolved, it became not only a compelling perspective for many Americans, but a concept accepted globally as a means of enhancing international understanding.

Chapter 2 presents the history and growth of diversity in the United States and responses of Americans to diverse groups. From the earliest days, religious diversity challenged the colonial population, and ultimately the decision to protect religious liberty was declared in the First Amendment to the U.S. Constitution. Yet Americans continued to be ambivalent about religious diversity, while they experienced increasing racial and ethnic diversity due to changing immigration patterns. The forces opposing and approving of this increased diversity battled into the 20th century until a racially restrictive immigration law was passed in 1924 and remained the law of the land until 1965. The chapter concludes with a description of how the 1965 reform has resulted in immigrants once again adding significantly to the diversity of the nation.

The next two chapters examine how diverse groups achieve their economic and political goals in a democratic society. Chapter 3 begins with the view of some scholars that America's founders included support for and protection of diversity in the U.S. Constitution and in their writings about democracy. Studies in political science often have described how diverse groups have taken civic actions to achieve their goals and why this is consistent with the freedoms associated with a democratic society. Chapter 4 addresses the more recent debate over affirmative action, reviewing some of the major arguments from those who want to eliminate it as well as those who believe affirmative action is still necessary.

Chapter 5 explores the issue of identity and the role of group memberships in establishing a personal identity. Psychological studies have examined the significance of race, ethnicity, and other forms of group membership in shaping personal identity, and they also have raised the issue of the possibility for a new American identity that accommodates diversity rather than requiring everyone to conform to a uniform image of our national identity.

Chapter 6 discusses multicultural education as an attempt to promote pluralistic attitudes among the diverse students attending our schools. The chapter describes some curricular and pedagogical issues related to implementing a multicultural approach in classrooms, especially the use of culturally responsive teaching as an effective strategy to enhance the academic achievement for all of the students attending American schools.

Chapter 7 addresses how the recent phenomenon of globalization has created new challenges with regard to human diversity, and how the growth of democracy worldwide appears to be promoting pluralistic attitudes and actions in response to global diversity. Diversity is not a choice; diversity is a global reality. Nations must choose (and are choosing) how to respond appropriately to the existence of diversity, not only within their borders, but also in their relations with other nations.

By the end of the book, it should be obvious that the central question in the diversity debate is not about the value of diversity but about what individual attitudes and actions and institutional policies and practices will enable a society to enjoy the potential benefits of a diverse population. Diversity between cultures around the world has been a historic fact, but contemporary diversity includes subcultures within the larger culture in most of the world's nations. All of these nations are struggling with the question of how to respect and gain the advantages of their diverse populations, but this question is not easily resolved. The Chancellor of Germany has declared that the country's efforts to create a multicultural nation have failed. Other European nations are experiencing increased antagonism by the majority toward a minority group such as the Roma or Muslims. Ethnic conflict continues to plague African nations, and around the world, diversity still represents more of a challenge than an advantage.

My belief is that this challenge ultimately will be met, and that most nations will be enjoying more of the benefits of diversity before the end of this century. In my 30 years of teaching diversity issues, I have witnessed the changes students exhibit when their assumptions are challenged respectfully, and when they are provided with accurate information about diverse groups. I have read and experienced the positive outcomes from interfaith social activities and other intergroup efforts. This book is my attempt to contribute to the ongoing need to challenge assumptions while providing accurate information regarding diversity issues, especially for an American audience.

The United States appears to be the most diverse nation among the family of nations. For that reason, Americans have a special responsibility to think carefully about the unique diversity that exists within our borders. If we choose to affirm our diversity, we will redefine who we are as a nation and what we stand for. The United States could become a model for other nations looking for ways to deal effectively with diversity and gain its benefits. America, with its incredibly diverse population, could be a leader in promoting pluralistic attitudes, policies, and practices that should enhance mutual understanding among groups in individual societies and among nations.

CHAPTER 1

The Diversity Debate

Life is already fragmented, and the practical problem facing us as living creatures is to go beyond the fragment. . . . Somehow, we have to live together. That is a practical problem which confronts us at every level, as members of families, neighborhoods, countries and increasingly simply as members of a world-wide human race.

—Keith Graham, 1996, p. 135

Across the globe and across time, groups of human beings consistently have categorized other groups of human beings based on perceived similarities or differences. Differences have not automatically defined a particular group as an enemy, but have meant the group was "the other" and was to be regarded with a certain amount of suspicion and mistrust. Creating categories of "others" has led to frequent conflicts ranging from local and regional disputes to global confrontations, and for the more thoughtful members of society, the history and persistence of such conflicts have always been a challenge to confront the stereotypes and prejudices involved in such categorization. In the past, some chose to emphasize our similarities as human beings. In the 17th century, John Comenius wrote: "We are all citizens of one world; we are all of one blood. To hate someone because he was born in another country, because he speaks a different language or because he takes a different view on a subject, is a great folly." (Durant & Durant, 1961, p. 582). Others who have been attracted to such an idea have continued to advocate it to this day.

THE ADVOCACY OF HUMAN SIMILARITIES

The argument that all human beings are similar has found advocates throughout the centuries, and in the 20th century two global wars produced even more advocates for ignoring human differences by focusing on human similarities. The fledgling science of anthropology contributed to this point of view by carefully studying diverse world cultures. Even though anthropologists described differences, they also identified common human needs addressed by indigenous cultures as well as by modern or "advanced" cultures. Among cultural similarities in anthropological accounts, culture itself was identified as a commonality linking all human beings. As Menand (2001) has noted: "Human beings produce culture in the same sense that they produce carbon dioxide: they can't help it" (p. 407). Stressing similarities of human needs and desires, and the creation of culture to address them were meant to challenge people to reject the fragmentation of humankind and to think of each person as a citizen of the world, as Comenius declared, or as a member of the global human race, as stated in Graham's comment. Some advocates insisted that certain human values were universal because they were replicated in all cultures, but trying to create unanimity by ignoring cultural differences and emphasizing cultural similarities did not prove to be a successful strategy.

Anthropologists could identify cultural similarities, but to describe particular cultures accurately required careful documentation of their cultural differences. In the early 1960s, Laura Bohannan (1966) was living in West Africa and studying the Tiv people. She was fascinated by storytelling as one of the most significant ways the Tiv articulated and sustained their cultural values. On one occasion, Bohannan shared a Western story with them. Based on her assumptions that there were universal human truths and that William Shakespeare was one of the greatest writers in expressing these truths, she related the story of Hamlet, but problems began from the beginning. The Tiv did not understand why Hamlet was upset that his Uncle Claudius married Gertrude, his dead brother's widow. In Tiv culture, it was considered moral for a younger brother to marry his brother's widow and raise his brother's children. The audience rejected the part of the story where Hamlet's father appeared as a ghost to accuse Claudius of his murder, because the Tiv believed that the dead could not appear in any form after they died. When Hamlet scolded his mother for marrying his uncle, the audience expressed strong disapproval; based on Tiv values, sons should never scold their mothers. Further, since Claudius poisoned Hamlet's father, they accepted the need for Hamlet to avenge the father's death, but not his intent to kill his uncle. A Tiv man would get his friends to do the killing because it was considered a great evil for a son to engage in violence against his uncle (and step-father).

Bohannan's experience illustrates the difficulty of emphasizing our common humanity and ignoring differences—cultural differences matter; ignoring such differences will produce a skewed or distorted description of the particular human beings who represent a particular culture. The work of anthropologists not only has documented the existence of *diversity*, but has helped define the term: "the presence of human beings with perceived or actual differences based on a variety of human characteristics" (Koppelman, 2011, p. 15). However, anthropologists' study of diverse cultures has not resolved the issue of how people should respond to human differences as a global phenomenon or within our own society.

VALUING HUMAN DIFFERENCES

By the middle of the 20th century, advocates for diversity were challenging those emphasizing our human similarities. Cultural pluralism is a perspective that values diversity, advocating for the perpetuation of differences within the boundaries of an institution, a nation, or the world (Pai & Adler, 1997). Parekh (1996) identified shared assumptions in Western cultures and argued that these assumptions had to be debunked before these cultures could understand and accept cultural pluralism. The assumptions included:

1. Human nature everywhere is the same.
2. Although some human differences exist, similarities between humans are more significant than differences.
3. Human nature has been consistent and transcendent; although differences appear to exist historically in different cultures, it has always been the same.
4. Human nature can be described as a consequence of rigorous, rational investigations.

With regard to the first assumption, Parekh admitted that human beings share many similarities, but he argued that people are also cultural beings whose desires and needs are shaped by a different history and a different environment that produce distinctly different ways of life. This was the insight that Bohannan illustrated in her work with the Tiv, and that many anthropologists have corroborated. As for the second assumption, Parekh refers to another Western assumption—that human beings have free will. He argues that it is contradictory to the assumption of free will to assert that every human being chooses to express his or her humanity in an identical manner. Instead, Parekh (1996) asserts that one of the obvious realities about people around the world is that "men and women are human in their own unique ways" (p. 133). As for the third assumption, that human nature is consistent and transcendent, Parekh says this would require people to ignore the complex and often contrasting ways that belonging to a cultural group tends to influence one's perceptions, values, and behaviors. Menand (2001) addressed this point in arguing that although people are individuals, "[they] belong to groups. They take their identities from groups, and it tends to be as members of groups that they pursue the goods they desire" (p. 377). Finally, the assumption about being able to understand human nature can be affirmed only by having a simplistic view of human nature as a static combination of specific components and ignoring the complexity of subjective human beings trying to identify innate qualities they all possess. In debunking these assumptions, Parekh rejects the similarity advocates and asserts that Western thought historically has been so focused on universal human truths that it has evolved into an anti-pluralistic perspective.

THE ORIGINS OF CULTURAL PLURALISM

Alluding to historical philosophical systems, Bevir (2007) stated that the dominant perspective was based on certain "fixed principles" to which all rational people were supposed to agree, but today there is more emphasis on the reality and complexity of diversity, affirming Parekh's analysis. The emphasis on complexity was the basis for the concept of cultural pluralism. Although there were many harbingers of the concept, the ideas that influenced and shaped the definition of cultural pluralism were being articulated in the late 19th and early 20th centuries by the anthropologist Franz Boas, sociologist Arthur Bentley, and philosopher William James. Even though James struggled with the ambiguities of pluralism, Skillen (1996) placed him "on the flagship of that movement" (p. 33), and James would turn out to be especially influential.

In a study of sensory thresholds, Boas discovered that differences in perception were not innate but derived from an observer's experiences and expectations. He argued that perception was a situational phenomenon, and differences in perception were learned behavior that was influenced by culture. In 1887, based on his ethnographic studies, Boas asserted "that civilization is not something absolute, but that it is relative, and that our ideas and conceptions are true only so far as our civilization goes" (Menand, 2001, p. 384). In 1908, Bentley's book *The Process of Government* rejected simplistic descriptions of the political process and promoted the radical thesis that interests of diverse political groups cannot be "fixed" in certain terms because those interests are not static; political groups constantly observe other groups and redefine their interests.

As for William James, he believed that each person had a unique individual perspective, but a perspective inevitably including "blindness" to perspectives of others, causing misunderstandings and even conflicts when one person's "truth" differed significantly from another's (Skillen, 1996). In 1909, James published *A Pluralistic Universe* based on the Hibbert Lectures he had delivered the previous year at Manchester College in Oxford. In the book, James described a pluralistic view of the world: "Nothing includes everything, or dominates over everything. The word 'and' trails along after every sentence. Something always escapes" (Menand, 2001, p. 378). Although Oxford students flocked to James's lectures, the Oxford professors made little or no response to them. James was challenging their conventional ideas by claiming that there could be no single vocabulary or discourse that would be adequate for every situation. However, belief in "a discourse that covers every case is one of the oldest dreams of philosophy. It was a dream philosophers were not willing to give up" (Menand, 2001, pp. 378–379).

Despite being ignored by his peers, James continued to argue the case for pluralism. He believed each individual could perceive and understand a portion of reality, and yet be completely unaware of another individual's perception and understanding of reality. If one person's understanding contradicted another person's, both could believe their perception was grounded in truth. In such cases, conflicts would occur when one individual failed to acknowledge the different but legitimate perceptions of another, insisting that his or her perception and understanding were the only "true" ones (Skillen, 1996). For extreme cases, in the words of King Lear: "That way madness lies." G. K. Chesterton (1942) understood and illustrated this issue in his biography of Charles Dickens, first published in 1906:

> The lunatic is the man who lives in a small world but thinks it is a large one; he is the man who lives in a tenth of the truth, and thinks it is the whole. The madman cannot conceive any cosmos outside a certain tale or conspiracy or vision. . . . The more plain and satisfying our state appears, the more we may know that we are living in an unreal world. For the real world is not satisfying . . . the real world is not clear or plain. The real world is full of bracing bewilderments and brutal surprises. (p. 110)

FORMULATING THE CONCEPT OF CULTURAL PLURALISM

Despite the contributions of Bentley and Boas, Lynch (1998) claimed that the concept of cultural pluralism originated in the academic discipline of philosophy. William James provided the intellectual foundation, but it was a Harvard graduate student named Horace Kallen who first defined and used the term *cultural pluralism*. Kallen was assigned to George Santayana as a teaching assistant, but he enrolled in several classes with James, and according to Menand (2001), Kallen regarded himself as a disciple of William James and his philosophical heir. Much of Kallen's thinking about cultural pluralism was intended to provide an alternative to the popular melting pot concept. Because the United States included so many nationalities, Kallen believed that America must become a "federation of nations" (Appleton, 1983, p. 72), but he found few supporters when he first introduced his ideas in a presentation entitled "Democracy Versus the Melting-Pot" at the 1914 meeting of the American Philosophical Society. Resistance to the term continued and it was not widely used in Kallen's lifetime, but cultural pluralism eventually was incorporated into many other fields, including psychology, anthropology, sociology, educational theory, political science, history, and even physics.

Kallen did not begin his college career as a pluralist, just the opposite. As an undergraduate at Harvard, Kallen did not want to be regarded as a Jew but as an American. When Barrett Wendell, an English professor, asked Kallen why he could not be an American and a Jew, Kallen began considering the idea of a dual identity. After entering graduate school in 1906, Kallen cofounded the Harvard Menorah Society, an organization that fostered pride in Jewish culture and religion, and encouraged Jewish students to incorporate this pride into their identity as Americans (Menand, 2001). Because Kallen had felt pressure to renounce his own culture, he was aware of how intensely this pressure was directed at immigrants. He rejected the expectation that immigrants should give up their ethnicity and be Americanized. Kallen (1924/1970) was convinced that immigrants could assimilate while maintaining their ethnicity, and with the passage of time their ethnicity would nurture their self-esteem: "The wop changes into a proud Italian, the hunky into an intensely nationalist Slav. They learn, or they recall, the spiritual heritage of their nationality. Their cultural abjectness gives way to cultural pride" (p. 106).

Kallen denounced the melting pot idea primarily because of its implications for uniformity; he argued that there was no single model for an American citizen. He asked whether the melting pot had produced the cowboy of the west, the farmer of the Midwest, or the Puritan descendants who lived in eastern cities. Americans were not a uniform people, so it was absurd to demand conformity, and it was unnatural: "Uniformity is superimposed, not inwardly generated. Under its regimentation the diversities persist; upon it and by means of it they grow . . . for Nature is naturally pluralistic" (1924/1970, pp. 178–179).

Kallen's criticisms of the melting pot were largely his own, but he did not generate his concept of cultural pluralism without assistance. As a freshman at Harvard, Alain LeRoy Locke enrolled in Kallen's class on the Greek philosophers, and the two quickly became friends. Kallen later would state that it was during Locke's senior year when he first began using the term *cultural pluralism* as they discussed America's ethnic diversity. Locke agreed with Kallen about the need to create a dual identity, and both opposed cultural separatism because it reinforced the dominant society's subordination of ethnic groups. Yet Locke disagreed with Kallen's contention that ethnicity was an immutable aspect of an individual's identity; Locke did not believe it was necessary to preserve one's racial or ethnic identity. Menand (2001) paraphrased Locke's position: "If it is a mistake to cling to ethnic identity, it is also a mistake to abandon it. The trick is to use it to overcome it" (p. 398). Influenced by Boas, Locke did not view human differences as genetically determined, but as largely the consequence of cultural differences.

As he prepared to graduate, Locke would become the first African American to be awarded a Rhodes scholarship–it is likely that the scholarship committee did not know his race until after the awards were announced. The committee did not withdraw the award, but when Locke went to Oxford the following fall, five of its colleges refused to admit him. He would spend the next 4 years in England and Europe, taking classes at Oxford and in Germany before returning to take a teaching position at Howard University, presenting his ideas about cultural pluralism in a series of lectures in the spring of 1915. He wanted to expand these lectures into a course, but the leadership at Howard viewed the subject matter as too controversial (Menand, 2001).

Just before Locke delivered his lectures, Kallen's ideas from his 1914 presentation were published in an essay in the *Nation*. By this time Kallen had graduated from Harvard and accepted a position at the University of Wisconsin. In 1924, Kallen published *Culture and Democracy in the United States*, where the term *cultural pluralism* first appeared in print. Kallen argued for the immutability of ethnicity and the need for immigrants to create a dual identity, and he explained why Americans should reject conformity and value diversity. Yet, Kallen retreated from his prior assertions that it was "necessary for the U.S. to become 'a federation . . . of nationalities' in order to ensure cultural democracy" (Fuchs, 1990, p. 74). Instead, Kallen

(1924/1970) introduced the term *cultural pluralism* and explained why this concept was appropriate for a democratic society:

> Cultural growth is founded upon Cultural Pluralism. Cultural Pluralism is possible only in a democratic society whose institutions encourage individuality in groups . . . whose program liberates these individualities and guides them into a fellowship of freedom and cooperation. (p. 43)

To illustrate the potential for peaceful yet productive relationships between diverse groups living in one nation, Kallen used the metaphor of an orchestra. Each ethnic group represented a section of instruments and these instruments produced different sounds, but the music that they created together was unlike anything that any one section could produce on its own. As exemplars of cultural pluralism, Kallen referred to the four nationalities constituting the population of Great Britain (English, Scottish, Welsh, and Irish) and Switzerland, whose population included three nationalities (French, German, and Italian). Kallen argued that both nations achieved harmony despite their diversity by asking for cooperation from each group to strengthen the nation, and he claimed that "Switzerland is the most successful democracy in the world" (p. 122). The book would attract few disciples to cultural pluralism.

Kallen's failure probably didn't surprise him. In the same year that his *Nation* essay was published, President Woodrow Wilson discussed the idea of immigrants maintaining their ethnic heritage to create a dual identity: "America does not consist of groups. . . . A man who thinks of himself as belonging to a particular national group in America has not yet become an American" (Menand, 2001, p. 406). Many Americans agreed with Wilson, and that prompted Kallen to address this issue in his 1924 book. Kallen referred to John Dewey's support for the dual identity illustrated by "hyphenated Americans," and Kallen included Dewey's caveat: "The point is to see to it that the hyphen connects instead of separates" (1924/1970, p. 132). Dewey believed that teachers should try to achieve this goal if they were working with children of immigrants—teaching those from different groups to respect one another. Like Kallen, Dewey argued that the uniqueness of the American people was that they represented diverse nationalities from around the world and yet lived peacefully together in America. The rejection of Kallen's ideas about diversity was best illustrated by the immigration reform passed the same year that Kallen's book was published. The Johnson-Reed Act of 1924 was intended to diminish the diversity of future immigrants by restricting immigration primarily to those who looked like the majority of Americans—White European ethnic groups.

FROM CULTURAL PLURALISM TO MULTICULTURALISM

During the 1930s and 1940s, concerns about immigration and ethnic diversity diminished considerably. Immigration declined dramatically as the Great Depression forced people around the world to focus on economic survival, and World War II inspired all Americans to proclaim their patriotism to the nation, not their native land. After the war, there was renewed attention to ethnic diversity as movies and books examined the horrors of the Holocaust and denounced anti-Semitism; in 1947, the first American to win the Nobel Prize for Literature addressed America's racial prejudices. In Sinclair Lewis's novel, *Kingsblood Royal,* a White man discovers that he has a Black ancestor. After confessing to neighbors and friends, a man who has always been regarded as White (and acceptable) becomes a pariah.

Although Americans appeared to be more willing to accept human diversity, fears of communism intervened as the Cold War demanded conformity as proof of patriotism; however, in time the Cold War would challenge Americans to be more accepting of the nation's diverse population, especially people of color. For the United States to defeat communism, neutral nations had to be persuaded to be our allies, and most consisted of people of color. Our leaders knew that the country would have to address racism to be successful in the pursuit of allies because Communist propaganda focused on racism in the United States. Military and political leader George C. Marshall argued: "The moral influence of the United States is weakened to the extent that the civil rights proclaimed in our Constitution are not fully confirmed in actual practice" (Lind, 1995, p. 106).

Horace Kallen (1956) advocated for pluralism in his book *Cultural Pluralism and the American Id* where he claimed that American immigrants had rejected the old assimilation models emphasizing uniformity. Instead, the new form of assimilation involved "the processes by which the diverse learn to know, to understand and to live with one another in equal liberty" (p. 97). Yet, even as he promoted "the union of the diverse," a footnote in Kallen's book would highlight the difficulty of advocating anything appearing to be radical. The footnote concerned a 1951 incident involving two reporters from the *Capitol Times* of Madison, Wisconsin. The reporters created a petition consisting of excerpts from the Declaration of Independence and the Bill of Rights. Out of 112 people they approached, only one person signed the petition, and some people denounced the petition as "communist stuff." Wondering if this was merely a rural phenomenon, two *New York Post* reporters created their own petition using excerpts taken exclusively from the Constitution and the Bill of Rights. They approached 161 New Yorkers, but only

19 would sign the petition. The story got national attention, and in response President Truman argued that the climate of fear created by the Cold War was responsible (Kallen, 1956, p. 63).

It was not until the early 1960s as the Civil Rights Movement gained momentum that academics reconsidered Kallen's ideas, but while Kallen had focused on the right of immigrants to maintain their ethnic heritage, the new cultural pluralism advocates wanted to expand the concept to include racial groups (Lind, 1995). This was the origin of *multiculturalism*, a political and educational movement promoting a general respect for human rights and the acknowledgment of and respect for cultures represented by diverse racial and ethnic groups in the United States (Feagin & Feagin, 2003). Multiculturalists focused on the diversity represented by five groups—African Americans, American Indians, Asian and Pacific Island Americans, Hispanic Americans (Latinos), and White Americans. Like Kallen, multiculturalists rejected the melting pot theory and the expectation of conformity for American immigrants to assimilate successfully into society. Multiculturalists asserted that these five human groups represented distinct cultural communities, and they expected new immigrants to assimilate into one or another of them (Lind, 1995).

According to Moghaddam (2008), most multiculturalists did not advocate cultural separation; instead, they encouraged individuals to share their culture with members of other cultural groups to increase cross-cultural understanding and to promote appreciation for cultural differences. Based on this rationale, multiculturalists successfully lobbied colleges and universities to offer courses in racial and ethnic studies. Multiculturalists argued that in a democratic society, individuals should have the freedom to maintain their diverse cultures, and that those in power had a duty to propose and implement policies and practices affirming these diverse cultures.

Critics of multiculturalism tended to view its advocates as engaged in a blatant effort to gain power at the expense of the White majority. Multiculturalists were denounced for having an anti-Western bias, and critics staunchly opposed the proliferation of racial and ethnic studies courses on college campuses because such courses diluted the academic rigor of the traditional Western curriculum. In response, multiculturalists argued that a multicultural society required a multicultural curriculum to accurately describe it. Some critics of multiculturalism acknowledged the importance of diversity while maintaining that there was an overriding American culture derived from Western traditions that should be emphasized. As historian Arthur Schlesinger, Jr. (1992) stated: "It is not that the Western cultures are superior to other cultures as much as it is—for better or worse—our culture" (p. B2).

FROM MULTICULTURALISM TO PLURALISM

Multiculturalism would evolve into a global movement in the 1970s and 1980s, influencing policies and practices in emerging multicultural societies such as Germany, France, the United Kingdom, Australia, Canada, and the Netherlands. In the United States, the Women's Movement was emerging and lobbied for gender equity, the 1969 Stonewall Riots became the catalyst for the Gay Rights Movement, and disability advocates emphasized the need for legislation to ensure a better education for students with disabilities and to forbid job discrimination against adults with disabilities. The concept of cultural pluralism was now being broadened to include these groups whose diversity was defined by factors other than race and ethnicity. Pluralism advocates tended to focus on issues relevant to their particular group, but they recognized the array of oppressed groups actively advocating for civil rights because of their status as citizens of our democratic society. Over time *cultural pluralism* evolved into *pluralism,* whose meaning was defined by Pai and Adler (1997): "[The] equal coexistence in a mutually supportive relationship within the boundaries . . . of one nation of people of diverse cultures with significantly different patterns of belief, behavior, color, and in many cases with different languages" (pp. 107–108).

This broader concept of pluralism was consistent with its philosophical roots, for it involved not only a respect for human diversity, but a recognition of the significance of a multiplicity of perspectives and truth in the world. As Lynch (1998) has stated, "Pluralism is the idea that there can be more than one story of the world; there can be incompatible, but equally acceptable, accounts of some subject matter" (p. 1). Each group encompassed by the term *pluralism* was trying to tell its own story and its own truth, and advocates wanted their perspective acknowledged and understood. Critics of pluralism accused them of being "cultural relativists" who rejected universal moral values by insisting that truth was relative. Pluralistic advocates responded that it was not relativism to think that a person was capable of understanding and appreciating the values and behaviors of people from other groups. After asserting that pluralism "is not relativism," Berlin (1991) described the process of studying and understanding a group other than one's own:

> They may find [their] values unacceptable, but if they open their minds sufficiently they can grasp how one might be a full human being, with whom one could communicate, and at the same time live in the light of values widely different from one's own, but which nevertheless one can see to be values, ends of life, by the realization of which men could be fulfilled. (p. 10)

As Berlin suggested, being a cultural pluralist was an intellectually challenging task. Lynch (1998) admitted to the difficulty inherent in examining worldviews other than one's own, but unlike Berlin, Lynch believed there were limits on a person's ability to comprehend the worldview of another group. Understanding that was sufficient to permit a credible evaluation of an alternative worldview could occur only if there was some common ground in the form of shared concepts between the evaluator and the worldview of the group being evaluated. Lynch argued that it was impossible to comprehend a worldview that was "totally *alien* to one's own" (p. 148, emphasis in original). Yet, even if individuals cannot evaluate a worldview, they can acknowledge the truths held by those whose lives are shaped by an alternative worldview. This was the insight Stephen Crane offered in his poem, "A Man Saw a Ball of Gold in the Sky" (1967, p. 943):

> A man saw a ball of gold in the sky;
> He climbed for it,
> And eventually he achieved it—
> It was clay.
> Now this is the strange part:
> When the man went to the earth
> And looked again,
> Lo, there was the ball of gold.
> Now this is the strange part:
> It was a ball of gold.
> Aye, by the heavens, it was a ball of gold.

Philosophical pluralists do not argue that a conceptual framework creates objective reality, but rather argue that an objective reality exists and conceptual frameworks are created to interpret reality in a way that makes sense of it. Lynch (1998) illustrates this point using the metaphor of measuring temperature: One group uses a measurement system to report that the outside temperature is "0" but another group using a different measurement system reports that the outside temperature is "32." Those who understand both measurement systems recognize that there is no disagreement. In some cases, however, there may be disagreements. Look at the following figures and answer this question: "How many of these figures are alike?"

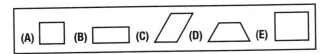

One person could answer that (A) and (E) are alike because both appear to be squares. Another might argue that (A) and (B) and (E) are alike because they are four-sided polygons having right angles. A third person could argue that all five are alike because they are all quadrilateral figures (the sum of the angles = 360°). All three answers accurately reflect an objective reality; they differ because of the meaning attributed to the word *alike*.

Similar to this analysis, contemporary pluralists insist that individual perspectives are shaped by the worldview or conceptual framework of the group to which the individual belongs. Further, since most people belong to multiple groups based primarily on differences of race, gender, ethnicity, socioeconomic status, sexual orientation, and disability, they have multiple perspectives by which they interpret objective reality. Having multiple perspectives adds to the complexity, but it also provides a basis for understanding perspectives other than one's own because it makes finding common ground more likely. A White male may not understand an African American's worldview, but since the worldview of Black males also is influenced by gender, their male perspective can serve as the common ground for communication and lead to a broader understanding. Most pluralists agree that the best way to achieve that broader understanding is through education, yet even education presents a paradox. Said (2007) addressed this issue:

> The fundamental paradox of education is that [a student] must submit to authority—the authority of tradition, of learning itself, of the scholars and scientists who went before you and in a sense made you possible—and at the same time you must somehow remain critical, even defiant. (p. 32)

Said argues that developing a critical consciousness is essential, especially for citizens in a democratic society who must employ critical thinking skills when listening to politicians, business leaders, religious leaders, and even messages broadcast in television programs and advertisements.

ARGUMENTS OPPOSING PLURALISM

The opponents of pluralism argue that it is "regressive" because the perpetuation of diverse cultural perspectives results in perpetuating forms of inequality embedded in cultures (Freeman, 2002). Squires (2002) specifically addresses the conflict between certain cultural groups and feminism, arguing that these cultural perspectives are opposed to the gender equity goals for which feminists advocate. Said (2007) responded by arguing that cultures are not static but dynamic. Cultures evolve and change in monocultural societies, and the same is true for a subordinate culture in a multicultural society because there inevitably will be conflicts, leading to cultural change to resolve them. Focusing on the dominant culture of the United States, Parekh (2002) illustrates this point by examining America's valuing of free speech based on a shared belief that every individual has the right to express his or her opinions. For some Americans this includes the right to burn the American flag or copies of the Constitution, while other Americans denounce such actions as unpatriotic speech that should not be permitted. As another example, the American culture places a high value on human life, yet while some want to protect human life from the moment of conception, others believe a fetus does not achieve the status of a human being until it reaches the point of development where it could survive outside the womb. In any culture, such complex issues are not easily resolved, but in time it is likely that some accommodation or consensus will be achieved.

There is ample evidence that the cultures in the United States have changed in significant ways from the cultures that existed in the immigrants' native lands. After the Vietnam War ended, the Hmong left Laos and migrated to the United States in large numbers. They were a rural people whose cultural practices included arranged marriages of teenage couples. After living in my community for a decade, Hmong high school students wrote and performed a play narrating their community's story beginning in Laos and including the impact of the Vietnam War, migration to the United States, and the problems of assimilation. The Hmong youth addressed the issue of arranged marriages negotiated by families, and the play expressed their desire to end this cultural practice. They wanted to have the freedom of their American peers in making their own selection of a marriage partner. In the play, the conflict was unresolved because it had not yet been resolved in their culture, but after another decade arranged marriages are no longer the norm in the Hmong community; instead, young people individually select their marriage partners with the family's approval.

Some anti-pluralism critics claim that if the United States endorses pluralism, the multitude of accommodations for members of diverse cultures will create a fragmented and chaotic society. Caney (2002) disagreed and provided several examples of reasonable accommodations that have already been implemented:

> Exempting Sikh males from rules prohibiting facial hair at the worksite when facial hair does not prevent them from doing the job, since their religion requires that they not cut their hair and facial hair.

Exempting religious institutions from the rule against using religious affiliation in hiring employees.

Excluding Muslim children from required attendance in the lunchroom during the month of Ramadan because it is more difficult for them to fast (as required by their religion) when surrounded by other children eating their lunches. (pp. 83–87)

Yet Caney also admitted that some accommodations might not be easy to implement. He discussed a workplace safety rule requiring all workers to wear a hard hat at construction sites and how the rule interferes with Sikh workers whose religion requires them to wear a turban. In the United States, this exemption has been denied to Sikhs because the requirement is regarded as a safety issue that must be maintained for the protection of workers. In the United Kingdom, Sikhs have been exempted from this requirement, but by choosing to wear a turban instead of a hard hat, they will be less likely to receive the same level of compensation for an injury as a worker wearing a hard hat.

Although Parekh (2002) agreed that cultures are dynamic and evolving, he also argued that no cultural tradition is or should be exempt from internal or external criticisms. Such criticisms have challenged members of a cultural group to rethink traditional beliefs and practices to determine whether they still serve a valid function in a contemporary context. Lynch (1998) argued that even when individuals embrace pluralism, they should regularly examine cultural beliefs and practices to ensure that they continue to provide adequate explanations of or responses to the individuals' objective reality, and should modify those aspects of their beliefs and practices that no longer seem satisfying. The same is true for the dominant culture. Skutnabb-Kangas (2000) noted that in the majority of the world's nations, bilingual or multilingual speakers are the norm; yet the United States continues to be a monolingual society and people in the English-only movement are trying to keep it that way. Americans need to respond to this criticism that monolingualism is no longer a viable condition for nations participating in global interactions.

Finally, some critics of cultural pluralism argue that any society needs to be based on a single, well-defined culture. Without a strong cultural center based on a consensus about beliefs and values that produce a shared objective reality, there is no glue to hold a society together. They view a shift toward pluralism as traveling down a precipitous path leading to cultural annihilation and the chaos described by the poet Yeats (2002):

Things fall apart; the centre cannot hold;
Mere anarchy is loosed upon the world. (p. 80)

Lynch (1998) has acknowledged that a commitment to pluralism involves some risk-taking and that pluralism is a challenging concept because it appears to eliminate the possibility of objectivity or an objective search for truth: "Pluralists, like overly permissive parents, always seem to be on the brink of allowing anything to be true—of saying that anything goes" (p. 1). Yet Lynch went on to frame the problem and clarify the nature of the risk-taking involved: "It is the problem of allowing for *different* truths without slipping into the nihilistic position that there is no truth at all" (p. 1, emphasis in original).

FIXED PRINCIPLES OR MULTIPLE PERSPECTIVES

Said (2007) described dynamic cultures as characterized by an ever-shifting center—old authorities are rejected and replaced by new ones, and ideas of new authorities are debated, revised, and perhaps discarded. Bevir (2007) argued that modern societies have moved beyond a belief in "fixed principles" that are true for all, because even fixed principles are subject to interpretation. Kane (1994) illustrated this point by using the fixed principle of the Old Testament's sixth commandment—Thou shalt not kill. Throughout history Christians and Jews have made exceptions to this principle, and, as Kane argued: "Once exceptions are admitted (for example, in cases of self-defense or war), it becomes problematic where the line on excepting is to be drawn (capital punishment? abortion? euthanasia?)" (p. 6).

American author Herman Melville described the difficulty of behaving according to fixed principles in *Moby Dick* (1851/1964). Ishmael, Melville's narrator, decides that his behavior should be guided by the New Testament passage in Luke 6:31—"And as you wish that men would do to you, do so to them." The Golden Rule is a particularly interesting fixed principle because it seems to exist in one form or another in the world's major religions, but what guidance does it provide? Ishmael is forced to share a room with a stranger as they wait for the Pequod to sail. The stranger's name is Queequeg, and he is a "savage" harpooner, a foreigner and a worshipper of idols. Despite their differences, they become friends. One night Queequeg invites Ishmael to participate in his idol-worshipping ritual. Ishmael knows this offer is made from the purest motives of friendship and affection, and he does not want to offend Queequeg, but he knows that Christians are not to worship any other gods—another fixed principle from the Ten Commandments. Using the Golden Rule, Ishmael resolves his dilemma:

> I was a good Christian, born and bred in the bosom of the infallible Presbyterian Church. How then could I unite with this wild idolator in worshipping his piece of wood? But what is worship? thought I. Do you suppose now, Ishmael, that the magnanimous God of heaven and earth—pagans and all included—can possibly be jealous of an insignificant bit of black wood? Impossible! But what is worship?—to do the will of God—that is worship. And what is the will of God?—to do to my fellow man what I would have my fellow man to do to me—*that* is the will of God. Now, Queequeg is my fellow man. And what do I wish that this Queequeg would do to me? Why unite with me in my particular Presbyterian form of worship. Consequently, I must then unite with him in his; ergo, I must turn idolator. (p. 85)

Melville suggests that having fixed principles does not mean they will have only one meaning; rather, different interpretations will lead to alternative individual choices or behaviors. We live in a complex world, but acknowledging that complexity does not mean that the world is inevitably chaotic. The limitations on the human ability to perceive what is true in our objective reality should not be exaggerated into having no ability. Lynch (1998) asserts that most educators would agree that there is no one best way to teach all children, yet they also would agree that it is possible to identify ineffective teaching methods. Within the limitations of our ability to perceive truth, individuals in a multicultural society engage in research and other activities to provide information about objective reality so we can identify problems such as disparities of income by race and gender, unequal opportunities based on social class, and a host of others. Based on a commitment to ideals of social justice, the information is used to foster social change in policies and practices. Should individuals evaluate and criticize a culture other than their own? Pluralists believe it is possible to study another culture and achieve understanding; therefore, once the culture is understood, an evaluation or judgment becomes credible. Caney (2002) described such a credible evaluation: "We should not judge cultures as indivisible entities that can be deemed worthy or unworthy. Rather cultures will include some features that are rewarding and fulfilling and others that are not" (p. 98). This assumption also must be made in evaluating our own culture. In a pluralistic society, a great deal of diverse behavior will be acceptable, but some behavior legitimately will be subjected to criticism. As Berlin (1991) explained: "Both liberty and equality are among the primary goals pursued by human beings through many centuries; but total liberty to wolves is death to the lambs, total liberty of the powerful, the gifted, is not compatible with the rights to a decent existence of the weak and less gifted" (p. 12).

People worldwide have been migrating as never before, and one consequence is that pluralism is gaining ground as the perspective most viable for those societies experiencing increased diversity from immigration. Yet there is still resistance from those seeking the comfort of certainty from fixed principles. As a professor at the Sloan School of Management at MIT, Thomas Vargish was teaching a seminar to senior corporate executives representing five different continents. In a discussion of values that drive behavior in corporations, one participant interrupted by standing up and identifying himself as a Christian:

> He stated that for him there could exist only one source of ethical authority and that source was God's will as represented in the New Testament. He implied that therefore what his co-participants (and of course the Professor of Management) were saying could in the end have little influence with him unless it went to support his Christian definition of authority. (Vargish, 2007, p. 118)

When the man's statement ended, no one spoke. Vargish felt compelled to break the silence and revive the previous discussion. He reminded everyone of the basic assumptions of an academic dialogue, especially in an advanced seminar such as this one. These rules required an open discussion with freedom for participants to express themselves; therefore no particular idea or belief could be granted priority over another. No single system of fixed principles or absolute truths could be granted a dominant role in the discussion. The man's response surprised Vargish:

> The Christian participant then brilliantly claimed that I had excluded his system, which could not exist except as an absolute system, from the forum, and therefore that I was ruling in contradiction of my own principles of open discussion. He had in fact carried out an impressive and technically correct deconstruction of the system of dialogue. (p. 118)

The participant had posed an intriguing dilemma—can an individual who believes in absolutes be accommodated in a discussion based on assumptions about diverse truths and the legitimacy of multiple perspectives? Vargish understood the attraction of an absolute system of beliefs because they provided certainty, assurance, and answers to many of life's biggest problems. Yet Vargish also believed that the global diversity of our contemporary world made systems of absolute truths dysfunctional. Vargish responded by telling the Christian participant that he was welcome to bring his system of absolute truths to the table, but that it was "a seminar table, not an altar" (p. 132). A seminar table required discussion, negotiation, and, when possible, consensus. A participant could bring any worldview to the table and perhaps take it away from the table unaltered by the experience, but at the table, participants would need to recognize and respect the right of other participants to engage in discussion based on their particular worldview. This response appeared to be acceptable to the Christian executive, who not only remained at the table, but actively engaged in the subsequent discussions.

GLOBAL DIMENSIONS OF PLURALISM

Lynch (1998) has asserted that "the problem of how to incorporate multiple viewpoints into one culture . . . is one of the most important political issues of our age" (p. 3). The political context for Lynch's comment is not simply national but global. Vargish's anecdote illustrates the extent to which pluralism has become the preferred perspective of most multinational corporations. For many corporate leaders, the obligation to promote diversity is pragmatic rather than idealistic. From a premise that corporations have an ongoing responsibility to increase their profits, corporate executives argue that a diverse workforce helps a corporation to be more competitive and to increase its profits; therefore, corporations that promote diversity "are being socially responsible as well as fulfilling a moral obligation" (Hopkins, 1997, p. 21).

Promoting diversity in corporations is not necessarily limited to hiring and promoting people of color, women, or other minority employees within the organization; it has implications beyond the organization. In 1993, the Apple Computer Company offered to build a new customer support center near Austin, Texas. In return for bringing 1,450 new jobs into the area, Apple requested a $750,000 tax break, but the county commissioners noticed that Apple's benefits policy included gay domestic partners. The commissioners refused to approve the tax cuts, arguing that the domestic partnership policy contradicted the values of people living in this area. When Apple canceled its plans to build the center, public pressure forced the commissioners to vote again, and they approved the tax break. Apparently having a good job was a higher regional value than keeping gay men and lesbians out of the community (Hopkins, 1997).

The European Union has more multinational corporations than the United States, and for over 2 decades many have advocated for issues of inclusion and human rights. In describing the new European vision of the future, Rifkin (2004) has noted, "Human rights are all about inclusion. They speak to the rights of women, minorities, cultural groups, the disabled, children, our fellow creatures, to all have their interests equally included" (p. 280). In contrast, the United States has not consistently played a leadership role in human rights. Niezen (2004) reported on the U.S. refusal to ratify the international *Convention on the Elimination of All Forms of Discrimination Against Women*, which calls for increased access and equity for women in such areas as education, employment, health care, marriage, and divorce. In addition, the United States and Somalia are the only two nations that have not endorsed the United Nations *Convention on the Rights of the Child.*

America's reluctance to participate in such global commitments may yet have consequences. As Rifkin (2004) argued, in the emerging global society, nations must "be willing to listen to and accommodate the interests of others.... One can choose not to play at all, but the price of not participating is isolation" (p. 281). Meanwhile, new technologies are attracting new participants in the global conversation, as indigenous people increasingly are using the Internet to preserve their language and their cultures (Niezen, 2004).

Colleges and universities worldwide have acknowledged the significance of increasing diversity in the United States and globally. Scholars from various disciplines have pursued issues related to diverse groups, and their efforts have created new fields of research, beginning with racial and ethnic studies and women's studies, and, more recently, queer studies and disability studies. Although initially there was some resistance among American academics, Said (2007) described this exploration of historic experiences and contemporary issues affecting minority groups as "the unraveling of the grand narrative of a unitary American history" (p. 26). The new narrative of American history will be addressed in the next chapter.

CHAPTER 2

The Growth of Diversity and Pluralism
The Impact of Immigration

Once we appreciate the importance of culture, we also appreciate its inescapable plurality.

—Bhikhu Parekh, 1996, p. 134

In his title for the essay that became his final book, John F. Kennedy proclaimed that the United States was *A Nation of Immigrants.* In the book (published posthumously in 1964) he wrote that the nation was and always had been a diverse society because of immigration, and that immigrants were continuing to contribute to the development and prosperity of the nation. Yet Americans have always exhibited an ebb and flow of sentiments in support of immigration and its diversity countered by hostile reactions based on viewing immigrants as a threat. Before examining how immigration has shaped our diverse society, we must acknowledge the indigenous peoples whose lands were purchased or taken by force to create space for immigrants to fill. In addition, some immigrants did not come voluntarily—Africans brought in chains to serve as slave labor, and Mexicans in Texas and the southwest whose presence in the United States was part of the spoils of war. Yet they were part of the diversity of those who came to America, and they would contribute to the character of the new nation that would emerge after the American Revolution.

COLONIAL DIVERSITY

Of every hue and caste am I, of every rank and religion,
A farmer, mechanic, artist, gentleman, sailor, quaker,
Prisoner, fancy-man, rowdy, lawyer, physician, priest,
I resist any thing better than my own diversity.

—Walt Whitman, 1983, p. 36

27

America's first great poet was also one of the first to celebrate our nation's diversity in his quintessentially American poem, *Leaves of Grass.* From the earliest days of the colonial era, there is evidence of diversity in its settlements. As early as 1643, a French Jesuit visiting New Amsterdam reported hearing 18 different languages (Daniels, 2002). French immigrant Crèvecoeur in his *Letters from an American Farmer* wrote: "No sooner does a European arrive . . . [than] he hears his language spoken, he retraces many of his own country manners, he perpetually hears the names of families and towns with which he is acquainted" (1912, p. 56). Some historians suggest that Crèvecoeur and the French Jesuit were exaggerating, but New Amsterdam became New York City, which exhibited the pattern of port cities containing diverse immigrant populations. According to Chernow (2004), just prior to the Revolutionary War not only was New York the second largest colonial city (after Philadelphia) with 25,000 people, but the diverse New Yorkers spoke at least 14 different languages.

Some historians argue that despite some diversity in the colonies, the population was largely homogeneous. Kaufmann (2004) asserted that the vast majority of the immigrants colonizing this British territory were White, and that at the time of the American Revolution, 80% of the White population had emigrated from Great Britain (60% of them from England), and 98% of the people were Protestant. Yet Protestants were intensely sectarian at this time, and even Kaufmann admits that it would be erroneous to regard the Protestant population as a unified body. As late as 1775, almost 90% of colonial Protestants were not even members of a specific church and rarely attended (Lippy, 1994). The remaining 2% of the colonial population included Catholics and Jews. Lord Baltimore wanted Catholics to settle his Maryland colony, but even the first boatload of immigrants had a minority of Catholic families. When Lord Baltimore proclaimed religious liberty in Maryland, it was primarily intended to ensure a safe place for the Catholic minority.

The first Jews to come to America were living in Brazil under a tolerant Dutch government when Portugal regained control of the land in 1654. Along with other "heretics," 23 Jews were expelled and sailed to the American colonies to settle in New Amsterdam. They hoped to encounter the same Dutch tolerance in New Amsterdam, but the colony's governor, Peter Stuyvesant, was not in a tolerant mood. According to Gaustad and Schmidt (2002), Stuyvesant firmly believed that the colony already had too much diversity in terms of religions, languages, and nationalities, so he met with the Jewish immigrants and asked them to leave, "in a friendly way" (p. 76). The Jews petitioned the Dutch West India Company, and its response was to affirm its policy of tolerance and grant their request to settle, travel, and trade in New Amsterdam. The presence of Jewish shareholders in the Dutch West India Company also may have been a factor in the Company granting their request (Daniels, 2002). Jews coming to the colonies tended to settle in port cities. The first synagogue in America was built in New York in 1729; 4 years later the next one was built in Savannah. In 1747, a synagogue was erected in Philadelphia, and 2 years later one was built in Charleston. Yet in 1790, the first U.S. census would record a total of only 1,200 Jews living in the new nation (Gaustad & Schmidt, 2002).

Peter Stuyvesant was not alone in his concern over diversity in his colony. According to Meacham (2006), immigrants to the Massachusetts colony who were not Puritans were told to leave. Puritan minister Nathaniel Ward wrote that religious liberty meant the "liberty to keep away from us" (p. 48). When Quakers refused to heed these warnings, Puritans arrested and tried them; four Quakers were hanged between 1659 and 1661, causing London authorities to insist that any Quakers who were arrested must be sent to England for a proper trial (Miller, 1976). At about the same time, the colony of Virginia passed a law making it a crime if parents did not baptize their children in the Anglican Church (Meacham, 2006).

The initial promotion of religious pluralism in America began in three colonies—Maryland, Pennsylvania, and Rhode Island. Maryland managed to maintain its commitment to religious liberty even after the Anglican Church was named the colony's established church in 1702. After trying unsuccessfully to persuade Puritans in Massachusetts to accept other faiths, Roger Williams was forced into exile and founded the colony of Rhode Island. People from diverse faiths came to new colony, eventually prompting Cotton Mather to compare Rhode Island to a cesspool or a latrine containing "a variety of religions together on so small a spot of ground . . . [including] everything in the world but for Roman Catholics and real Christians" (Gaustad & Schmidt, 2002, p. 70). Later Mather again harangued Rhode Island for allowing Jews to settle in Newport. The Jews remained and in 1763 built a synagogue that is the oldest existing synagogue building in the United States. Roger Williams welcomed the Jews, but Quakers represented a real challenge to his commitment to religious liberty. As Quaker migration to Rhode Island increased, Williams expressed vehement criticisms of their beliefs and practices, yet he stopped short of demanding their expulsion from the colony. Before his death, Williams would see the Quakers become the largest religious denomination in Rhode Island.

Under the leadership of William Penn, the Quakers in Pennsylvania engaged in the most significant attempt to foster religious liberty in the colonies. Penn believed that a secular government should never interfere with a person's religious faith or practices; he believed that God gave humans the ability to think in order to make decisions about what faith was right for them. As a consequence, Penn initiated his "holy experiment" by inviting diverse faiths and nationalities to settle in his colony, and they came. Fuchs (1990) described the variety of diverse faiths that immigrants brought to Pennsylvania—Amish, Anglicans, Anabaptists, Baptists, Catholics, Calvinists, Lutherans, Jews, Mennonites, Methodists, Pietists, Presbyterians, and, of course, Quakers. Although most came from Great Britain, the immigrants included Africans, Dutch, and Germans. Several thousand Germans speaking "Deutsche" settled in the southeastern part of the colony. They were called the "Pennsylvania Dutch" by their Anglo neighbors, and the label stuck (Daniels, 2002).

Scholars tend to agree that Pennsylvania's was the most ambitious experiment to promote religious liberty, and what made the achievement especially notable was that the colony experienced impressive economic growth. The Pennsylvania experiment suggested that religious liberty also might facilitate economic progress, attracting attention beyond the colonies. In *The Wealth of Nations*, Adam Smith wondered whether Pennsylvania's prosperity occurred despite its religious diversity, or whether "such success was a result of the disestablishment of religion and the pursuit of an open religious marketplace" (Gaustad & Schmidt, p. 94).

New York and New Jersey inadvertently would stumble into promoting religious pluralism because diverse nationalities and faiths settled in both colonies without the guidance of any plan or laws to protect the rights of diverse groups. Assessing the presence of the diverse religions in New York and New Jersey at the end of the 17th century, Gaustad and Schmidt (2002) concluded: "Freedom in religion there, never complete, arrived in spite of efforts to prevent it and in spite of theories that condemned it. As in so much of American history, diversity itself set the agenda" (p. 74). As the 18th century began, religious liberty was established in five colonies, and attitudes in support of religious pluralism were beginning to develop. The stage was set for the religious transformation known as the Great Awakening.

Although the people colonizing America were largely Protestant, they were clearly not unified by their faith because Protestant churches were sectarian and contentious. In the early 1700s, a movement toward greater unity began as certain New England ministers began to question the genuineness of people's faith. One of them, Jonathan Edwards, had always emphasized the importance of reason in choosing one's faith, but now he recognized that reason alone was not enough, that reason without emotion created a sterile faith. Edwards believed that Protestants needed to infuse more passion into their knowledge and beliefs if they were to have a faith that animated their choices and actions. His sermons argued that behaving like a Christian was more important than one's Protestant denomination.

Edwards and other New England ministers shared these ideas, incorporating them into sermons and other writings. In 1740, the arrival of a preacher from England reinforced their efforts. George Whitefield was a charismatic speaker who turned down offers to preach in church pulpits in favor of preaching in open fields where he attracted huge numbers of people. His message was blunt and passionate as he told audiences that what was required of Christians was to be so committed to their faith that it could be seen in their everyday lives, and that belonging to a particular denomination was not significant.

The Great Awakening created greater tolerance for faiths other than one's own, but it did not extend to Catholics, Jews, or others. For that reason, Kaufmann (2004) argued that this event did not establish any form of genuine religious pluralism. However, even though the tolerance achieved was limited, the Great Awakening did establish a foundation for having a pluralistic attitude toward diverse faiths. As Gaustad and Schmidt (2002) noted: "An eventful experiment with religious pluralism took place that was at once deliberate, fortuitous, and turbulent. That very diversity, if largely Protestant in its contours, is a reminder that Protestantism itself was far from homogeneous" (p. 74).

INVOLUNTARY IMMIGRANTS TO COLONIAL AMERICA

As this fledgling form of pluralism regarding Protestant faiths developed, there was no corresponding development with respect to the diverse nationalities in the United States. The concept of cultural pluralism was more than a century away. Descriptions of "ethnicity" among Americans during the colonial period usually exclude one immigrant group that was not the first to be established on American soil. Yet, in a discussion of the earliest settlements in the United States, it is important to include the Mexican pioneers who settled Texas and the American southwest. In 1598, the first settlement in the southwest was established in Santa Fe—9 years before the first British settlement in Jamestown. By the late 1600s, there were many Mexican settlements in Texas and California, including one near San Diego established in 1769 (Daniels, 2002).

After the United States annexed Texas in 1845, the Mexican-American War would result in the cession of lands making up the current states of

Arizona, New Mexico, Utah, Nevada, and California, and parts of Colorado and Wyoming. Most of the Mexicans chose to stay on their land, thus becoming the first Mexican Americans. Shorris (2001) paraphrased their perspective: "We didn't cross the border; the border crossed us" (p. 37). There were early indications in Texas and elsewhere in the southwest that Mexicans were not going to be accepted or treated as real Americans. Perhaps the most significant illustration was the response of the U.S. Congress to New Mexico's bid for statehood. Two years after being annexed to the United States in 1848, residents in the New Mexico territory submitted a statehood proposal to Congress. The territory had a population of approximately 60,000 people, and it met all the criteria for statehood, but according to Daniels (2002), Congress did not regard the territory's population as sufficiently American. For the next 62 years, New Mexico would not be granted statehood status; in 1912 Congress finally voted to admit both New Mexico and Arizona into the union.

Another group often overlooked in discussions of early American immigration is the African people, involuntary immigrants brought here to work as slaves. Although a few Blacks immigrated to the United States voluntarily and a few former slaves earned their freedom, their numbers are dwarfed by the 10–12 million Africans who managed to survive the Middle Passage and the 5–6 million who did not (Franklin & Moss, 2000). Those who justified slavery claimed that Blacks were inferior to Whites and would benefit from slavery if well treated, but some Whites denounced the South's "peculiar institution." Observing a slave auction for newly arrived Blacks, Crèvecoeur (1912) described Africans: "Arranged like horses at a fair, they are branded like cattle and then driven to toil, to starve, to languish. . . . Are not these blacks . . . [God's] children as well as we?" (p. 161). To those who claimed that the Africans derived some benefits from slavery, Crèvecoeur said that the masters "look not upon them with half the kindness and affection with which they consider their dogs and horses" (p. 161). The first Abolitionist organization was established in Philadelphia in 1775, and many more soon formed in other northern cities.

Although claiming to be products of the enlightenment, leaders such as Thomas Jefferson and James Madison owned slaves. During the Revolutionary War, Washington rejected Alexander Hamilton's suggestion that slaves be recruited into the military in return for their freedom. Hamilton believed they would be especially good soldiers because they would be fighting for their own freedom. Hamilton's argument below illustrates why he would join the New York Abolitionist organization founded in 1785:

The contempt we have been taught to entertain for the blacks makes us fancy many things that are founded neither in reason nor experience. . . . An essential part of this plan is to give them their freedom with muskets. This will secure their fidelity, animate their courage, and, I believe, will have a good influence upon those who remain by opening a door to their emancipation. (Chernow, 2004, p. 122)

Although Hamilton's arguments did not persuade Washington, Hamilton predicted that if the Continental Army did not recruit slaves, the British army would. When the British did begin to recruit slaves, Washington agreed to allow recruitment of free Blacks; however, colonial militias eventually would recruit numerous slaves for the war effort (Chernow, 2004). Although the Blacks were good soldiers, their success on the battlefield did not change White attitudes of Black inferiority, nor end the practice of slavery. That would require another war.

ESTABLISHING THE PRINCIPLE OF PLURALISM

Winning the War for Independence was almost easier than creating a government for the nation. In 1781, the Articles of Confederation tried to establish a union of states bound together by a common purpose, and a year later *E Pluribus Unum* became the national motto to emphasize the unified nation. Yet it soon became obvious that this model was not working. Leaders reconvened in Philadelphia to draft a new Constitution, and it was soon clear that the new model was a secular one. The only reference to religion appeared in Article VI declaring that no religious test should be required of anyone seeking public office. Although many in attendance agreed with Connecticut's William Williams that a person unwilling to swear allegiance to Christianity should not be involved in government, a majority disagreed (Meacham, 2006). When questioned about the omission of any reference to God in the Constitution, Alexander Hamilton responded, "We forgot" (Chernow, 2004, p. 235). In reality, participants at the Convention were aware of the religious diversity debate in Virginia 3 years earlier.

Patrick Henry brought a resolution to the Virginia legislature for a tax to support Christianity. The most appealing aspect of the proposal was that no single Christian faith would be the recipient of tax funds; each taxpayer would designate the particular faith his tax dollars should support, and those with no faith could have their taxes go to a general education fund. Initially, the majority of legislators seemed supportive of the bill until James Madison launched a writing campaign opposing it. One of Madison's primary arguments was that if the government was given the power to favor Christianity over all other religions today, then tomorrow the government could decide to favor a particular Christian faith over all others. Agreeing with Madison, Baptist minister John Leland argued that the government's role was not to promote religion but to protect it: "Let every man speak freely without fear . . . [and] worship according to his own faith, either one God, three gods, no God or twenty Gods; and let government protect him in doing so" (Meacham, 2006, p. 32). Christians from minority faiths vigorously lobbied legislators to vote against the bill, and it was defeated (Waldman, 2006).

In its place, Virginia passed a slightly modified version of Thomas Jefferson's proposed Statute for Religious Freedom. This law protected Virginia's citizens from "the impious presumption of legislators . . . [who] have assumed dominion over the faith of others," and concluded that "truth is great and will prevail if left to herself . . . [if not] disarmed of her natural weapons, free argument and debate" (Jefferson, 1786). When asked about his Statute, Jefferson was adamant that he wanted to protect "the Jew and the Gentile, the Christian and the [Muslim], the Hindoo and infidel of every denomination" (Meacham, 2006, p. 11).

This law established religious liberty in Virginia and influenced the language of the First Amendment requiring the federal government to protect all religions and not interfere with individual religious beliefs or practices. Since religious diversity represented the most volatile form of diversity in the new nation, the First Amendment was a major achievement in the progress toward pluralism. Although the Protestant majority did not often adhere to the principle of religious pluralism on the domestic front, in international affairs the United States presented itself as a secular government. In the 1790s, Barbary pirates stopped and boarded American vessels, stealing trade goods. Diplomats dispatched to Tripoli negotiated a treaty stating that the United States respected all faiths and had no quarrel with Muslim beliefs or practices, and in Article 11, the treaty asserted that "the government of the United States of America is not in any sense founded on the Christian religion" (Roediger, 2005, p. 103). In Senate hearings to consider ratification of the treaty, there is no record of a debate over Article 11.

The First Amendment's guarantee of religious liberty was a necessary precondition to achieving religious pluralism. By the end of the 19th century, with the hindsight of more than 100 years of history under the Constitution and the Bill of Rights, Robert Ingersoll praised the principle of religious liberty that the founders established:

Our fathers founded the first secular government that was ever founded in this world. . . . The first government that said every church has exactly the same rights and no more; every religion has the same rights, and no more . . . [they] were the first men who had the sense, had the genius, to know that no church should be allowed to have a sword; that it should be allowed only to exert its moral influence. (Meacham, 2006, p. 33)

DIVERSITY ISSUES CONFRONTING THE NEW NATION

During the Constitutional Convention, some participants expressed concern that the diversity of nationalities would make it impossible to meld the states into a single nation, but Alexander Hamilton argued that the melding was already occurring: "From New Hampshire to Georgia, the people of America are as uniform in their interests and manners as those of any [nation] established in Europe" (Chernow, 2004, p. 265). Yet the diverse nationalities also contained the potential for conflict. Tocqueville (2004) recognized the problem and warned: "If America ever loses its liberty, the fault will surely lie with the omnipotence of the majority, which may drive minorities to despair and force them to resort to physical force" (p. 299). How could the new nation avoid the "tyranny of the majority" and yet present a united front in dealing with other nations? In a letter written to a friend, Tocqueville described the dilemma of a country that consisted of "people differing from one another in language, in beliefs, in opinion," and he asked, "How are they welded into one people?" (Takaki, 2002, p. 30).

The Constitutional Convention resolved several issues related to diverse groups within the union, but its major failure concerned slavery. The participants debated how to count slaves, and the political implications of this debate were evident in Virginia where slaves constituted 40% the population and in South Carolina where slaves outnumbered Whites (Chernow, 2004). Northerners yielded to southern pressure and adopted the compromise of counting each slave as three fifths of a person. To appease opponents of slavery, the Constitution prohibited the importation of slaves beginning in 1808, but said nothing about when slavery would be prohibited, and the number of slaves continued to grow. In 1790, the first census reported that Africans were the second largest group in the United States, constituting almost 20% of the nation's population.

The Constitution addressed diversity issues that related to immigration, such as naturalization, citizenship, and residency requirements. It required residency for 7 years before immigrants could seek office as a member of the House of Representatives, and 9 years before they would be eligible for a seat in the U.S. Senate. Immigrants were banned only from serving as President or Vice President. According to Daniels (2002), being able to hold all but the two highest offices in the land represented an unusually liberal attitude toward immigrants. Although the Constitution did not establish naturalization guidelines, it charged Congress with this responsibility.

During Washington's first term, Congress approved a naturalization law apparently opposed to diversity since it restricted citizenship to White immigrants; Fuchs (1990) argued that it was a liberal law, especially generous for its time because it created no restrictions to citizenship based on such factors as religion or national origin and required only 2 years of residency. Further, the law addressed only the foreign-born, saying nothing about non-Whites born in the United States, an omission that later would be addressed in the 14th Amendment. Although the residency requirement was increased to 5 years during Washington's second term, and then up to 14 years during John Adams's Presidency, the 5-year residency was reinstated after Thomas Jefferson was elected President and it has remained so ever since.

Although the naturalization law seemed to accept diversity among White immigrants, the American people regarded immigrants as Americans only if they conformed to Anglo norms. The pressure to conform existed throughout the colonial period and was reflected in the changing names. A Pennsylvania Dutch family known as Rittinghuysen became Rittenhouse, and a descendant of French immigrants called Revoire would be known to later generations of Americans by an Anglified name—Paul Revere (Kaufmann, 2004). The 1790 census documented Anglo dominance—those of English origin constituted 49.2% of all Americans. Africans were almost 20% of Americans, and other nationalities had small shares of the population: Germans (7%), Scots (6.6%), Scotch-Irish (4.8%), and Irish (3%). Groups constituting less than 2% of the population included Dutch, French, and Swedes (Kaufmann, 2004). As for religion, of more than 3,900,000 Americans in the 1790 census, approximately 25,000 were Catholics and 1,200 were Jews (Gaustad & Schmidt, 2002).

The dominant Anglo group insisted that immigrants should want to become Americans, and that they could achieve this by "absorbing American English, American liberty and American Protestantism and, ultimately, by intermarrying with Americans" (Kaufmann, 2004, p. 19). Thornton (2000) reported Thomas Jefferson expressing a similar attitude while meeting with Indian representatives. He urged them to become farmers, adopt White ways, and marry Whites so that "you will become one people with us; your blood will mix with ours, and will spread with ours over this great island" (p. 149).

Although most White Americans did not support encouraging intermarriage with Indians, ethnic intermarriage was a factor in people from diverse groups being regarded as Americans. Crèvecoeur (1912) described one American family: "I could point out to you a family whose grandfather was an Englishman, whose wife was Dutch, whose son married a French woman, and whose present four sons have now four wives of different nations" (p. 43).

Yet ethnic conflicts occurred during the colonial era and they persisted. The mocking phrase "Dutch treat" reflected a stereotype about the stinginess of the Pennsylvania Dutch. Many political leaders expressed concern about the numbers of Germans immigrating to America who settled in segregated communities instead of assimilating. Benjamin Franklin wrote to a friend that the Germans would "shortly be so numerous as to Germanize us instead of us Anglifying them" (Feagin, 1997, p. 18). The ethnic group encountering the most prejudice was the Irish. Irish immigrants were distributed throughout the colonies, but even when they created ethnic enclaves in cities like Boston and New York, their numbers couldn't protect them from the pre-existing Anglo prejudice. Some political leaders believed that the best strategy for resolving ethnic conflicts was to pretend there was no ethnic diversity in the United States. Daniels (2002) quoted John Jay in an essay from *The Federalist Papers*:

> Providence has been pleased to give this one connected country to one united people—a people descended from the same ancestors, speaking the same language, professing the same religion, attached to the same principles of government, very similar in their manners and customs. (p. 108)

The diversity of immigrants made this "ethnic-blind" approach patently absurd. Although immigration declined drastically during the War of 1812 (customary during wartime), afterward it rapidly accelerated, but with a declining number of English immigrants. From 1820 to 1850, only 20% of immigrants were English, as the German share went up to 25% and the Irish increased to 35%. During this 30-year period, of the 2.5 million immigrants who settled in America, about 600,000 were Germans (Kaufmann, 2004). Because many German immigrants were Catholics, antagonism against them stemmed from religious as well as ethnic prejudices; Irish immigrants faced the same antagonism, but German economic success helped them to avoid conflicts. Crèvecoeur believed that German success in the United States was a consequence of their ethnic solidarity and their passion to preserve their language and culture by re-creating Germany in their new home. He described the arrival of German immigrants:

Their astonishment at their first arrival from Germany is very great—it is to them a dream . . . they observe their countrymen flourishing in every place; they travel through whole counties where not a word of English is spoken; and in the names and the language of the people, they retrace Germany. (1912, pp. 61–62)

From 1820 to 1850, more than 1 million Irish immigrated to the United States. Some people of Scotch ancestry were especially concerned about the Irish immigration. Because many of them migrated to Ulster before coming to America, they were considered Irish. By the 1830s, the group had coined the term "Scotch-Irish" to distinguish themselves from the much maligned Irish. The negative attitude toward Irish immigrants was illustrated in an ad from the *New York Evening Post* on September 4, 1830: "Wanted. A Cook or Chambermaid . . . must be American, Scotch, Swiss or African—No Irish" (Daniels, 2002, p. 131). People in the southern states often hired Irish workers for dangerous construction projects rather than risk the lives of valuable slaves. According to Daniels (2002), just before the Civil War many Irish workers were killed during construction of the "New Canal" in New Orleans.

Although ethnic prejudices fueled the antagonism toward German and Irish immigrants, another primary source of the animosity was the Protestant prejudice against Catholics, which intensified as the numbers of Catholics in the United States increased. Much anti-Catholic activity occurred in urban areas where Catholics settled, such as Philadelphia, Boston, and New York. Public schools became a source of conflict because many textbooks and teachers expressed anti-Catholic attitudes. When Catholics established their own schools, Protestant leaders such as Lyman Beecher demanded that Catholic children be required to attend public schools so that they could be properly educated. Protestants like Beecher hoped that if Catholic children went to public schools, they might convert to Protestantism (Kaufmann, 2004).

Mainstream media frequently expressed anti-Catholic attitudes, and by the 1830s an overtly anti-Catholic press was firmly established. By 1860 it included 25 newspapers, 13 monthly or quarterly magazines, and more than 200 anti-Catholic books produced by American publishers (Hunter, 1991). One of the most popular books was published in 1836: *Awful Disclosures of the Hotel Dieu Nunnery of Montreal* by Maria Monk. The book described a secret passageway between a residence for priests and a convent that provided access to the nuns to satisfy the priests' sexual desires. The Mother Superior murdered any babies produced by these liaisons. The author claimed to have been one of the nuns at this convent who was seduced by a priest and became pregnant, but escaped to protect the life of her unborn child. In reality, Maria

Monk had never been a nun and never lived in a convent. The only truthful aspect of this exposé was that Maria was unmarried and pregnant. Although the author (and the publisher) made a lot of money from the book's success, Maria squandered her share and ended up in a brothel; eventually she was arrested as a pickpocket and died in prison (Daniels, 2002).

The numerous anti-Catholic newspapers, magazines, and books fanned the flames of Protestant fears that as more Catholic immigrants became naturalized citizens, they would gain enough political power to expand their influence. Some Protestants known for secular achievements used their fame to reinforce anti-Catholic attitudes. Samuel F. B. Morse, inventor of the electric telegraph and the Morse code, warned American Protestants about a Catholic conspiracy to gain political power (Myers, 1960). Alarmed by such predictions, anti-Catholic organizations such as the Christian Alliance and the American Alliance were established to monitor Catholic activities; they attracted the largest membership in cities containing significant numbers of Catholics (Hunter, 1991). One minister who believed that only a Protestant could be a true Christian preached a sermon entitled "The Duty of Christian Freemen to Elect Christian Rulers" and sent a copy to President Andrew Jackson. Although Jackson knew this minister was one of his political supporters, he wrote back: "Among the greatest blessings secured to us under our Constitution is the liberty of worshipping God as our conscience dictates" (Meacham, 2006, p. 111).

The potato famine (1845–1851) caused a surge in Irish immigration of 1.5 million people and that became a factor in the sudden emergence of the Know-Nothing Party. Two of the party's legislative goals included preventing Catholics from running for public office and extending the residency requirement to 21 years before an immigrant was eligible for citizenship. Because of its anti-Catholic and anti-immigrant rhetoric, the party experienced political success in the 1850s, electing nine governors, 104 of the 234 members of the House of Representatives, and eight of 62 U.S. Senators (Myers, 1960). Despite this success, the party split on the issue of slavery, causing its supporters to look elsewhere for political representation. Many of those who were opposed to slavery would join the newly formed Republican Party.

With the election of Abraham Lincoln, the nation had its first President who was not a member of any particular church, reflecting the status of most Americans, only 20% of whom were members of a church (Lippy, 1994). Lincoln believed that "a non-sectarian Christianity [was] the faith of the nation" (Littell, 1968, p. 35). The two holidays that Lincoln established—a day of Thanksgiving and Memorial Day to honor the dead—were implicitly Christian yet non-sectarian. After the Civil War, anti-Catholicism declined significantly, perhaps because Catholic soldiers fought alongside Protestant soldiers and many gave their lives to the country. As Nord (1995) has written: "The politics of race and Civil War put the politics of anti-Catholicism to rest" (pp. 73–74). Although many Americans would cling to anti-Catholic sentiments, this prejudice would never be the force it once had been.

INCREASING DIVERSITY AFTER THE CIVIL WAR

In 1860, people of British descent were still the majority in America, with 53% of the population, and Germans in second place with 31%, but both groups declined after the Civil War. By 1890, their combined share of the U.S. population was less than 64%, and by 1920 they would barely exceed 25% (Daniels, 2002). Increasing ethnic diversity contributed to the decline of anti-Catholicism because the immigrants arriving after the Civil War wanted to preserve their ethnicity along with their faith, and that meant the presence of churches exclusively for particular immigrant groups. Catholic churches were established for groups such as Italians, Poles, and Lithuanians; Lutheran churches were identified as Danish, Swedish, German, Norwegian, Icelandic, or Finnish. According to Hudson (1973) there were at least 24 different Lutheran immigrant churches.

From 1820 to 1914, 30 million people came to the United States, creating the largest migration of people that the world had yet seen (Chua, 2007). The immigrant churches were unable to meet the needs of these people, causing two Christian organizations to be transplanted from England. The Salvation Army addressed poverty problems for families, and the Young Men's Christian Association (YMCA) focused on unmarried men (Hudson, 1973). To provide these men with an enjoyable indoor activity during winter, one YMCA director named James Naismith invented a game he called "basketball" (Gaustad & Schmidt, 2002).

Increasingly, Jews were migrating to the United States. Most Jews already in America were Reform Jews and most were German, but in the late 1800s Jewish immigrants were coming from southern and eastern Europe, especially Russia. Many were Orthodox, but the majority were secular Jews (Gaustad & Schmidt, 2002). Jewish communities provided financial support to the new arrivals—partly from ethnic solidarity but partly for fear that the new Jews might provoke anti-Semitic reactions unless they quickly could become economically stable.

Although many Swedes immigrated to the Midwest to become farmers, more than 150,000 had settled in Chicago by 1900, making it the largest

Swedish city in the world except for Stockholm. Since only 3–4% of Norway's land was tillable soil, the increasing population forced Norwegians to immigrate. Many came to America in search of cheap farmland and settled in the Midwest. Poles tended to settle in urban areas; more than 100,000 descended on Pittsburgh and New York, while 400,000 chose Chicago (Daniels, 2002).

Finally, over 4 million Italians came to America at this time, more than any other ethnic group, but most were young men who returned to Italy. Immigrants coming to urban areas often would settle in an ethnic enclave, described by Daniels (2002) as "a place where the language and customs of the old country were transplanted, however inexpertly" (p. 170).

Even when they lived in ethnic enclaves, immigrants were not safe from discrimination. Many Armenian immigrants went to California and settled in or near Fresno. They belonged to the Greek Orthodox Church, and when they established their own town near Fresno, they called it "Yettem," which means "Eden." Although they were Christian, Fresno's Christian citizens soon established restrictive covenants on their property to prevent Armenians from purchasing their homes. The Armenians also were excluded from many social organizations—even the YMCA (Daniels, 2002). Yet immigrants continued to establish ethnic enclaves or took over enclaves already established, as when Chicago's "Swede Town" was transformed into "Little Sicily." Despite their choice to live in ethnic enclaves, the word *ethnic* had little meaning for most immigrants; native-born Americans were more likely to use the term. As sociologist Richard Senett explained: "Most European peasants who migrated here had no consciousness when they came of being 'ethnics'"; their sense of ethnicity developed in response to "the badges of inferiority" that native-born Americans projected upon immigrants (Roediger, 2005, p. 18).

German immigrants had the longest history of preserving their cultural heritage while maintaining a dual identity as both Germans and Americans. Because of their economic success and their reputation as hard workers, states made accommodations for them. Daniels (2002) reported that Pennsylvania and other states with large numbers of German residents passed laws allowing public schools to provide instruction in German if a certain percentage of parents requested it, usually 50%. Other immigrant groups such as Poles, Chinese, Japanese, Scandinavians, Jews, and Italians tried to preserve their cultures by establishing language schools that their children attended before or after going to public school. By the late 19th century, opposition to German language in public schools was first expressed in Illinois and Wisconsin, both of which passed laws to regulate academic instruction in German and to mandate English instruction in reading, writing, arithmetic, and U.S. history. In Wisconsin, any school that didn't adhere to the law would not be considered a legitimate school, meaning that attending students would not be in compliance with compulsory education laws. Yet German remained the language of choice in many communities. Before World War I, nearly 25% of all high school students in public schools were enrolled in German language classes (Daniels, 2002).

In response to critics accusing immigrants of not being willing to assimilate, a Polish newspaper editorial said: "It is deplorable that so many Americans object so much to foreign customs. . . . It is not quite at all in accordance with American ideals of freedom." An Italian newspaper agreed: "Americanization is an ugly word [if] it means . . . making the foreign born forget his mother country and mother tongue" (Fuchs, 1990, p. 65). Yet opposition was growing as political leaders such as Teddy Roosevelt were openly critical of "hyphenated Americans." German Americans continued to claim a dual identity until Germany became America's enemy in World War I. Opposition to all things German verged on hysteria as sauerkraut became "liberty cabbage" and German fries were transformed into "American fries" (Kallen, 1924/1970).

German Americans tried to keep a low profile and hoped that life would return to "normal" after the war, but in 1919 the Nebraska legislature banned the teaching of all foreign languages in public schools. When the case of *Meyer v. Nebraska* came before the U.S. Supreme Court, the justices expressed sympathy for the legislature's stated goal of creating a homogeneous citizenry embracing American ideals, but they ruled against the state because of their responsibility "to rule based on upholding the freedoms guaranteed to individuals by the Constitution even when those freedoms contributed to the perpetuation of ethnic or religious diversity" (Fuchs, 1990, p. 70). In this ruling, the court supported the principle of cultural pluralism, even though that term had not yet been defined.

RESPONSES TO DIVERSITY

What had been defined in the early 20th century was the concept of America as a "melting pot." Foreshadowing this concept was a frequently expressed yet ambiguous notion of America as a place where diverse groups interacted with one another and in the process became Americans. Crèvecoeur (1912) said of his adopted country, "Here individuals of all nations are melted into a new race of men, whose labours and posterity will one day cause great changes in the world" (p. 43). Tocqueville (2004) observed: "As Americans mingle, they assimilate. Differences created by climate, origin, and institutions diminish. Everyone comes closer and closer to a common type" (p. 444). In 1908, a Jewish immigrant from England named Israel Zangwill defined and popularized the concept when his play "The Melting Pot" opened in Washington, D.C., to enthusiastic audiences. The play described American immigrants being mixed together in "God's crucible," and one character commented on the result of this "melting" process: "God is making the American" (Zangwill, 1915, p. 33).

The popularity of the concept was not merely in the public mind but in the views of government leaders. An article from the Department of Interior's *Americanization Bulletin* described the United States as a nation that was "fashioning a new people . . . we are doing the unprecedented thing in saying that Slav, Teuton, Celt, and the other races that make up the civilized world are capable of being blended here" (Fuchs, 1990, p. 61). Yet, as with Zangwill's play, people of color were absent from this description. Their exclusion caused many people of color to be critical of the melting pot concept, even before anti-immigrant voices rejected the idea. Congressman Albert Johnson, who would sponsor a racist immigration bill, argued that the melting pot idea was a failure because the foreigners in America were not being Americanized. In a popular book entitled *The Melting Pot Mistake*, Henry Pratt Fairchild argued that efforts to promote assimilation had failed because "the deepest feelings of love and affection of immigrants lay understandably with their ancestral homelands" (Fuchs, 1990, p. 61).

It is not surprising that the search for an alternative to Americanization would bear fruit in Chicago. In 1880, Chicago consisted of about a half a million people, but that number doubled by 1890 and doubled again in the next decade. Of the 2 million people living there in 1900, 75% were foreign born (Kaufmann, 2004). University of Chicago professors such as anthropologist Franz Boas and educator John Dewey were arguing that immigrant cultures were a valuable asset and should be preserved. Jane Addams of Hull House and other leaders of the Settlement House Movement agreed. They viewed immigrant cultures as a "gift" and engaged in conscious efforts to assist immigrants to preserve their language and culture. Dewey argued that if immigrant cultures were preserved, America would benefit by gaining "the best that each [group] has to offer from its tradition and culture . . . so that it shall surrender into a common fund of wisdom and experience what it especially has to contribute" (Kaufmann, 2004, p. 101).

Those rejecting such arguments insisted that immigrants should conform to American ways and accused Dewey, Boas, and others of advocating cultural separatism, but philosopher Horace Kallen refuted this charge. Kallen promoted the idea of "cultural pluralism" as an alternative to the uniformity implied in the melting pot concept. Kallen (1924/1970) rejected the assumption that immigrants needed to be Americanized, which he defined as "the adoption of the American variety of English speech, American clothes and manners, the American attitude in politics. Americanization signifies, in short, the disappearance of external differences" (p. 79). Arguing from a pragmatic perspective, Kallen said that attempts to Americanize immigrants would fail because ethnicity was so deeply engrained: "Men may change their clothes, their politics, their wives, their religions, their philosophies to a greater or lesser extent; they cannot change their grandfathers" (Menand, 2001, p. 392). Kallen rejected the idea that uniformity produced national loyalty, arguing that being an American should mean valuing individuality and human differences. Kallen said immigrants should develop a dual identity by incorporating their cultural heritage into their emerging American identity.

Kallen's arguments, as well as those of John Dewey and others, were not persuasive to most political leaders, and not to many in the general public, in large part because immigrants in the late 19th and early 20th centuries were so different from previous years. By 1910, about 15% of U.S. residents were foreign born, the highest percentage in American history (Eck, 2001), and White Americans did not consider many of the recent immigrants, such as Italians, Slavs, and Jews, to be "White." Immigrants were also more concentrated than ever. At a time when 75% of Americans were rural and only 8% lived in large cities, almost two thirds of the new immigrants settled in cities—one third of them in cities with more than 100,000 people (Kaufmann, 2004).

Although still a small group, by 1910 the number of Jews in the United States had increased to nearly 2 million, and anti-Semitism increased as well. Ancient stereotypes of Jewish pawnbrokers, greedy merchants, and usurious bankers found their way into Broadway plays, popular literature such as the Horatio Alger books, and even school textbooks (Miller, 1976). Mainstream media published numerous articles denouncing Jews as "aliens" incapable of assimilating into American society. Some landlords posted "To Let" signs on available apartments with two additional words—"No Jews." Successful Jews attempting to leave their ethnic neighborhoods encountered Christian homeowners refusing to sell to them because of restrictive covenants. If a prosperous Jewish family was allowed to purchase a home in a wealthy neighborhood, family members could not be members of and were denied admission to country clubs, social organizations, and resorts (Hunter, 1991).

On the west coast, immigrants of Asian descent were the biggest concern. Passed in 1882, the Chinese Exclusion Act ended immigration from

China for 10 years and was renewed for another 10 years; in 1902, Congress made the exclusion permanent. Japanese immigrants came until President Teddy Roosevelt negotiated the Gentleman's Agreement with Japan in 1908. Many Japanese immigrants initially were hired as agricultural workers until they began to purchase farmland; by 1920 they controlled 450,000 acres of land and provided 10% of California's produce (Daniels, 2002). In 1913, the California legislature passed the Alien Land Law, which prohibited anyone not eligible for citizenship from owning or purchasing land, but the Japanese farmers found a solution in the 14th Amendment (Takaki, 1993).

Passed by Congress in 1866 and ratified in 1868, the 14th Amendment was intended to protect the rights of former slaves by declaring that "persons of African descent" were eligible for citizenship, and that "all persons born or naturalized in the United States . . . are citizens of the United States and the state wherein they reside." This statement revised the naturalization law by allowing any resident regarded as non-White to claim citizenship for his or her American-born children. Awarding citizenship to children of foreign-born parents was not a new concept. According to Schuck (2003), it originated in English common law as the legal concept of *jus soli* (law of the soil), but Schuck acknowledged: "The American version of this is probably the world's most liberal" (p. 96). Because the 14th Amendment made citizens of all children born in the United States to Japanese immigrants, Japanese farmers designated their children as landowners. Those with no children paid another family for the right to use their child's name.

In 1920, California's legislature would pass a revised Alien Land Law prohibiting the designation of children as owners or purchasers of land (Takaki, 1993), but the 14th Amendment's guarantee of citizenship for children of all non-White immigrants would encourage the growth of ethnic diversity in the United States. At this time there were 105 million people residing in the United States; 14 million were foreign-born adults with 22 million children who were born in America to at least one foreign-born parent. These parents and children combined constituted one third of the U.S. population (Daniels, 2002).

As for religious diversity, anti-Catholicism persisted into the 20th century. In 1922, Oregon's legislature passed a law that outlawed private or parochial schools and required students to attend public schools. The law was perceived as an attempt to eliminate Catholic schools, but in *Pierce, Governor of Oregon et al. v. the Society of Sisters*, the state argued that its goal was to bring immigrant and native children together in a public school setting where teachers could foster a homogeneous citizenry and promote patriotic attitudes. In its decision, the court asserted that patriotism would be more likely to flourish among immigrants and naturalized citizens if they were free to maintain their faith, their ethnic traditions, and their native language. In affirming the right of Americans to send their children to non-public schools, the justices also affirmed diversity: "In what are essentially private matters, . . . diversity is protected by the Constitution" (Fuchs, 1990, p. 71).

Although some historians regard the 1915 revival of the Ku Klux Klan as an example of heightened anti-Catholicism, others attribute its revival mainly to its anti-immigrant activities. KKK membership declined from a high point of 2 million in 1925 to a mere 100,000 at the time of the 1928 election, and its numbers would continue to decline (Myers, 1960). In 1928, the Democratic Party was confident enough to nominate Al Smith, a Catholic, for President of the United States. Analyzing votes cast in that election does not suggest that Smith's religion was a major factor in his loss. According to Hudson (1973), Smith received more votes than the Democratic candidates for President in 1920 and 1924, and he received a higher percentage of votes (40%) than a majority of Democrats who ran for Congress in that election. After Franklin Delano Roosevelt's election in 1932, Catholics would become visibly engaged in politics and government at all levels—an indication of the growth of religious pluralism in America.

There were too few advocates for cultural pluralism to counter the anti-immigrant activities throughout the United States. The voices of pluralism advocates went largely unheard beyond academic circles and Settlement Houses, but as unions struggled to organize for the protection of workers, they demonstrated an appreciation for the ethnic diversity of their members. Craft unions like the American Federation of Labor (AFL) tended to be anti-immigrant, or at least certain kinds of immigrants. Supporting literacy tests in 1902, AFL leader Samuel Gompers insisted that the desired immigrants—British, Irish, Germans, French, and Scandinavians—wouldn't be affected, but that such tests would eliminate "a considerable number of Slavs and [others] . . . more undesirable and injurious" (Roediger, 2005, p. 81). By contrast, industrial unions made a significant contribution to promoting a greater acceptance of ethnic diversity. Roediger (2005) provided an example from the early 1900s describing the conclusion of a union meeting where members were asked to air their grievances:

> The crowd, described as black and white, Polish, Bohemian, Irish, Croatian and Hungarian, was silent for a time; then a "morbidly shy black girl" rose to say [that] a Polish girl was always taunting her on her color. The two young women were told to stand together. The Polish worker explained, "Well, I did tease her, but she called me a Polack, and I won't stand that." A "hearty, good natured"

collective laugh cleared the international atmosphere. "Ain't you ashamed of yourselves?" the [union] President asked. "Now shake hands and don't bring any more of your personal grievances here." (p. 87)

THE TRIUMPH OF ANTI-IMMIGRANT FORCES

As anti-immigrant lobbying in Washington intensified, it was inevitable that Congress would address this issue. They needed to assuage the fears of many White Americans who were concerned that American society could not continue to absorb races from around the world. The concept of "race" encompassed a much broader range of categories than it does today. People talked about the Irish race, the Greek race, or the Italian race, but when these groups reached the third generation, the belief that such groups constituted a race disappeared (Roediger, 2005). People of color were the only ethnic groups that continued to be viewed in racial terms. A Republican from the state of Washington, Albert Johnson, co-sponsored an immigration bill and lobbied unambiguously concerning the need for it:

> Today, instead of a well-knit homogeneous citizenry, we have a body politic made up of all and every diverse element. . . . Our capacity to maintain our cherished institutions stands diluted by a stream of alien blood, with all its inherited misconceptions respecting the relationships of the governing power to the governed. . . . The United States is our land . . . the day of indiscriminate acceptance of all races has definitely ended. (Daniels, 2002, pp. 283–284)

When Congress passed the Johnson-Reed Act in 1924, it was the nation's first comprehensive immigration law. Also called the National Origins Act, it established quotas based on the national origins of current American citizens. Although European immigration was limited to 150,000 people annually, using current national origins of Americans resulted in preferential treatment for some groups. The law provided generous quotas for immigrants from England, Germany, or the Scandinavian countries, but immigration from most other countries was reduced. Immigration from Japan was prohibited, and Asian immigration in general was virtually excluded (Schuck, 2003). The intent of the law was to limit people with darker skins from immigrating to the United States, including Italians, Slavs, and Greeks. Since the law did not establish quotas for nations in the Western Hemisphere, Mexicans and Filipinos could freely enter the United States. Since the Philippines was now an American territory, Filipinos had the advantage of entering the United

States as "nationals." Attempts were made to restrict immigration from Mexico, but business interests desiring cheap Mexican labor were successful in opposing such efforts (Daniels, 2002).

The 1924 immigration law controlled the flow of immigrants for the next 5 years until the stock market crashed and immigration declined to its lowest levels since the nation began keeping track. Newly elected President Franklin Roosevelt showed little desire to encourage immigration. As Daniels (2002) observed: "There was no New Deal for immigration" (p. 296). From 1932 to 1935, more immigrants living in the United States returned to their native countries than the numbers immigrating to America. Not until the end of World War II would the United States admit at least 100,000 immigrants in a single year.

Despite the lack of immigrants competing for jobs, unemployment remained high, and was even more severe among African Americans. By the end of the 1930s, Blacks living in northern urban areas were twice as likely to be unemployed as Whites, creating a racial disparity that has been sustained or exceeded to the present day (Roediger, 2005). The New Deal didn't do much to address race except for American Indians, and that effort primarily concerned ending a failed approach to the "Indian problem." From the earliest years, the goal had always been to regard Indians as a people needing to become civilized. The first Bible published in America in 1663 was in the Algonquian language (Fraser, 1999). Americans expected Indians as well as immigrants to adopt the language, manners, and customs of the dominant society. When the first census was conducted in 1790, although only American Indians who paid taxes were counted, they were included with White taxpayers. It was not until the 1870 census that Indians were counted as a distinct group (Thornton, 2000).

Several generations of Indian children were taken from their parents and educated in boarding schools where they not only learned the curriculum that White children learned, but learned to dress, talk, and behave like White children (Adams, 1995). In 1928, the Meriam Report concluded that boarding schools and other attempts to "Americanize" Indians had failed; yet the report's authors concluded that the "Indian problem" still could best be addressed through education. Thornton (2000) perceived the Meriam Report as "a turning point" because it initiated a new educational direction by mandating that educational objectives be "more sympathetic to American Indians . . . [by incorporating] aspects of American Indian history and culture into the curricula" (p. 151). Despite the federal government's decision to change its policies and practices toward American Indians, FDR's New Deal did not address Indian issues. In the 1930s, boarding schools declined and more Indian children attended public schools, where the curriculum did not include Indian history and culture.

THE IMPACT OF WORLD WAR II ON DIVERSITY

Once World War II began, there were contradictory messages about diversity. Black and Asian soldiers were in segregated units, but "Brown" soldiers such as Italians and Mexicans were integrated with White soldiers, even though Italy was one of our enemies. Although Germany and Japan were also enemies, German Americans did not attract the kind of hostility they experienced during World War I, but Japanese Americans were regarded with suspicion. In response to President Roosevelt's Executive Order 9066, more than 120,000 Japanese residents were forced to abandon their homes and businesses and kept in relocation camps for the duration of the war, even though two thirds of them had been born in the United States and were American citizens. Almost 40 years after the war, a Presidential Commission concluded that FDR's executive order "was not justified by military necessity" but resulted from "race prejudice, war hysteria, and a failure of political leadership" (Daniels, 2002, p. 303).

Demonstrating the injustice of the negative attitudes toward Japanese Americans, the all-Japanese military unit known as the 442nd Regimental Combat Team emerged as not only the most highly decorated unit in the war, but the most highly decorated unit in U.S. military history. All races and ethnicities sacrificed and served the country well during the war, and their achievements seemed to influence the attitudes of political leaders. In 1943, Republican Presidential candidate Wendell Willkie publicly praised American minority groups:

> Minorities are rich assets of a democracy . . . minorities are the constant spring of new ideas, stimulating new thought and action, the constant source of vigor. Our way of living together in America is a strong but delicate fabric. It is made up of many threads. . . . It serves as a cloak for the protection of poor and rich, of black and white, of Jew and gentile, of foreign- and native-born. Let us not tear it asunder. (Kaufmann, 2004, p. 178)

During the war, numerous events strengthened a sense of unity among the American people regardless of race, faith, or ethnicity. In 1943, a German U-boat torpedoed the Dorchester, a ship carrying American troops. It was so badly damaged that it sank in 20 minutes, listing so severely that many lifeboats were inaccessible and only about 200 of the 904 troops were saved. Although the sinking of the Dorchester was a tragedy, it also would be remembered for the actions of four military chaplains—two Protestants, a Catholic, and a Jew—who gave up their life jackets to save soldiers and were arm in arm when the ship went down. In 1948, the U.S. government commemorated this incident on a postage stamp (Meacham, 2006).

The war also would have its share of ironies. Removing Japanese Americans to relocation camps created a need for more agricultural workers, especially in California, so the federal government negotiated an agreement with Mexico to send workers to the United States to replace the Japanese. Called the Bracero Program, it would continue long after the war ended. Another irony occurred in 1943 when the federal government modified the 1924 immigration law to placate China, one of our allies in the war. The amendment to the law set a quota of 105 Chinese immigrants annually, and they were allowed to become naturalized citizens (Daniels, 2002).

As the horror of the Holocaust became known after the war ended, anti-Semitism was addressed in books and films like *Gentleman's Agreement*— winner of the Academy Award for Best Picture in 1947. Yet some Americans were still not willing to accept religious diversity, especially as fears of "godless communism" grew. In the late 1940s and early 1950s, evangelical Christians lobbied to get a reference to Jesus Christ added to the Constitution and failed, but Congress voted for "In God We Trust" as the nation's motto and for adding "under God" to the Pledge of Allegiance (Meacham, 2006).

Motivated by fears of communism, many Americans regarded a certain amount of conformity as patriotic. The melting pot perspective reached the height of its popularity and frequently appeared in school textbooks (Kaufmann, 2004). Yet in 1955, sociologist Will Herberg published *Protestant–Catholic–Jew: An Essay in American Religious Sociology* declaring that Americans were becoming more accepting of the nation's religious diversity, and that the glue holding all three faiths together was their belief in the Judeo-Christian God. Herberg argued that an "Americanization of religion" had occurred, meaning that members of all three faiths exhibited a considerable overlap in values and perspectives on social issues. Herberg admitted that the majority of Americans still harbored anti-Semitic attitudes, but he argued that it was no longer acceptable to act on them.

This assertion of religious pluralism would be tested in 1960 when the Democratic Party again nominated a Catholic for President of the United States. John F. Kennedy knew he would have to talk to Protestant voters about his faith if he was to win the election. His message to both Catholics and Protestants was that they should not vote for him or against him based on his Catholic faith. His message to Protestants focused on his history of service to America: "Little or no attention was paid to my religion when I took the oath as senator in 1953—as a congressman in 1947—or as a naval officer in 1941. Members of my faith abound in public office at every level except the White House" (Gaustad & Schmidt, 2002, p. 344). Following Kennedy's narrow victory, two U.S. Supreme Court cases would affirm the principle of religious pluralism.

In 1961, Supreme Court justices unanimously rejected a provision in the Maryland Constitution requiring that an individual declare his or her belief in God as a prerequisite for holding office. When this provision was written, it was regarded as liberal since it allowed Catholics and Jews as well as Protestants to hold public office. The Supreme Court ruled that not only did the prohibition in Article VI against a religious test for those seeking public office refer to requiring candidates to belong to a certain faith, but requiring candidates to believe in God violated the Constitutional rights of Americans. Two years later in *Abington v. Schemp*, the Supreme Court heard arguments that priority should be granted to Christianity as the dominant faith in America, as long as tolerance was extended to other faiths, but the justices rejected the argument, saying the Constitution mandated "the extension of evenhanded treatment to all who believe, doubt or disbelieve" (Katz & Southerland, 1968, p. 272).

THE REVIVAL OF CULTURAL PLURALISM

When the racially and ethnically diverse veterans came home from the war, they expected society to change in recognition of the sacrifices that they had made during the war. As with religious pluralism, court cases addressed unequal treatment based on race or ethnicity. In 1946, California courts ruled in *Mendez v. Westminster School District* that it was unconstitutional for public schools to segregate Mexican American children. In 1954, the U.S. Supreme Court reinforced the California ruling in its unanimous decision against racial segregation in *Brown v. Board of Education*. In 1955, Rosa Parks defied Jim Crow segregation, and a year later the successful Montgomery bus boycott ended when the U.S. Supreme Court upheld a federal court ruling against racial segregation in public transportation. With the leadership of the Reverend Martin Luther King, Jr., and the courageous actions of thousands of African Americans, the Civil Rights Movement gained momentum as racial and ethnic diversity provoked some of the most critical issues covered in newspapers and among broadcast journalists.

The efforts of those in the Civil Rights Movement were seen as culminating in the Civil Rights Act of 1964 and the Voting Rights Act of 1965. The success of the Civil Rights Movement would inspire other groups to draw attention to discrimination against their members as they formed organizations lobbying for women's rights, gay rights, and disability rights. Although these groups have experienced some success in their pursuit of social justice and respect for diversity, perhaps the most significant event in the evolution of pluralistic attitudes in American society received far less notice when it occurred in the mid-1960s–the passage of the Immigration Reform Act.

As the 1960s began, the racist 1924 immigration law, with national origins quotas, was still in place. Congress had modified it in 1952 by passing the McCarren-Walter Act over a Presidential veto. Truman's objection was the failure to eliminate the national origins quotas. Congress argued that the more important issue was that the McCarren-Walter Act addressed racism by ending the exclusion of any racial or ethnic group from immigrating to the United States, a critical change if we were to persuade other nations to join America in the Cold War. After Congress overturned his veto, President Truman immediately appointed a Commission on Immigration and Naturalization. In its final report, the Commission recommended the elimination of national origins quotas, but the report came out shortly before the election of Dwight D. Eisenhower. The new president felt no obligation to implement recommendations from a commission appointed by his predecessor (Daniels, 2002).

Although Eisenhower ignored the national quotas issue, a Presidential aspirant in the Senate named John F. Kennedy wrote an essay entitled *A Nation of Immigrants*, criticizing national quotas and calling for immigration reform. After Kennedy's election, 2 years passed before he submitted a proposal for immigration reform to Congress, and he would be assassinated before it was passed. President Lyndon B. Johnson lobbied vigorously for the passage of Kennedy's bill. After some minor modifications, Congress passed the Immigration Reform Act in 1965. It abolished the national origins quotas and established new limitations: a limit on the number of immigrants from each country outside the Western Hemisphere, an overall limit on immigrants from countries in the Western Hemisphere, and an annual ceiling of 290,000 for all immigrants.

The primary change Congress made in the new immigration law was to include an emphasis on family unification by exempting from immigration requirements the spouses, minor children, and parents of American citizens. Although the scholars disagree, some have argued that the exemptions to promote family unification were implemented because many legislators assumed that this provision would benefit the White majority and ensure that the majority of immigrants would continue to be White (Schuck, 2003). If that was the intent, their assumption was mistaken. The law not only resulted in increased numbers of immigrants coming to the United States, but in dramatic increases in the number of Latino and Asian immigrants.

Fifteen years after the implementation of immigration reform, Congress had to revisit immigration issues because of the increasing number of refugees seeking admission to the United States. The Refugee Act of 1980 permitted 50,000 refugees annually to settle in America, but the law also gave the President, in consultation with Congress, the power to admit refugees in excess of this limit. According to Daniels (2002), the limit of 50,000 refugees annually has been exceeded every year. As the 20th century was ending, because of exemptions for family unification and the provision allowing refugees to exceed their limit, the United States was admitting almost 1 million immigrants every year (Moghaddam, 2008). Even with the increased numbers, Shuck (2003) cited historian Jill Lepore reporting that in 1990 the percentage of people in the United States who were non-native English speakers was smaller than it was in 1790.

Why was the 1965 immigration law regarded as a dramatic change in the history of American immigration? For the first 75 years of our nation's existence, the United States denied citizenship to the majority of people around the globe who might have wanted to immigrate here. For another 70 years Asian immigration was limited or excluded. From 1924 to 1965, a racist immigration law ensured that the overwhelming majority of U.S. immigrants would be White people. In the 1965 law, these blatant racial and ethnic restrictions were eliminated, and the consequences were immediate. During the 1960s, 33% of all immigrants were Europeans, 40% were Latinos, 12% were Asians, and the rest were Canadians. By 2000, Europeans accounted for only 12% of immigrants, while 52% were Latinos and 32% were Asians (Schuck, 2003). This changing pattern of immigration has created such a dramatic increase in racial, ethnic, and religious diversity in the United States that Shuck (2003) argued that the 1965 immigration reform law should be regarded as "one of the great turning points in American history" (pp. 75–76).

Although more attention has been given to legislative achievements of the mid-1960s, in 1972 Congress addressed past racist practices in the Indian Education Act. In addition to a provision requiring the inclusion of Indians in affirmative action programs, this law stipulated that Indian tribes possessed certain attributes of a nation; therefore, they had the right to be treated as nations with sovereignty to exercise certain governmental duties and powers over their members, superseding the power of state or local governments. This law mandated that the federal government and federal courts honor provisions of past treaties between the federal government and Indian nations, and stipulated that if treaty language was ambiguous enough to call for interpretation, a court's interpretation should be favorable to Indian nations (Fuchs, 1990).

Beginning with the 1990 census, the federal government permitted people to self-identify as American Indians and no longer required them to produce a tribal number as proof of tribal membership. Compared with the 1970 census, the number of people claiming to be Indian in 1990 tripled, "an increase far beyond what was generated by either migration or births" (Sandefur et al., 2000, p. 41). In Alabama alone, the percent of people self-identifying as Indians increased by 118% from 1980 to 1990 (Kosmin & Lachman, 1993). Some insist that the increased numbers fulfilled the Congressional intent to encourage individuals to reclaim their Indian heritage, but others argue that the increased numbers include many Americans with no cultural connections to a tribe but a genetic connection they are exploiting to make them eligible for affirmative action programs.

In 1970, people of Spanish descent had been allowed to self-identify for the census, and in 1980 the Census Bureau coined the term "Hispanic" to include Mexicans, Cubans, Puerto Ricans, Central and South Americans, and anyone whose family had immigrated from a Spanish-speaking nation (Shorris, 2001). As the number of Hispanics increased, members of this diverse group became more politically active and lobbied to eliminate obstacles that had curtailed their political participation in the past, such as poll taxes, gerrymandered districts, and English literacy requirements. Their success was demonstrated initially by the increasing use of bilingual ballots and by the results of aggressive campaigns to register Hispanics and encourage them to vote. Political activities have been especially effective in states with large Latino populations such as Florida, Texas, and California. In the 1980 election in Texas, 39% of eligible Mexican American voters cast their ballots as compared with only 35% of eligible White voters (Fuchs, 1990). In the 2002 Texas primaries, both Democratic gubernatorial candidates agreed to have a debate in Spanish and another in English (Schuck, 2003). Increasing numbers of Hispanics have been elected to public office. Looking back to the 1950s, Sandefur and colleagues (2000) noted: "With the exception of New Mexico, the number of Hispanic elected officials at the state and federal level could be counted on one hand" (p. 117), but in just 4 decades, more than 5,000 Hispanics have been elected to public office, including 68 mayors. Although the percent of Hispanics in public office doesn't match their share of the U.S. population, Hispanic activism is expected to continue in the 21st century.

Not all Americans have welcomed the political and social changes related to America's increased diversity. In 1981, the Select Commission on Immigration and Refugee Policy issued a report recommending three major goals for overall immigration policy, one of which was that the cultural diversity of immigrants should reflect a cultural diversity consistent with national unity. Even though the statement stopped short of invoking the former national origins quotas, many believed it was intended to encourage the admission of more immigrants from traditional White ethnic groups to offset the large increases in the Latino and Asian populations (Schuck, 2003).

In the 1990s, Congress passed legislation establishing negative consequences for legal immigrants who had not yet become naturalized U.S. citizens, such as laws facilitating deportation of legal immigrants for a variety of causes. By the late 1990s, the number of eligible immigrants seeking naturalization increased significantly, resulting in over 400,000 naturalized citizens each year (Daniels, 2002). As the 21st century began, Schuck (2003) reported that 90% of legal immigrants were coming from nations that permit dual citizenship, and that this influenced the decision of recent immigrants to pursue American citizenship.

Perhaps the most difficult aspect of increased diversity among immigrants today has been the increase in religious diversity. By the 1960s, Americans seemed to have accepted religious diversity and embraced religious pluralism in their attitudes and actions toward members of other faiths, but the "other faiths" were part of the Judeo-Christian tradition. Immigrants since 1965 have represented numerous religions, with only Muslims having a connection to the Judeo-Christian faiths. Chinese Americans have been in the United States for over 100 years, longer than any other Asian immigrants, but most of the Buddhist institutions in America have been built since 1965 (Eck, 2001). According to Schuck (2003), by 2002 there were more than 1,000 Buddhist study centers in the United States serving over 4 million Buddhists.

Some Asian immigrants are Christian, as illustrated by the over 2,000 Korean Christian churches in the United States (Gaustad & Schmidt, 2002), but Asian and Southeast Asian people who have settled here identify with diverse world religions, and their numbers include Hindus, Sikhs, Jains, Muslims, Buddhists, Bahais, and other faiths less well known. Muslims represent the fastest growing faith, with believers coming from Middle Eastern, Asian, and Southeast Asian nations. Although it is difficult to get a precise number, it has been projected that the number of Muslims in the United States today is over 6 million people, surpassing Jews to become the second largest religion in America. As with Buddhist buildings, 80% of the 1,400 mosques in the United States have been established since 1965 (Eck, 2001).

Accepting the diverse faiths of immigrants today is especially difficult for Americans who have always viewed religion in a Judeo-Christian context. Religion has always been an important aspect of American society. For over 60 years, polls consistently have reported that well over 90% of Americans believe in God, about 40% of them attend religious services every week, and more than 30% read the Bible at least once a week (Schuck, 2003). Many Christians are uncomfortable with non-Christians in their communities, and with the increasing presence of non-Christians at the national level. In 1996, the U.S. Navy commissioned its first Muslim chaplain, and that same year the White House hosted a ceremony at the end of the month of Ramadan to recognize the holy day of Eid al-Fitr—the Festival of Fast Breaking (Eck, 2001). Two years later President Bill Clinton sent a letter to the Sikh community applauding their faith's emphasis on human equality and expressing his belief that the increasing diversity of religions was having a positive influence on Americans: "Religious pluralism in our nation is bringing us together in new and powerful ways" (Eck, 2001, p. 7).

According to Gaustad and Schmidt (2002), not all Americans shared the President's view. They quoted an Illinois woman at a public meeting expressing resentment in response to the announcement that a mosque was about to be built in her community; she said that America was "one nation under God, and that's a Christian God. These people have absolutely no right to be here" (p. 418). Other Christians share her sentiments and reject the call for tolerance of diverse faiths. A few Christians have argued that the United States has become hostile to people who believe in a (Christian) God, but Schuck (2003) quoted Michael Kinsley's rhetorical question in response to this contention: "Does anybody really think it is harder to stand up in public . . . and say 'I believe in God,' than it is to stand up and say, 'I don't'?" (p. 288).

One positive response to such religious conflicts can be seen in the number of individuals and churches engaged in interfaith activities; another source of understanding could come from the increased numbers of Americans involved in interfaith marriages. Similarly, the increasing number of interracial marriages may have a positive influence on Americans' attitudes about racial and ethnic diversity. In California, almost two thirds of interracial marriages involved a Latino partner, and demographers predict that by 2050 40% of Latinos in the United States will be multiracial, as will 14% of all Americans (Schuck, 2003). Perhaps children from interracial or interfaith marriages could be a bridge between groups and a model for accepting diversity. Some Americans view President Barack Obama as such a model since he was the child of an interracial marriage and was raised by his White mother and White grandparents. But before attitudes toward racial and ethnic diversity can change, Americans must address long-standing issues that stem from our history of intolerance for diversity.

LEARNING FROM THE PAST—LOOKING TOWARD THE FUTURE

Observers of the American experiment in democracy from the earliest years of the nation until today have wondered how a sense of unity and patriotism could be created from such diverse elements in our population. Tocqueville (2004) observed that European patriotism usually stemmed from an appreciation of the customs and heritage of the country where an individual was born, but with so many foreign-born people in the United States, American patriotism had to be fashioned on a more rational basis:

> How is it that in the United States, whose residents, leaving customs and memories behind, came only recently to the land they now inhabit, where they met as strangers for the first time and where, to put it bluntly, it is scarcely possible for a patriotic instinct to exist—how is it that everyone in the United States takes an interest in the affairs in his town, county, and state as though they were his own? The answer is that, within his own sphere, each person takes an active part in the government of society. (p. 271)

Many Americans in the past and present expect immigrants to conform to a White, middle-class ideal, and one of their main concerns has always been the tendency of immigrants to settle in clusters. In the 1980s, thousands of Salvadorans fled their country to escape the infamous death squads and settled along several blocks in Los Angeles, eventually constituting the largest concentration of Salvadorans in the world except for El Salvador's capital (and largest) city, San Salvador (Daniels, 2002). From the 1980s until the present the Hmong from Laos continue to cluster in communities in the Midwest and in California. Yet Fuchs (1990) argued that clustering was one of two distinct immigrant patterns, and not the more common one, and that neither pattern prevented immigrants from engaging in the process of becoming American:

> A minority of immigrants and their children would separate themselves from the mainstream and live in small ethnic enclaves for at least two or three generations.

A large majority, after establishing ethnic churches, fraternal and mutual aid associations, and ethnic economic networks, would begin to participate in the wider economic marketplace and in the arenas of American politics, and become strongly patriotic in the process. (p. 29)

Fuchs (1990) believes the unifying culture of the United States has always been the "civic culture" established by the founders and based primarily on three principles:

1. Average adults electing representatives to govern them.
2. Everyone in a political community having equal access to participation in public life.
3. Individuals having the freedom to choose how to conduct their private lives (e.g. they are free to choose their religion). (p. 5)

Of particular interest is the third principle since it promotes the idea of cultural pluralism, although Fuchs prefers the term *voluntary pluralism*. Pluralism exists in any society where immigrant families may choose to maintain their cultural traditions while participating in the civic culture of society. Because immigrants were allowed to maintain their cultural and religious identifications while transitioning into the larger society, Fuchs argued that this unofficial pluralism fostered immigrant feelings of patriotism toward their new country.

America's contradictory attitudes toward immigration and diversity are perhaps best captured in the evolution of the Statue of Liberty as a symbol. The statue was first erected in 1886, and at the inaugural ceremony President Grover Cleveland said nothing about the statue as a symbol for immigration (Perea, 1997). The statue was more widely regarded as representing the guardian of the nation's purity, making it a more likely candidate to be an anti-immigrant symbol (Kaufmann, 2004). It was not until 1903 that an Emma Lazarus poem written 20 years earlier and specifically referencing immigration was attached to the statue. Georgina Schuyler, a Lazarus admirer, donated a plaque with the final five lines of "The New Colossus," and it was placed in a somewhat obscure location on an interior wall of the statue. As the poem became increasingly popular with visitors and began appearing in children's textbooks, those wanting to redefine the meaning of this statue as a symbol of America welcoming immigrants lobbied for its relocation (Kaufmann, 2004). In 1945, a new plaque that contained the entire Lazarus poem replaced the original, and it was placed over the main entrance into the statue where it has remained, welcoming newcomers to our shores and reminding all Americans of our history of immigration.

Although the United States receives the most diverse array of immigrants of any nation in the world, diversity is not an issue in the United States alone. In the last decades of the 20th century, Finland's foreign-born population quadrupled; the foreign-born population doubled in Austria, Denmark, Italy, Portugal, and Spain; and in Germany it increased by 64% (Daniels, 2002). Anti-immigrant attitudes in Europe usually are directed at Arabs and Muslims, but American targets are usually Asians or Latinos (Huntington, 2002). Among journalists and pundits, *Newsweek* columnist Robert J. Samuelson (2002) is not alone in complaining about Latino immigrants: "The United States cannot act as a sponge for Mexico's poor" (p. 218).

There are voices on the other side of the issue—people who still embrace John F. Kennedy's vision of America as a "nation of immigrants" that has progressed and prospered because of the people who came here to find a better life. Those Americans who accept the increasing diversity in the United States argue that we must value this diversity if we want our society to benefit from it. Eck (2001) believes that our nation's historic commitment to religious freedom requires Judeo-Christian Americans to be pluralistic in their attitudes toward other faiths, and she concludes with a challenge that encompasses all forms of diversity in the United States: "We must find ways to make the differences that have divided people the world over the very source of our strength" (p. 25). Her challenge is directed not merely at individuals but to Americans collectively who want our nation to continue as a global power in order to promote democracy and American ideals.

The challenge for each American is to develop a more inclusive view of what it means to be an American. Fischer (1999) provided a useful example when describing a trip to San Francisco where he observed a Columbus Day parade that included "Chinese girls wearing Scottish kilts." He concluded: "What could be more American?" (p. 219). On a deeper level, accepting the diversity in the United States is ultimately a question of justice. Americans should be committed to providing education and opportunity to all Americans regardless of group membership. We need to remember the advice given by Alexis de Tocqueville in the early years of our existence as a nation: "It is of great importance in a republic not only to guard society against the oppression of its rulers, but to guard one part of society against the injustice of the other part. . . . Justice is the end of government" (2004, p. 299).

CHAPTER 3

Pluralism and Democracy
Complementary or Contradictory?

As complexity increases . . . those in charge need more and more information to
avoid disaster, let alone arrive close to their chosen destination.

—R. A. Dahl, 1982, p. 52

Combining 13 individual states into one democratic union was a complex
undertaking, as illustrated by the demise of the Articles of Confederation. Yet
18th-century British statesman Edmund Burke claimed that the United States
simply was founded on English ideas and practices that were familiar to the
majority of Americans, whose ancestors came from England. Although few
disputed the truth of his assertion, Norton (1998) has pointed out that even
during Burke's time, the mixture of people in America was quite distinct from
that which existed in England, and became far more influential as the nation
developed, especially when compared with the history of Great Britain.

THE ATTITUDE OF THE FOUNDERS REGARDING DIVERSITY

As described in the previous chapter, the significant diversity in the population of the United States throughout the colonial period increased during the
first years of the new nation. Immigrants settling in cities or building farms
on Indian land represented many nationalities and spoke many different languages, and even those of "English ancestry" included a diversity felt more
strongly at that time among the Welsh, Scottish, and Irish. Immigrants came
from prisons and poorhouses, middle-class homes or upper-class estates, and
they included individuals with religious and political differences. According
to Torres (2006), the founders recognized that the nation's diversity would
need to be accommodated; therefore, their Constitution provided a framework that explicitly promoted religious pluralism and implicitly supported a
pluralist democracy.

Some scholars have disagreed. Berns (1998) argued: "The framers of our Constitution never spoke of multiculturalism, cultural pluralism, or, for that matter, even of pluralism. Such terms were not part of their political vocabulary" (p. 93). Yet there is evidence that the founders were familiar with this concept. Parini (2008) paraphrased a proposition by James Madison in *The Federalist Papers* arguing that shifting power from the states to a central government in the Constitution allowed "the passions of the majority" to be offset by "the forces of pluralism" (p. 41). Berns (1998) admitted that the First Amendment ensured the growth of religious diversity: "By separating church and state . . . the Constitution guaranteed a proliferation of religious sects" (p. 97), a proliferation that would force Americans of diverse faiths to co-exist with one another, a situation promoting religious pluralism. But with the exception of religion, Berns (1998) rejected the idea that the founders were aware of other forms of diversity, and he provided this quotation from *The Federalist Papers*: "Providence has been pleased to give us this one connected country to one united people—a people descended from the same ancestors, speaking the same language, professing the same religion" (p. 93). As noted in Chapter 2, the author of this passage was John Jay, and since there was ample evidence during Jay's lifetime to refute his claim that Americans spoke the same language and shared the same religion, one can only assume that Jay intentionally ignored the evidence, perhaps for political or diplomatic purposes.

In contrast to Berns, Schuck (2003) asserted that the Constitution was and is a source of support for diversity. In addition to promising religious freedom, the Constitution rejected a religious test for public officeholders, thus reinforcing the ideal of religious pluralism. The First Amendment not only promoted religious diversity, but also protected ideas and opinions expressed by those in the minority. Schuck (2003) argued that the founders were well aware of the diversity that existed "among states, regions, groups and interests, . . . and the Framers' constitutional design sought not only to reflect those diversities but to protect and even perpetuate them" (p. 34). Representation in the U.S. Senate was intended to achieve a greater balance of power between large and small states. Provisions related to taxes and matters of commerce prevented strategically located coastal states from using their economic power to exploit states located in the interior. Further, state constitutions were modeled after the federal Constitution, so they also reflected concern for diversity.

The confusion about the Constitution supporting diversity is due in large part to a lack of early enforcement of constitutional principles. For example, Lippy (2006) has explained that despite the explicit protection of the First

Amendment, the concept of religious liberty for Americans "denoted a reluctant and selective tolerance of others . . . [and] tended to refer almost exclusively to the variety of Protestant bodies that staked out a place for themselves on American soil" (p. 89). Religious pluralism developed slowly over the nation's first 2 centuries before Americans finally appeared to accept all three Judeo-Christian traditions—Jewish, Catholic, and Protestant (Herberg, 1955), but Lippy (2006) noted that this acceptance did not eliminate religious prejudice nor did it signify that Americans believed "that all religions somehow had a claim to being true in any absolute sense" (p. 89).

Since 1789 when the Constitution was first implemented, it has been amended to allow more people to participate in our democracy—amendments that granted citizenship to non-White people, that gave voting rights to women, and, most recently, that lowered the voting age to 18 so that those selected to fight our wars could vote for politicians who supported or opposed our involvement in such conflicts. The Constitution's protection of citizens' rights also has been reinforced by legislation such as the 1964 Civil Rights Act and the 1965 Voting Rights Act, with the latter having an immediate impact beyond voting. Torres (2006) reported that by the early 1980s, "unprecedented numbers of black people and Latinos had been elected to every level of government" (p. 168). Representatives from these diverse groups have attempted to shift the discussion from focusing only on individual rights to recognizing the importance of addressing group rights in a democracy. They have challenged the nation to become a more pluralistic democracy.

U.S. Supreme Court decisions also have produced judicial interpretations of our Constitution's concerns for diversity. Based on a review of selected Supreme Court decisions, Strike (2003) identified three emerging themes related to diversity: (1) freedom of conscience, (2) freedom of association, and (3) protecting the marketplace of ideas. The first theme relates largely to religious pluralism because freedom of conscience protects the right of individuals to reject authoritarian demands based on one's spiritual or intellectual beliefs. Whether the source is religious or secular, the commands of conscience can never be regarded as a matter of opinion: "No one's conscience would be greatly troubled by violating one of the Ten Suggestions" (Strike, 2003, p. 80).

The second and third themes relate to various forms of diversity, not just religious groups but racial and ethnic groups, political groups, and others. Freedom of association relates to developing an identity within a group context. In the past, opponents of pluralism demanded an Americanization process that stripped away an individual's sense of racial or ethnic identity, but people persisted in maintaining such an identity while also developing an American identity. For example, many male American Jews continued to wear a *yarmulke* (head covering), not from habit but because in the Talmud it was recommended and was regarded as an expression of humility before God. This practice was more deeply related to identity than simply maintaining ethnic foods or holidays. As Strike (2003) suggested, hearing someone say, "I wear a yarmulke because I am a Jew," is not analogous to hearing: "I like pasta because I am an Italian" (p. 81). Maintaining a sense of identity as part of a group requires a commitment to specific values, beliefs, and behavior.

The third theme is the broadest one, reflecting a concern for the free flow of ideas from all sources, yet with an implicit concern for minority voices. Boxill (1998) argued that a major challenge for culturally diverse democracies is to ensure that the majority does not impose its will on the rest of society to protect its own interests at the expense of one or more minority groups. Kelso (1978) identified pluralists as the people most likely to call attention to the "tyranny of the majority," referring to the abuse of minority rights by majority rule. The majority must be opposed if it denies individuals from minority groups such rights as free speech, free assembly, equal opportunities for employment, and fair housing practices.

INDIVIDUALISM AND PLURALISM

Torres (2006) insisted that all democratic societies have to be pluralistic to some degree because it is realistically impossible to have a completely homogeneous society. Even if racial or ethnic diversity does not exist, there will be other forms of diversity based on gender, socioeconomic status, religion, and ideology; individuals from such groups likely will express views that differ from those of the majority, and a democracy must offer a certain level of tolerance to achieve civic harmony. Only powerful authoritarian states could sustain a monoculture where "everyone has the same worldview, religion, language, eating habits, musical and artistic aesthetics" (Torres, 2006, p. 161). Boxill (1998) proposed that a dominant culture benefits from minority cultures because they are, as John Stuart Mill called them, "experiments in living" (p. 117). Subordinate cultures in a culturally diverse society may offer valuable lessons that could even influence legislation mandating social changes to benefit all citizens.

In the United States, the commitment of pluralists in the 20th century to advocate for minority perspectives has been viewed by opponents of pluralism as advocating group rights over individual rights, but this pluralist commitment has always reflected a concern for protecting individual rights guaranteed in our democracy. As Pai and Adler (1997) have written, one of the foundations of democracy is "a belief in the intrinsic worth of individuals and their unique capacities to become intelligent human beings" (p. 109). The freedom offered to individuals in a democracy is the freedom to develop their intellect and abilities by taking advantage of opportunities the society provides to its citizens. Yet critics have maintained that pluralism stands in opposition to democracy because a democracy consists of individuals not groups. We vote as individuals; we pay taxes as individuals; we run for office as individuals to protect and preserve our individual rights as guaranteed in our democracy. These critics have insisted that when groups are emphasized, individual rights are secondary to group rights, and that group rights could even impair individual freedom if a group demands conformity from its members. The result is that individuals are forced to choose "between democracy that maximizes individual autonomy or pluralism that protects the autonomy of the group" (Appleton, 1983, p. 66).

Appleton described this claim as a false dichotomy since contemporary pluralists do not advocate group autonomy over individuals but advocate for what Fuchs (1990) called *voluntary pluralism*. When Horace Kallen first coined the term *cultural pluralism*, he was arguing for the right of ethnic immigrants to maintain their ethnic identity, but most pluralists today emphasize the right of individuals to choose how much of their ethnic heritage or how much influence from other groups they choose to retain as part of their identity. Appleton (1983) argued that it is as wrong to denounce third-generation Mexican Americans for not being sufficiently Mexican as it is to denounce them for not being sufficiently American. Individuals should not be forced to relinquish their sense of identity or coerced into maintaining an identity that they no longer regard as meaningful. Pluralists believe that citizens of a democracy should have the freedom to control the evolution of their individual identity.

Since differences are a critical aspect of an individual's sense of identity, pluralists promote valuing differences. As Berlin (1991) has written:

> There are many things which men have in common, but that is not what matters most. What individualises them, makes them what they are . . . is what they do not have in common with all the others. Differences, peculiarities, nuances, individual character are all in all. (p. 39)

When individuals identify with a group, pluralists view this as an issue of identity, not conformity. Hoover (2003) argued that identity historically began as a function of birth, with individuals placed in a hierarchical arrangement, but insists this has changed because democracy tends to eliminate hierarchical categories; therefore, people living in democratic societies "experience their identities not so much as something projected onto them by their society but as something inner directed and more individualized" (p. 27).

In a democracy, a person's identity is not established at birth but develops through interactions with others, and that includes people who do not belong to one's identity group. Hoover (2003) does not use the term *identity group* to refer to groups based on a particular ideology or cause, or groups whose members are determined simply by race, ethnicity, gender, and so on. An individual pursues membership in an identity group based on feelings of affinity for the group's values and beliefs, and this affinity is influenced by shared everyday elements such as language, appearance, food rituals, and a framework for living in the world. Hoover (2003) argues that such identity groups "produce unique 'cultures' that give expression to these identities" (p. 26).

Although studies show a tendency for American immigrants to lose much of their cultural heritage and fluency in their native language by the third generation, immigrants still attempt to preserve their culture and their language. In the United States today, 25% of all K–12 students live in a home where a language other than English is spoken, and more than three fourths of them are Spanish speakers (Gort, 2005). Latino parents interviewed by Villanueva (1997) wanted their children to be bilingual so they could continue to communicate with grandparents and other family members. In support of a bilingual approach, Salas (2006) reported that a review of research on bilingual education programs found students in such programs "do as well as or better on standardized tests than students in comparison groups of English-learners in English-only programs" (p. 34). Despite the research, federal policies still emphasize English-only programs for English language learners (ELLs) rather than the more pluralistic bilingual approach.

Many Americans have found it difficult to accept pluralism because they historically have believed that our solidarity as a people is based on a shared national identity. Some have demanded that English be declared the "official language" of the United States, claiming that a growing number of immigrants don't learn English. Crawford (2000) reported on an investigation of an English-only organization that found evidence of a commitment "to resist racial and cultural diversity in the United States" (p. 23). Baron (2000) argued that such organizations have a history that "often masks racism and certainly fails to appreciate cultural difference" (p. 447). Accusations of xenophobia have been raised since Arizona passed its new immigration law in

2010 and banned ethnic studies. These controversies illustrate the ongoing tension over issues of immigration, identity groups, and a national identity.

Over the years, the American belief in the need for a national identity has been reinforced by the melting pot metaphor and by Americanization efforts. When some citizens seem to emphasize their ethnic identity instead of a shared national identity, many Americans view this as being unpatriotic, even anti-American, because they don't understand the role of identity in locating an individual along the human spectrum. Yet there will always be people for whom broad labels such as *human* or *American* are not adequate for creating a satisfying sense of identity.

Hoover (2003) believes that identity begins where it has always begun, with family and neighborhood. Later religion and ethnicity are added, and later still nationality, profession, and even ideology, with the "primary anchors" for identity tending to come from one's affinity with "middle-sized groups" based on religion and ethnicity. Identity groups have always influenced how individuals understand reality and respond subjectively to it. Although the diversity created by identity groups also may result in conflicts, Berlin (1991) explained why there are people who adamantly advocate for maintaining diversity: "To crush all diversity and even conflict in the interest of uniformity is, for them, to crush life itself" (p. 46).

GROUPS IN A DEMOCRACY TAKING CIVIC ACTIONS

In his observations of the new nation, Tocqueville noted that the American way of responding to problems was to have individuals "form a group to do something about it" (Fuchs, 1990, p. 345). Kelso (1978) agreed, asserting that advocates for a pluralistic democracy assume that individuals will form, join, or support groups to lobby for their goals and protect their interests. Fuchs (1990) provided historical evidence that immigrants from diverse racial and ethnic groups tended to form organizations for the purpose of engaging in civic actions. With the availability of the Internet, it has become even easier for an individual to contact and work with groups of like-minded people.

According to Fuchs (1990), the civic actions of ethnic groups have created an alternative process of Americanization that rejects pressures to conform or to be subsumed in a melting pot. He described an alternative process consisting of three stages: (1) forming ethnic or religious organizations to ensure group solidarity, (2) forming other organizations to focus on achieving economic goals, and (3) working with other organizations to develop strategies to increase their political power (pp. 343–344). At each stage, pluralistic attitudes are blended with democratic ideals about the need for active participation in the nation's social and political issues. It is the third stage—the pursuit of political influence—that has been the most controversial. Just as the demand for "Catholic power" in the 1840s aroused Protestant fears, the call for "Black power" in the 1960s aroused White fears. Yet Fuchs has concluded that such political efforts have been both logical and necessary for the Americanization of ethnic groups in our culturally diverse democracy.

Similar to Fuchs, Dahl (1982) argued that "relatively autonomous organizations . . . are a necessary element in a large-scale democracy" (p. 36). Dahl described historical evidence from the aftermath of World War II as democratic forms of government were instituted to replace totalitarian regimes in Italy, Germany, and Japan. As these societies demonstrated, a pluralistic democracy inevitably will have organizations representing the will of diverse groups of people within the society. This same pattern appeared in the former nations of Yugoslavia and Czechoslovakia, as well as Portugal and Spain. Groups with representative organizations in a pluralistic democracy could include identity groups (e.g., based on race, ethnicity, or gender), economic organizations (e.g., business associations, labor unions, or farmers associations), or groups promoting a certain cause (e.g., human rights violations, environmental problems, or poverty issues). Because a pluralistic democracy values diversity, governmental policies and practices will be initiated in response to these diverse groups.

According to Dahl (1982), a primary dilemma for the central government in a pluralistic democracy is to determine an appropriate response to disparate and often conflicting voices competing for resources and governmental actions. Government leaders must respond to diverse organizations without contradicting or violating what they perceive as the general will of the people. The dilemma for diverse groups in a pluralistic democracy is to make their organization effective enough so that their voice is heard and their issues are brought to the attention of the central government. One of the easiest ways to create an effective organization is to adapt organizational models from groups that have already been successful. Fuchs (1990) has described how the National Association of Arab-Americans and the Arab-American Anti-discrimination Committee were modeled after similar groups created by Jewish immigrants.

Although the purpose of these organizations is to speak for the group with one voice, the emergence of competing identity groups may stem from a commitment to different strategies. In the U.S. census, Asian Indians had always been classified as Caucasian/White, but the Association of Indians in America (AIA) successfully lobbied to have the classification of "Asian

Indian" placed under the "Asian/Pacific Island" category for the 1980 census. The new classification gave minority status to Asian Indians, and the AIA firmly believed that Asian Indians could benefit in such areas as employment, housing, and health services. This campaign by the AIA was opposed by the Indian League of America, which feared that being labeled a minority group might arouse hostility against Asian Indians not only from Whites, but from other minority groups (Fuchs, 1990).

Despite such internal conflicts, the history of group organizations lobbying for their constituents has clearly established this mechanism as part of our pluralistic American democracy, but critics do not believe this is the democracy Americans want. Wolfe (2006) acknowledged this debate: "The question Americans face is not whether their society will be democratic but what kind of democracy it will be" (p. 22). Wolfe described the opposite of pluralistic democracy as a diverse society where a dominant group views its own perspective as the only credible point of view and excludes perspectives that are not consistent with its assumptions and goals. Such a narrow ideological framework repudiates pluralism and imposes the will of the dominant group on diverse groups, thus contributing to their disempowerment and oppression. By contrast, a pluralistic democracy attempts to empower individuals belonging to diverse groups. As Kelso (1978) explained: "Pluralism is a form of liberal democracy that seeks to enhance the opportunities for people to participate in politics at the same time that it protects the basic liberties of the individual" (p. 78).

PLURALISM AND DEMOCRACY

Beginning in the 1960s, multiculturalists built the foundation for contemporary pluralism by reviving Horace Kallen's challenge of the assumption that homogeneity was necessary in a democratic society. They rejected a socially constructed concept of race, replacing it with an emphasis on culture. Multiculturalists advocated eliminating the racial hierarchy of privileges and power and challenged Americans to be committed to equal opportunities for all our citizens. Critics of multiculturalism argued that a major flaw in multiculturalists' thinking was their identification of large groups as one culture rather than as consisting of many groups representing diverse cultures. Ceasar (1998) explained that Franz Boas developed the concept of culture to replace the unscientific concept of "race" with a more scientifically defensible term based on observations of the customs and mores of diverse human groups. Using this anthropological concept of culture, Ceasar questioned how one could speak of an "Asian American culture." While admitting that groups such as Chinese Americans and Japanese Americans did represent subcultures in the United States that had blended aspects of their native cultures with American culture, Ceaser said it was absurd to speak of an Asian American culture if one accepted the concept of culture that Boas developed.

Although critics of multiculturalism recognized groups based on differences of race, ethnicity, gender, sexual orientation, and other factors, and even acknowledged that their shared goals and beliefs influenced the identities of group members, most of the critics rejected the idea that group coherence was sufficient for identity groups to claim that they represented a "culture." The response from many multiculturalists was that they simply were recognizing the influence of identity groups and subcultures on individuals, and they advocated that such groups be valued and respected for their contribution to the American mosaic of diversity.

Building on such arguments, pluralists have broadened the mosaic of diversity to include more identity groups in our democratic society. They argue that pluralism is intrinsic to democracy since democratic governments should be committed to individual rights and responsibilities, especially the right of individuals to choose their beliefs, their occupation, and their lifestyle. As Pai and Adler (1997) maintain, pluralism strengthens democracy by promoting "equality of opportunity for all people, respect for human dignity, and the conviction that no single pattern of living is good for everyone" (p. 102). Fuchs (1990) agrees and proposes that the efficacy of pluralism in the United States is documented in the history of immigrant groups engaging in political activities. In achieving their objectives, they also enhanced their loyalty to the nation, prompting Fuchs (1990) to conclude:

> No nation in history had proven as successful as the United States in managing ethnic diversity. No nation before had ever made diversity itself a source of national identity and unity. No nation in history had so eroded the distinction between naturalized and native-born citizens or had made it so easy for aliens from vastly different cultures to become citizens. (p. 492)

American pluralists also have promoted respect for global diversity. Historically, pluralism initially was based on the recognition that human beings had objectives, goals, and values that were shaped by different cultures, and the concept later was expanded to encompass individuals from diverse groups living in a multicultural society. Yet, even though they emphasize diversity, pluralists understand that human differences are not infinite and they recognize aspects that constitute our common humanity. As Berlin (1991) said of human nature, it "must possess some generic character if it is to be called human at all" (p. 80).

The primary difficulty that many Americans have with the presence of diverse groups stems from the historical desire that all Americans share a national identity. Strike (2003) suggested that instead of insisting on a shared national identity, Americans should regard U.S. citizenship as a commitment to a specific set of democratic principles that promote equal justice for all. This notion of citizenship would permit greater diversity of opinion and action, while still respecting all citizens as Americans. "We know that Jehovah's Witnesses who will not salute the flag can still be good citizens . . . that African Americans who work primarily for the betterment of their race are still good citizens" (Strike, 2003, p. 93). Based on this shared commitment to democratic principles, any activity whose goal is to address problems related to people being denied equal justice should be regarded as the noblest act of good citizenship.

Americans have not yet taken this direction. Greeley (2006) described the current situation: "There is more ethnic diversity than ever, and on the other hand more suspicion of strangers among us. . . . The diversity they represent is an affront to our American patriotism" (p. 5). Schuck (2003) also addressed this dilemma, saying of Americans:

> We welcome (or at least tolerate) different ways of speaking, dressing, eating, praying, working, and living. . . . At the same time, however, we increasingly hive ourselves off into gated residential communities and other enclaves where uniformities of economic class and lifestyle mute, conceal, and even banish these differences. It is as if we like the *idea* of diversity more the less we have to *live* with it. (emphasis in original, p. 315)

Although Americans are not yet comfortable with diversity, the nation, as Appleton (1983) stated, is "an interdependent society where the actions of one group affect the well-being of many others" (p. 151). If the United States is to become an authentic pluralistic democracy, the concerns of diverse groups must be heard as a multitude of voices attempting to influence the future of the nation.

The role played by the central government will be a critical factor in achieving a pluralistic democracy. Wolfe (2006) has argued that if benefits and policies controlled by the central government are perceived as largely directed toward one group (e.g., corporate interests) or a few groups (representing those with the most wealth and power), then people will not regard the central government as exhibiting fairness. When diverse groups are valued, their perspectives and concerns are taken seriously. If that is achieved, governmental policies and practices should reward a wider array of its constituents. Wolfe (2006) argued that pluralism was essential for a democracy because "it represents the most effective way to deliver fairness" (p. 117).

Pluralistic theory acknowledges the competitive nature of political activities in a democracy. Torres (2006) described the importance of political participation: "Changing notions of who is entitled to participate politically are critical, as the political arena is an important place in which new groups obtain access to public goods" (pp. 176–177). Groups can be marginalized because of lack of resources (e.g., low-income families), lack of members (e.g., Native Americans), or lack of a cohesive organization (e.g., Latinos). Marginalized groups will encounter greater difficulties in pursuing their political goals even in a pluralistic democracy. The existence of marginalized groups is a problem in any democracy, but it needs to be openly addressed in a pluralistic democracy.

The success of advocates to gain better education for children with disabilities illustrates what can happen when a marginalized group becomes empowered. Instead of being enrolled in public schools, most American children with disabilities historically were kept at home or sent to segregated institutions. From 1930 to 1960 the number of children with disabilities increased dramatically, which led to more research on their needs. From 1948 to 1956, the number of public schools providing special education programs increased by 83% (Osgood, 2005). In the 1960s, researchers coined the term *learning disability* and identified conditions that interfered with a child's ability to learn. Parents and other advocates for children with disabilities pursued legal remedies, resulting in favorable court decisions and state legislation.

In 1975, the federal government passed the Education for All Handicapped Children (PL 94-142) Act, which required public schools to educate students with disabilities in the "least restrictive environment." Studies reported that students with physical and mental disabilities had higher academic achievement when they were integrated into regular classes than when they were taught in separate classes (Hines, 2001; Kochhar, West, & Taymans, 2000). Yet many schools still resisted change, and segregation for special education students persisted.

In the 1990s, disability advocates began arguing for the merger of regular education and special education in schools and in preparation programs for teachers. They used the term *inclusion* or *full inclusion* to lobby for total integration of students with disabilities in regular education classrooms (Kavale & Forness, 2005). Their efforts were assisted by a series of court decisions that cited civil rights laws to rule in favor of families that had children with disabilities, ordering schools to adapt regular classrooms to meet the needs of these students (Osgood, 2005). Despite court rulings, the debate over how to educate students with disabilities has continued, but advocates representing the disability community have gained both knowledge and skills in the process and continue to be effective as they pursue their goals.

PROBLEMS OF PLURALISM IN A DEMOCRATIC SOCIETY

Many Americans express some version of the belief that we are a nation of immigrants, but Vickers (2002) has written that Americans are comfortable with this assertion only when "the consequences of migration do not include the dilution of their sense of the nation" (p. 22). Further, assumptions about the need for homogeneity, combined with the abuse of such democratic principles as equality and majority rule, have resulted in a form of democratic racism that has perverted a major goal of a democracy—to provide a just society for all citizens. In response, racial minorities formed organizations to confront racism, to promote pluralism, and to challenge our democracy to live up to its ideals. Identity groups that represent women, gays and lesbians, people with disabilities, and others have taken a similar approach.

Opponents of pluralism have insisted that these identity groups should be focused on individual rights instead of demanding group rights. Yet the history of ethnic groups in the United States reveals that immigrants have always formed organizations to lobby for rights and resources for their group (Fuchs, 1990). In response to critics who blame pluralists for perpetuating "the problem of diversity," pluralists argue that diversity is a reality that must be accepted and that the larger issue is the need for our diverse, democratic society to value multiple perspectives in order to gain the benefits of that diversity. Although these advocates have acknowledged the historic pattern that ethnic Americans tend to maintain less of their cultural heritage from one generation to the next, they also recognize that ethnic individuals typically retain some connection to their group. Pluralists support this choice by advocating for the value of diversity and rejecting demands for conformity.

Berns (1998) has asserted that the views of some groups cannot be reconciled with Western values. He criticized Muslims for not upholding the principle of free speech for those who are critical of Islam or its prophet Muhammad. Berns referred to the denunciation of Salman Rushdie, who faced death threats for his irreverent depiction of Muhammad in his novel *The Satanic Verses.* Muslims also have been criticized for their violent response to cartoons satirizing the Muslim faith and Muhammad that appeared in newspapers in Denmark before being reprinted in dozens of other countries.

What Berns and other critics often have not acknowledged is that Islam, like other world religions, includes adherents with diverse views. In visiting a variety of American Islamic websites, such as the Islamic Society of North America, the Islamic Supreme Council of America, the American Islamic Congress, and the Muslim Student Association, one finds comments supporting diversity and expressing the willingness of Muslims to be part of a pluralistic society. These websites all denounce terrorism, with one site arguing that most of the deaths resulting from terrorism have been Muslims. The websites address other issues, such as explicitly denouncing violence, encouraging assimilation not separatism, advocating for tolerance and peace, encouraging mutual respect for those of other faiths, and promoting inter-faith activities.

Many of the criticisms Berns (1998) expressed with regard to a multicultural society would seem to apply more to hate groups than to minority groups. Because of the plethora of hate groups in the United States, it is important not to confuse them with identity groups. Identity groups do not advocate causing harm to other groups, but are committed to preventing harm to their own group members and creating a safe space for them to function in the world. Hate groups like the Ku Klux Klan or the Aryan Nation may appear to offer a sense of identity, but such groups go beyond affirming the identity of their members. By engaging in verbal and physical attacks on members of other groups, such as Blacks, gay men and lesbians, Jews, and immigrants, hate groups contradict a critical purpose of identity groups by denying to others the safe space they claim for themselves.

Hoover (2003) criticized other so-called identity groups that may not engage in violence but still inflict harm on other groups. The "Sons of Confederate Veterans" insist that their group is intended only to honor their ancestors' struggle against a perceived threat to southern views about states' rights, and that their purpose is largely to maintain a sense of pride in southern cultural history and military achievements. Yet if they are to be credible in claiming not to be racist, they cannot condone or promote displaying the Confederate flag in public buildings and public spaces. Hoover (2003) observed that celebrating a symbol that so blatantly represents slavery and racism to African Americans was a malicious and harmful act.

Other problems for pluralism in a democracy relate to the access groups have to all aspects of society. Dunne (2003) discussed how diverse groups operate in different societal spheres, such as schools, the economy, communications media, health services, organized sports, and religious institutions. These spheres are largely autonomous because each has unique attractions, functions, and demands. If a diverse society is pluralistic, members of diverse groups will participate in each sphere, but injustice occurs in any sphere where their needs are not equitably served. For example, Dunne (2003) wrote that when corporations control communications media or when politicians serve the interests of business to the detriment of consumers, the needs of many people are not served. Such conditions violate not only pluralism but democratic principles. As Dunne (2003) observed:

> Democracy is endangered when the same people come to wield influence in all spheres—as happens when the rich may use their wealth to purchase political patronage (irrespective of persuasion), and better health care (irrespective of need), and a better education for their children (irrespective of need, interest or talent). (p. 109)

To be effective, organizations representing diverse groups must operate successfully in all the different spheres; if they fail in this, it could lead to injustices. Dahl (1982) suggested that failure could occur if: (1) individuals have unequal access to representative organizations; (2) some organizations have a disproportionate share of resources, affecting their influence on decisions; or (3) organizations with a large membership have more influence than smaller organizations (pp. 82–84). Such problems could result in a majority group denying the rights of a minority group despite the efforts of the organization representing the group. Reinforcing Dahl's point, Boxill (1998) has argued that a major challenge for a culturally diverse, democratic society is to ensure that a majority group does not impose policies or practices that protect its own interests at the expense of one or more minority groups. In such cases, Dahl (1982) believes that the central government must intervene. The intervention could be legislation, an executive order, or a court decision, but the purpose should be to protect democratic principles and affirm the autonomy and value of minority groups.

As Kelso (1978) has noted, pluralists in the United States have been primarily responsible for drawing attention to the "tyranny of the majority" in terms of the abuse of minority rights by majority rule. Yet some opponents of pluralism have claimed that minority groups have managed to impose their will on the majority. These opponents have denounced affirmative action, bilingual education, and other programs intended to promote access and opportunity for minority group members. They have accused such programs of violating the American ideal of meritocracy, resulting in incompetent

individuals being hired for jobs or enrolled in colleges because of a mis-
placed concern for group rights over individual achievement. Such programs
have been accused of unfairly rewarding minorities, leading to divisiveness
among the American people. Some pluralists have responded by noting that
the evidence for such accusations is largely anecdotal rather than based on
statistical analysis. They question the claims of power and advantage for minority groups since the definition of a "minority group" describes a lack of
power relative to the majority. Pluralists argue that the larger issue is the use
of power by the majority, and the need to oppose the actions of the majority
if they deny individual rights to members of any group.

The concept of a pluralistic democracy has been criticized as unrealistic
because wealthy corporations and individuals inevitably will have a disparity of power and will use their resources and influence to their benefit. Kelso
(1978) has pointed out that this is not just an issue for pluralistic democracies: "The problem of overcoming cultural norms that reflect and reinforce
disparities in power among different elements in society is not a difficulty
unique to any one form of democracy" (p. 166). Wolfe (2006) emphasized
one of these disparities: "Americans have begun to experience a rather dramatic shift toward injustice in recent years as income inequality has risen
sharply" (p. 139). Harvard psychologist Howard Gardner has stated the point
bluntly: "Tell me the ZIP code of a child and I will predict her chances
of college completion and probably income" (Schuck, 2003, p. 298). Wolfe
(2006) argued that the growth of poverty and inequality was perhaps the biggest threat to achieving a more pluralistic democracy in the United States.
He also observed that the trend toward increased inequality was a result of
policies enacted by both Democrats and Republicans, but that Republican
policies arguably had a greater impact.

Group disparities regarding income and resources are one outcome of
discrimination against certain groups, and Torres (2006) argued that when
such inequities exist, a pluralistic democracy must pay attention to group
rights. Identity groups exist to advocate for a group's interests and to confront negative actions toward the group from those in power. Yet some critics
claim that the goal of justice is lost in the pursuit of resources. Levy (2009)
affirmed this point:

> Identity politics isn't much concerned with abstract ideals, like justice. It's
> a version of the old spoils system: align yourselves with other members of a
> group–Irish, Italian, women or whatever–and try to get a bigger slice of the
> resources that are being allocated. (p. 80)

Most White Americans are reluctant to acknowledge the function that identity groups serve; instead, they still persist in the assumption that to reduce conflicts we must de-emphasize identity groups and focus on individuals. Hoover (2003) suggested that the United States needs a new framework that recognizes competition and potential conflict between groups and provides processes to resolve conflicts without resorting to violence. Any proposal for such a new framework must include a clearly defined role for government.

THE ROLE OF GOVERNMENT IN A PLURALISTIC DEMOCRACY

Although Schuck (2003) agreed that maintaining one's ethnic heritage is an acceptable goal, he argued against that goal being promoted by government policy or in public schools. When immigrant children attend school, Schuck believes they must learn how to become citizens, and that requires a focus on enhancing their English language abilities, receiving accurate content on American political institutions, and understanding fundamental civic principles of American society. By contrast, Dunne (2003) argued that the state must not be neutral toward minority groups in a diverse society. If the state offers little protection for the beliefs, values, and aspirations of a minority group, it is inevitable that a dominant group will implement oppressive policies and practices. If a diverse nation wants to become pluralistic, it must offer minority groups not only moral support, but resources. Without such support, minority groups may succumb to assimilation demands that often lead to a loss of power, cohesiveness, and identity.

This argument can be traced back to the founding of the nation. In *The Federalist Papers* (No. 10), Madison argued that the proposed Constitution would protect the people from "an interested and overbearing majority" who might impose their "superior force" on one or more minority groups in the society (Parini, 2008). When a central government affirms minority groups, it provides them a sense of safety and security. Dunne (2003) observed that if minority groups felt secure, their members would be more likely to engage in critical reflection about their sense of identity, creating more openness toward other groups and a greater receptivity in general to outside influences. Dunne (2003) concluded: "Responsiveness to differences is the only way to worthwhile political unity; without it, the [diverse society] invites disaffection and fragmentation" (p. 108).

Many observers have noted the growth of pluralistic attitudes in the various spheres of American society. According to Schuck (2003), leaders in public and private spheres have expressed their acceptance of diversity and acknowledged the need to promote pluralism:

> Leading politicians in both parties as well as educational, corporate, and minority elites have mastered diversity rhetoric. . . . In the pantheon of unquestioned goods, diversity is right up there with progress, motherhood, and apple pie. (pp. 11–12)

As an illustration, Shuck cites the first inaugural address of President George W. Bush, a self-described "compassionate conservative." In this excerpt, Bush abandons traditional assimilation rhetoric to espouse a pluralistic interpretation of what it means to be an American: "America has never been united by blood or birth or soil. We are bound by ideals. . . . Every immigrant, by embracing these ideals, makes our country more, not less American" (Schuck, 2003, p. 12).

Yet even some people who accept pluralism are opposed to the idea of a pluralistic democracy because of problems they regard as inherent in this form of government. Dahl (1982) argued that the central government in a pluralistic democracy must acknowledge the inevitability of conflicts stemming from its defects and identify strategies to make good decisions in response to competing needs. Another major issue for a pluralistic democracy is the extent to which society supports centralization vs. decentralization of power and decision making. A pluralistic democracy requires decentralization of power in order to give a degree of autonomy to organizations representing diverse groups. Yet there must be sufficient power for the central government to intervene in situations where the democratic rights of certain citizens are denied or diminished by a majority group or by a coalition of groups. For example, if an organization representing the dominant group tried to establish new requirements related to citizenship, employment, or holding public office that explicitly or implicitly would create obstacles for equitable participation by individuals from one or more minority groups, the central government would need to intervene to restore these rights to the minority individuals.

In addition to protecting diverse groups, Kelso (1978) argued that government officials in a pluralistic democracy should be advocates for marginalized groups, "defending and even organizing interests for groups like the poor . . . who presently lack political clout" (p. 27). Such advocacy would require some government bureaus to assist groups in lobbying for political changes or to oppose legislative actions that were detrimental to the marginalized groups. Although blurring the line between public and private power, such actions would promote the ideal at the heart of the political process—a competition of ideas. American history provides examples of groups created and supported by the government that became effective organizations, such as the Chamber of Commerce—initiated by the Department of Commerce and Labor in 1912—and the Farm Bureau—initiated subsequent to a 1914 program disseminating agricultural information (Kelso, 1978).

According to Dahl (1982), conflict is inevitable in a pluralistic democracy because issues of self-interest and a cynicism toward government often will derail organized efforts to achieve social justice. Wolfe (2006) has argued that the majority in any democracy will not always support actions intended to promote social justice. At the local, state, and national levels, organizations representing diverse groups will articulate their demands for governmental action and resources, but in a weak pluralistic democracy a small number of organizations or groups may have far more resources and power than the others. A pluralistic democracy is strengthened when there is less disparity of power and resources between diverse organizations, allowing them to compete more effectively. In a strong pluralistic democracy, all organizations representing diverse groups would have access to government officials to ensure a fair competition in the marketplace of ideas. Under such conditions, a diverse democratic society benefits all of its members.

THE GLOBAL CONTEXT FOR A PLURALISTIC DEMOCRACY

In the history of the world, diverse cultures have always existed, alternating between peaceful co-existence and wars of conquest. In the 19th and 20th centuries, these nations found it increasingly difficult to respect their diverse traditions and live in peace, resulting in many conflicts, including two world wars in the 20th century. Shortly before World War I, British author G. K. Chesterton (1906/1942) explained how and why all nations should appreciate diversity:

> It is a great mistake to suppose that love unites and unifies men. . . . The thing that unites men and makes them like to each other is hatred. Thus, for instance, the more we love Germany the more pleased we shall be that Germany should be something different from ourselves. . . . But the more we hate Germany the more we shall copy German guns and German fortifications in order to be armed against Germany. The more modern nations detest each other the more meekly they follow each other; for all competition is in its nature only a furious plagiarism. As competition means always similarity, it is equally true

that similarity always means inequality. If everything is trying to be green, some things will be greener than others; but there is an immortal and indestructible equality between green and red. (pp. 179–180)

With the advent of the European Union (EU), these nations have gone beyond appreciating diversity to create an economic and political relationship based on a willingness to trust one another in order to compromise and collaborate for their mutual interests. Rifkin (2004) described the changes brought about by this new European vision that emphasizes "community relationships over individual autonomy, cultural diversity over assimilation, quality of life over the accumulation of wealth . . . and global cooperation over the unilateral exercise of power" (p. 3). The EU is the culmination of historic efforts that intensified after World War II to affirm the diversity represented by European nations.

The 18th-century German philosopher Johann Gottfried Herder was one harbinger of pluralistic thought. Focusing on diverse global cultures, Herder rejected arguments advocating for uniformity among people and nations based on a belief in a universal human nature. Instead, Herder argued that such a belief reduced human beings to the lowest common denominator and obscured the specific ideals that animated individual lives and dreams. "Herder and his disciples believed in the peaceful coexistence of a rich multiplicity and variety of national forms of life, the more diverse the better" (Berlin, 1991, p. 245). Reflecting Herder's ideas, the EU has promoted the acceptance of diversity within a broad concern for human rights, an acceptance perhaps more easily achieved because the EU nations consist of democratic societies. Schuck (2003) argued that totalitarian societies are more likely to view diversity as a problem, and in those societies minorities are more likely to be subjected to blatant oppression.

Accepting diversity has become a more critical human rights issue because of global migrations. Torres (2006) reported that in democratic nations, most of the changes pertaining to diversity reflect a pluralistic approach rather than a traditional emphasis on assimilation. Some scholars want to eliminate the term *ethnic group* as a useless category for dividing human beings (Young, 2003). Yet Hoover (2003) has observed: "It is commonly noted that even while political democratization appears to be on the march globally, there is also a groundswell of movements emphasizing distinctions and differences among humans" (p. 25). These human distinctions include not only race and ethnicity, but also linguistic, nationalist, and religious differences.

Hoover (2003) observed that some scholars are surprised by the increase in advocates for both democracy and pluralism because of their assumption that "as societies democratize (as equality of rights and access to decision making are maximized), distinctions between persons due to culture, race, faith or ethnicity will be deemphasized" (p. 25). As minorities in democratic societies persist in identifying with a particular group, this does not seem to be happening. Young (2003) predicts that pluralism will continue to gain more global adherents. As for Americans, Torres (2006) has predicted that the United States will evolve into a more pluralistic democracy: "There is good reason to believe that, despite contemporary obstacles, notions of who is entitled to have a voice in public affairs will continue to become more inclusive in the future" (p. 177).

CHAPTER 4

Diversity and Discrimination
The Argument over Affirmative Action

> In America, many marginally competent or flatly incompetent whites are hired every day—some because their white skin suits the conscious or unconscious racial preference of their employer. The white children of alumni are often grandfathered into elite universities in what can only be seen as a residual benefit of historic white privilege. Worse, white incompetence is always an individual matter, while for blacks it is often confirmation of ugly stereotypes.
> —Shelby Steele, 1997, p. 133

Affirmative action has aroused hostile responses from many White people (especially males) in part because it has drawn attention to the history of White male supremacy and unearned White privileges. This has pricked White guilt, provoking angry denials of a history heretofore shrouded in myths of the American dream. Critics have attempted to revive this dream by demanding that we re-establish the concept of rewarding individuals based on merit and hard work, as if in the past hard work was always rewarded.

The reality is that inequities related to race, gender, and social class already existed when the United States of America began its independent existence. They were created during a colonial period that included the enslavement of Africans, the use of deception and coercion to claim Indian land, the exploitation of workers (especially immigrants) living in poverty, and the denial of civil rights to women. One could argue that White privilege became official U.S. policy in 1790 when Congress passed the naturalization law restricting citizenship to people who were "White," leaving it up to the U.S. Supreme Court to decipher obscure terms and debate complicated racial theories to decide who was qualified to be "White." An understanding of this history is essential to appreciate the context in which affirmative action first was proposed as a necessary remedy.

EFFORTS TO COMBAT DISCRIMINATION

Former slave Frederick Douglass was one of the first proponents of affirmative action for Black people. Similar to Martin Luther King, Jr., Douglass often emphasized that Whites should focus on a person's character and not his or her skin color, but during the Reconstruction period, he also advocated for federal legislation to protect Black civil rights. In an article defending the 15th Amendment's protection of Black voting rights, Douglass sounded like a contemporary affirmative action advocate, expressing his hope that at some future time Blacks would "cease to require special efforts to guard their rights and advance their interests as a class. But that time has not yet come, and is not even at the door" (Rubio, 2001, p. 39).

After Black gains during Reconstruction, actions that ranged from poll taxes to lynching eliminated any hope for racial equity. In 1896, the U.S. Supreme Court added its approval of racial inequities in the *Plessy v. Ferguson* decision, which permitted Whites to have separate facilities far better than those available to Blacks, since the term "equal" in "separate but equal" did not refer to quality. If Black children and White children both had schools to attend, they were provided an "equal" education, despite differences in facilities and funding.

One of the earliest and most prolific scholars writing about the need to address racial discrimination in the United States was W. E. B. Du Bois. His Harvard doctoral dissertation on the slave trade was published in 1896, and 3 years later he published a study of Black people in Philadelphia. As the new century began, Du Bois greeted it with this prophecy: "The problem of the Twentieth Century is the problem of the color line" (Du Bois, 1903/2003, p. xli). After ten more books and countless articles, Du Bois was in pursuit of funding for an ambitious study of Black people throughout the United States, but he was pre-empted by the decision of the Carnegie Corporation to fund a study of race in American society, with a Swedish economist named Gunnar Myrdal selected to lead the research. Although Du Bois was not invited to work on the project, he recommended several young Black scholars who were chosen to be part of the research team that would produce Myrdal's *An American Dilemma: The Negro Problem and Modern Democracy*, published in 1944 (Lewis, 1993). The book established the foundations for subsequent efforts to address race problems at all levels of American society.

After World War II, the G.I. Bill rewarded veterans with unprecedented benefits that provided the opportunity to achieve middle-class status. Rubio (2001) noted that each veteran was eligible for "free college education, low-cost housing loans, a weekly unemployment benefit . . . and jobs in the federal government" (p. 118). Universities and colleges chose to reassert racism and White privilege by denying admission to Black veterans. The Veterans Administration (VA) guaranteed housing loans to veterans, but the banks rejected Blacks for Federal Housing Administration (FHA) loans. The prosperity achieved by White veterans while veterans of color were discriminated against exacerbated racial segregation in America, as could be observed in the growth of all-White suburbs, with Blacks being restricted to the central cities. In 1947 alone, the VA guaranteed 3,229 loans, but only two Black veterans received these loans (Katznelson, 2005). Examining the effects of FHA policies and practices, sociologist Charles Abrams said the FHA "undermined the old pattern of heterogeneous neighborhoods in communities from coast to coast where people of mixed races and mixed religions had been living nearby . . . without a qualm or a quibble" (Rubio, 2001, p. 123).

For many years after the war, veterans accounted for almost half of college enrollments (Rubio, 2001). In 1947, about 20,000 Black veterans attempted to enroll in college but could not find a campus that would accept them, and as many as 50,000 additional Black veterans who were qualified to enroll in college did not even try (Katznelson, 2005). As with other young Blacks, the best opportunity available to Black veterans was to enroll in Black institutions of higher education, yet most of these colleges were small—half of them enrolling fewer than 250 students and all of them accounting for only 3% of the enrollments in higher education (Katznelson, 2005). There were so many Black veterans applying that even Black institutions had to reject over half of them because of insufficient space. Meanwhile, White colleges and universities, especially state universities, had the resources to expand enrollments and accommodate returning White veterans.

Katznelson (2005) reported that the G.I. Bill spent over $95 billion to reintegrate 16 million returning veterans, mostly White, into the society and the economy. As White veterans were being rewarded for their service to their country, Black veterans struggled to find a job, just like other Blacks. In response to widespread unemployment among Blacks during a time of prosperity, the NAACP wrote to the American Federation of Labor, challenging them "to take *affirmative action* to end the various forms of racial discrimination" (Rubio, 2001, p. 125, emphasis in original). Analyzing the impact of the G.I. Bill, Katznelson (2005) concluded: "This legislation created middle-class America . . . but almost exclusively for whites" (pp. 113–114).

African Americans took hope from progress reflected in the 1954 *Brown v. Board of Education* decision, in which the U.S. Supreme Court overturned *Plessy v. Ferguson* and prohibited segregation, and in 1956 Black people were encouraged by the successful bus boycott in Montgomery, Alabama, as

Dr. Martin Luther King, Jr., and the Civil Rights Movement were propelled into the public eye. In 1961, as the Civil Rights Movement gained adherents of all colors, President Kennedy issued Executive Order 10925—prohibiting government contractors from discriminating against job applicants based on race, religion, or national origins. Every President since Franklin Delano Roosevelt had issued executive orders prohibiting discrimination by federal contractors, but they were largely ineffective since they relied on employees coming forward to file complaints, and most workers of color would not file a public charge of discrimination for fear of retribution. Comparing this Presidential directive to the earlier executive orders, Kellough (2006) noted that all them directed employers not to discriminate, but there was one critical difference: "Kennedy supplemented that approach by requiring employers *to take specific actions* to promote greater equality of opportunity" (p. 30, emphasis in original).

Employers with federal contracts were required to file compliance reports periodically and could be excluded from future contracts if they failed to comply with the executive order; in addition, the Department of Justice could prosecute employers for violating their federal contract. With Vice President Lyndon Johnson chairing the new Contract Compliance Committee, the emphasis was not on punishing employers but on encouraging them to engage in meaningful efforts to promote equal opportunity at the workplace (Kellough, 2006). Kennedy's use of the term *affirmative action* meant that eliminating discrimination would require more than promises not to discriminate. As Benokraitis and Feagin (1978) noted, affirmative action meant businesses taking aggressive actions "to remove all barriers, however informal or subtle, that prevent access by minorities and women to their rightful places in the employment" (p. 1). Unlike other executive orders, there was an immediate impact. Kellough (2006) reported that employment of African Americans in the federal government rose by 13.1% during the Kennedy administration.

In 1963, shortly after Martin Luther King, Jr., led the Birmingham March, President Kennedy filed a bill addressing racial discrimination that would become the Civil Rights Act. President Johnson would sign it on July 2, 1964, and the following month he filed the Voting Rights bill, which was passed by Congress 5 months later. Title VI of the Civil Rights Act prohibited job discrimination by any organization receiving federal funds, including federal contractors, and Title VII prohibited discrimination by private employers, labor unions, and employment agencies. The Civil Rights Act established the Equal Employment Opportunity Commission (EEOC) to enforce the implementation of affirmative action plans, but southern senators filibustered the bill for what was then a record 83 working days until EEOC was stripped of its cease-and-desist power and its authority to bring discrimination lawsuits against employers. The only role remaining was for EEOC to monitor job discrimination in public and private sectors and to be a conciliator (Sterba, 2003). In the first EEOC annual report in 1966, 60% of discrimination complaints alleged racial bias and 37% alleged gender bias (Rubio, 2001).

To address the enforcement deficiency of the Civil Rights Act, President Johnson issued his own Executive Order 11246 in September 1965, which restated Kennedy's affirmative action mandate and assigned enforcement responsibility to the Department of Labor (DOL). The DOL demonstrated its commitment to equal opportunity by sending representatives to college campuses with significant minority enrollments to recruit minority applicants. The DOL also contacted minority organizations and advertised its available positions in minority media (Kellough, 2006). Two years later President Johnson issued his Executive Order 11375 to eliminate an oversight by mandating the inclusion of women in Equal Employment Opportunity policy. EEOC was instructed to collect employment data on women as well as minorities to monitor the progress of both groups (Kellough, 2006).

IMPLEMENTING THE AFFIRMATIVE ACTION MANDATE

The ultimate goal of affirmative action was to eliminate blatant disparities between White males and minorities and between men and women with regard to employment, salaries, and occupational diversity. It affected private employers with 15 or more employees, labor unions, employment agencies, and federal, state, and local governments. Employers could not reject applicants, fire employees, or discriminate against employees based on race, religion, ethnicity, or gender. Employers could not segregate their employees or limit them in any way that adversely affected their employment status. Although preferential treatment was considered a legitimate strategy to redress past discrimination, Section 703(j) stated: "Nothing in [Title VII] shall be interpreted to require any employer . . . to grant preferential treatment to any individual or to any group." This rule applied even when the total or percentage of employees of color or of women was less than the total or percentage of people of color or of women available in the workforce of the community, state, or geographical area (Leiter & Leiter, 2002).

The construction industry was an early target of affirmative action efforts because of its history of blatant racial discrimination. The construction companies blamed the trade unions, whose history of denying membership to racial minorities was at least as bad as the dismal record of minority employment in the construction industry. As Kellough (2006) wrote: "Segregation was the norm for construction and trades unions, and [these] unions, which tended to supply workers for the larger government-funded projects, were openly discriminatory in their attitudes" (p. 38). Because of the blatant discrimination of both the industry and the unions and because of the building boom in the late 1960s boosted by billions of dollars for federal construction projects, enforcement of affirmative action focused on rewarding employers who achieved their minority employment goals. First implemented in Philadelphia, this approach was called "the Philadelphia Plan," but opponents quickly criticized this approach. As Rubio (2001) has pointed out, the initial demands to curb affirmative action came about 5 years after the law was implemented, just as evidence was emerging that the program was becoming effective at reducing workplace discrimination against women and people of color. White support for affirmative action, always tentative, eroded quickly.

President Nixon hoped that his promotion of "Black capitalism" would shift the focus away from the outrage over job discrimination that fueled some urban riots. Yet with the threat of George Wallace's candidacy for the White House, Nixon needed to assure White voters that he was on their side. He used several tactics, including his blunt opposition to using busing to desegregate public schools. Although President Johnson had abandoned the Philadelphia Plan to placate its opponents, the Nixon administration revived it. Many political observers believed that the reason for its revival did not reflect a commitment to an aggressive approach to affirmative action, but rather the Nixon administration's desire to pit two Democratic constituencies against each other—African Americans and the largely White unions (Rubio, 2001). Intentional or not, enough Democrats allied themselves with the Nixon administration to cause a standoff between the two parties in Congress. Further, the advocacy of goals and timetables during the Nixon years was mistakenly viewed as the implementation of quotas, and this belief was fixed in the public mind like a shipwreck.

This perception resulted in part from a 1971 U.S. Supreme Court decision followed by successful EEOC discrimination lawsuits. The Supreme Court case originated in Charlotte, North Carolina, where workers at Duke Power Company were organized into five departments—labor, coal handling, operations, maintenance, and laboratory/testing. Every job in the labor department paid lower wages than jobs in the other four departments (Kellough, 2006). For years, Duke Power had openly discriminated against Blacks, employing them only in the labor department—the only department that did not require a high school diploma for initial employment. After the

Civil Rights Act passed, Duke Power began to eliminate any policies that could be viewed as blatantly discriminatory. The company implemented a policy requiring a high school diploma for transfer from labor to another department, and satisfactory scores on two aptitude tests in addition to a high school diploma for *initial* employment in all departments except labor (Kellough, 2006). Thirteen Black employees accused Duke Power of engaging in racial discrimination.

In their arguments before the Supreme Court, the lawyers representing the Black employees successfully argued that disparities in educational opportunity offered to Blacks and Whites in Charlotte and the surrounding area made it far more likely for Whites to have a high school diploma (Kelly & Dobbin, 2001). The *Griggs v. Duke Power Company* decision prohibited employers from engaging in practices that had a "disparate impact" on the employment of minorities or women. The court did not object to the requirement of a high school diploma or test scores to be eligible for employment as long as such requirements were legitimate. The court ruled: "If an employment practice which operates to exclude Negros cannot be shown to be related to job performance, the practice is prohibited" (Kellough, 2006, p. 46). The court also said it didn't matter whether an employer did not intend to discriminate when implementing a policy or practice; if discrimination could be documented in terms of a disparate impact on women or minorities, the policy or practice was unconstitutional.

In 1972, the passage of the Equal Employment Opportunity Act reinstated the original power for EEOC to issue "cease-and-desist" orders and to bring lawsuits against employers appearing to engage in discriminatory hiring or promotion practices. With a legal staff increased from 40 to 222 attorneys, EEOC experienced early victories in landmark cases—first in 1973 against AT&T (the world's largest private employer at the time) and in 1974 against the steel industry (Rubio, 2001). The agreements reached in these two cases required these employers to establish minority goals and timetables in hiring decisions and for promotions. The monetary award given to female employees and workers of color who had been discriminated against totaled almost $50 million (Rubio, 2001). In 1970, less than 20% of employers had established affirmative action plans, but with the *Griggs* decision and the successful lawsuits, over 80% of employers had instituted such plans by 1976 (Kelly & Dobbin, 2001).

The Carter administration reorganized affirmative action in 1978, shifting more responsibility to the EEOC for encouraging timetables and goals for hiring women and minorities, but affirmative action made minimal gains. In 1980, following the election of Ronald Reagan, the new Republican administration reduced affirmative action, de-emphasized the use of goals and timetables, and made little effort to enforce affirmative action. This hands-off approach continued during George H. W. Bush's administration, causing policy analyst Linda Faye Williams to conclude: "The Reagan and Bush administrations virtually eliminated the threat of sanctions for discrimination in employment" (Rubio, 2001, p. 164).

AFFIRMATIVE ACTION AND THE U.S. SUPREME COURT

With a passive if not hostile administration, affirmative action was in the hands of the courts, especially the U.S. Supreme Court. From 1978 to 1987, the Supreme Court ruled on several significant cases that provided clarification on what did and did not constitute legitimate strategies for achieving affirmative action goals. In 1978, the high court ruled in *Regents v. Bakke* that setting a goal of a specific number of minority enrollments constituted a quota, and that wasn't acceptable. On the other hand, Justice Powell's majority opinion allowed universities to use race as one of the factors in admissions procedures based on the assumption that having a diverse student population enhanced the education of all students.

In the 1979 *United Steelworkers of America v. Weber* case, a White plaintiff was not chosen for a training program because the company's affirmative action plan mandated that Blacks be included in this program even though 90% of the workers were White and most had more seniority than Black workers. The plaintiff claimed reverse discrimination and argued that he was rejected solely on account of his race. The court ruled against the plaintiff, arguing that such strategies were necessary in order for affirmative action to provide employment opportunities for minorities, especially in occupations where they previously had been excluded (Leiter & Leiter, 2002). In the 1986 *Wygant v. Jackson Board of Education* case, Justice Powell once again addressed this issue: "As part of this Nation's dedication to eradicating racial discrimination, innocent persons may be called upon to bear some of the burden of the remedy" (Leiter & Leiter, 2002, p. 61).

Yet in 1984, the court voted in *Firefighters v. Stotts* to uphold the seniority system for laying off workers because there was no compelling evidence that Black employees being laid off had ever been discriminated against during their period of employment, and there was no evidence that the seniority system was designed to discriminate based on race. In other cases involving firefighters and state troopers, the courts approved affirmative action plans that mandated promoting one Black employee for every White employee as a necessary strategy to address a history of discrimination by employers (Leiter & Leiter, 2002).

By the time Reagan left office, he had appointed three justices to the U.S. Supreme Court, and in 1989 the court made decidedly anti-affirmative action rulings in *Ward's Cove Packing Company v. Antonio* and *Richmond v. Croson*. The *Croson* ruling struck down "set-aside" programs for minority businesses, and the *Ward's Cove* ruling reversed a precedent established 17 years earlier in the *Griggs* decision. The court asserted that employers could not be held responsible for unintended discrimination, and that plaintiffs must now prove that employer policies and practices were intended to discriminate against minorities or women (Kellough, 2006). Proving intent would be far more difficult than simply gathering data to document a disparate impact on women or minorities. In response, Congress passed the 1991 Civil Rights Act to restore the "disparate impact" principle as an adequate justification for affirmative action lawsuits. President Bush threatened to veto the bill, arguing that it mandated "quotas," but with the increased racial tensions caused by his controversial nomination of Clarence Thomas to the Supreme Court, there was sufficient pressure on him to sign the bill (Sterba, 2003).

In the 1995 *Adarand Constructors v. Peña* decision, the *Croson* ruling was reinforced as the justices called for "strict scrutiny" of how race was used to remedy past discrimination. Justice O'Connor's majority opinion not only rejected set-aside programs because they constituted quotas, but asserted that since the Constitution protected individual rights rather than group rights, activities intended to promote the rights of a group or class of people would be considered constitutional only if they satisfied a "strict scrutiny," meaning "only if they are narrowly tailored measures that further compelling government interests" (Leiter & Leiter, 2002, p. 71). Concerned by the implications of this decision, President Clinton appointed a team of experts to engage in a review of affirmative action at the federal level.

Their report on affirmative action programs concluded that these programs were responsible for numerous major achievements, including the effective integration of the military, 260,000 positions made available to women during just the preceding 3 years, dramatic increases in loans from the Small Business Association to qualified women and minority applicants, and private corporations attributing increased productivity and competitiveness in the global economy to the diversity they had achieved because of their affirmative action programs. Although these achievements documented that affirmative action was working, the experts also concluded that "there was still a need for affirmative action because of continuing racial and gender disparities in employment, income, and business ownership" (Clinton, 2004,

p. 663). In response to critics who insisted that affirmative action was being misused at times, the report included recommendations addressing that issue. President Clinton praised the report and implemented its recommendations for affirmative action programs. He described this action as an effort to "mend it" because it was not yet time to "end it."

CALIFORNIA REJECTS AFFIRMATIVE ACTION

These court rulings may have influenced the California Board of Regents in their decision to rescind affirmative action in 1995, followed in the fall of 1996 by California voters passing Proposition 209 to eliminate affirmative action programs in the state. The impact of affirmative action in higher education can perhaps best be understood by analyzing admissions data immediately after these two events. At the time, approximately 40% of California's population consisted of underrepresented minority groups. In 1995, members of these minority groups constituted 21% of freshmen enrolled at public universities in California, but following these two events, most of California's public universities experienced a major decline in minority enrollments. In 1998, only 15.5% of students enrolling in University of California schools were from underrepresented minority groups (Kellough, 2006). Even Ward Connerly, the African American who spearheaded the efforts to convince Californians to vote in favor of Proposition 209, expressed surprise at the extent of the enrollment decline (Laird, 2005). In the first few years after Proposition 209 passed, the state government and California's universities would spend almost half a billion dollars developing various legal strategies to counter the negative impact of this state mandate (Laird, 2005).

Critics argued that California was extending the racial segregation in its K–12 schools to its institutions of higher education. Enrollment figures for 1998 show students of color representing more than 88% of students in San Francisco's K–12 schools; in Los Angeles the figure was closer to 90%, and in Oakland's K–12 schools students of color were more than 94% of students (Laird, 2005). In response to accusations that they were promoting racial segregation in higher education, California's Board of Regents approved a policy in 1999 stipulating that the top 4% of the state's high school graduates would be considered eligible for enrollment at any University of California campus. Critics said the policy was cynically based on racial segregation—accepting the top 4% of high school graduates would make students from predominantly minority schools eligible for public universities. As Laird (2005) noted: "There was a theater-of-the-absurd quality to the public discussion, in that nearly everyone who supported [the policy] denied that building minority enrollment was one of its goals" (p. 153).

After the 4% policy was approved, minority enrollment increased. By 2002, it reached 19% (Kellough, 2006), but when Laird (2005) analyzed the enrollment data, he found increasing racial segregation on University of California campuses. Many students of color chose to attend campuses with less competitive enrollments, such as UC–Riverside and UC–Santa Cruz, while fewer attended selective institutions. For example, Laird (2005) found that students of color who had been turned away at UC–Berkeley and UCLA, while being accepted to less selective California public universities, had chosen to attend prestigious institutions such as Stanford, Harvard, and Yale.

According to Laird (2005), similar percentage plans in the states of Florida and Texas also have been criticized, for two primary reasons: First, students of color attending more competitive high schools may not graduate in the top 4% of their class even though they have the academic skills to be successful in college, as documented by the achievements of previous minority graduates from those schools. Since these students are being denied admission to university campuses where they would have been admitted in the past, many are forced to attend universities out of state. Second, students of color graduating in the top 4% from an academically weak high school may not have the abilities to succeed in higher education even if their campus has remedial programs to address academic deficiencies.

California, Texas, and Florida continue to struggle with the consequences of prohibiting overt racial preferences in admissions procedures at colleges and universities, and the states of Washington and Nebraska have followed California in eliminating affirmative action programs. Although these states may have ended affirmative action activities, they have not eliminated discriminatory practices; therefore the debate over affirmative action has continued.

THE AFFIRMATIVE ACTION DEBATE

Unlike previous antidiscrimination measures, affirmative action did not address individual behavior but societal biases in both public and private spheres. Because of the history of discrimination against individuals based on race, ethnicity, religion, and gender, affirmative action required taking steps to remedy the impact of such bias on individuals from these groups. Affirmative action goals included reducing discrimination and promoting integration of all people belonging to diverse groups in our nation's workplaces, public spaces, and public schools. Both critics and advocates of affirmative action agree that a legitimate goal of the federal government is to ensure equal treatment of all citizens. As Leiter and Leiter (2002) have written:

> In contemporary constitutional theory, equality is the fundamental principle of our democracy. At the moment of birth, every American-born person is deemed the equal of every other American in civil rights and obligations. (p. 24)

Critics insist that affirmative action has exceeded this goal by establishing preferential treatment based on an individual's race, ethnicity, or gender, resulting in discrimination against White males. Denouncing preferences is reflected in four of the major criticisms of affirmative action that Kellough (2006) identified:

1. In our democratic society, the focus should be on individual rights not group rights, and decisions concerning employment and admissions should focus strictly on merit and not on skin color or gender.
2. Preferences often benefit middle-class individuals who have the ability to achieve on their own talents and do not need preferences; further, women and minority applicants have been chosen despite the availability of more highly qualified White males.
3. Affirmative action discriminates against White males who have personally never engaged in discriminatory activities.
4. Affirmative action stigmatizes women and minorities receiving preferential treatment; their presence on a campus or at a work site is viewed as a consequence of preference rather than merit.

These four arguments have formed the basis for much of the debate over affirmative action, so it is important to be aware of the arguments in response to each one in order to develop a reasonable understanding of this debate.

Individual Rights Not Group Rights

Since its inception, opponents of affirmative action have declared it unconstitutional because they say its intent is to protect group rights whereas the Constitution emphasizes individual rights, and Justice O'Connor's majority decision in *Adarand* supported their contention. On the other hand, beginning with the 1886 ruling in *Santa Clara County v. Southern Pacific Railroad,* the U.S. Supreme Court affirmed a form of group rights to corporations by granting them the same equal protection rights as individuals. In 2010 that ruling was expanded to include the same free speech rights for corporations as for individuals, when the Court ruled in *Citizens United v. the Federal Election Commission* to allow corporations to use their own resources to purchase advertising promoting their preferred political candidates.

Advocates argue that affirmative action is a response to a well-documented history of White supremacy and patriarchy in the United States, and that this past discrimination requires efforts to ensure that women and people of color have the same rights and opportunities available to White males. As for the claim that affirmative action protected groups, Sterba (2003) rejected this argument, contending that affirmative action was intended to protect individuals who belonged to a group when there was documented evidence that members of that group had been and still were discriminated against. Black people have been and still are discriminated against because of their race, and women because of their gender. Affirmative action is similar to a class action suit in seeking to compensate individuals belonging to a group that has been disadvantaged.

Middle-Class Beneficiaries and Racism Against White Males

Those opponents who claim that middle-class minorities are the major beneficiaries of affirmative action often go on to suggest that a better way to confront discrimination would be to base affirmative action on class rather than race. For example, children and youth living in poverty, regardless of their race, should be encouraged to work hard in school, with a promise that if they graduate with good grades they will be rewarded with scholarships to enable them to attend college (Cohen, 2003). Advocates counter that if class discrimination justifies preferential treatment, why not racial discrimination as well? Reviewing the histories of middle- and upper-middle-class families of color has revealed evidence of blatant discrimination that drastically limited their financial achievements. The Black middle class has evolved largely since affirmative action was implemented, but Black people still had to contend with subtle and not-so-subtle barriers (Feagin & Sikes, 1994; Waller, 2001). Japanese American families worked hard to regain their economic position after being stripped of their homes and possessions while in the internment camps during World War II. In 1988, Congress concluded that they should be compensated for this racial injustice. Blacks and other Americans of color also have been victims of racial injustice. Why shouldn't they receive compensation?

In addition, trying to promote opportunities for people who are victims of class discrimination involves even more complexity. For example, Cohen

(2003) admits that students of color from low-income families are often so ill prepared academically for college that most of them are unlikely to be accepted under any admissions system, even when the university provides remedial courses. Nevertheless, Cohen and other critics object to using racial preferences to assist students of color from middle- and upper-middle-class families whose academic achievements make them qualified to compete for entry to prestigious law and medical schools.

As for denying opportunity to more-qualified White males, opponents of affirmative action denounce racial preferences for replicating the error it was supposed to correct. As Cohen (2003) wrote: "A wrong is not redressed by inflicting that same wrong on others" (p. 27). Because they don't want race-conscious solutions, those who complain about racial preferences offer no adequate solutions to compensate for the ongoing overt and covert racial discrimination directed against people of color. Sterba (2003) used an analogy to illustrate the absurdity of trying to avoid race in dealing with past and present discrimination based on race. He asks us to imagine a law that forbids the use of coercion: "Surely that law should not be taken to prohibit whatever coercion is necessary to correct for violations of the law itself. If it did that, then the law's prohibition of coercion would be unenforceable" (p. 318).

Bobo (2001) acknowledged that proponents of affirmative action often regard White opposition as simply racist—at best a reaction resenting a disruption of White privilege, at worst a reaction fueled by racial prejudice. Shaw (2003) expressed his skepticism about those who insist that any use of racial preferences is being racist:

> They believe that race consciousness is inherently dangerous and offensive. But why now, when the race-conscious measures they oppose are aimed at finally including those who have been excluded because of race? . . . Try as I might, I have never with certainty been able to separate the intellectual and ideological descendants of white supremacy proponents from the good faith affirmative action opponents. Even David Duke claims not to be a racist. (p. x)

As for women or people of color being selected for college admission or a job over more-qualified White males, affirmative action advocates challenge the objectivity of determining the "best qualified" person. On many campuses and work sites today, university leaders and employers have described the benefits to be gained by having diversity among their students or employees. After creating a pool of qualified applicants according to conventional criteria, an admissions officer or employer could legitimately view an applicant who was female or a person of color as the "best qualified" candidate based on the officer's or employer's beliefs about the value of diversity. From his research, B. R. Taylor (1991) quoted a Black worker who questioned the assumption that employers can objectively identify the "best qualified" applicant: "There is no such thing as any person who is best for a job. People may . . . approach jobs in different ways, but you can take any number of people and make [them] successful at any job" (p. 107). This worker also argued that to insist on hiring the "best qualified" person in reality promoted preferential treatment for White males because White males tended to have access to experiences and opportunities that were not as available to women or people of color.

Punishing White Males Who Have Not Discriminated

According to Sugrue (2001), opponents regard affirmative action as a "zero sum" solution to the problem of racial discrimination since gains made by workers of color were regarded as losses for White workers. Yet Bobo (2001) has argued that descriptions of White opposition to affirmative action often present a distorted view "that opposition to affirmative action among whites is monolithic. It is not" (p. 192). Bobo described affirmative action as a wide range of strategies, some of which—such as scholarships for students of color, outreach efforts, and job-training programs—are widely supported by Americans regardless of race. Based on his study, Bobo (2001) reported that about 30% of Whites agreed that affirmative action was helpful in keeping the United States economically competitive and rejected the statement that affirmative action was unfair to Whites.

Sugrue (2001) observed that White opponents who regarded affirmative action as a consequence of "identity politics" refused to acknowledge their own "identity politics" as reflected in their efforts to maintain a status quo that favored Whites. Has affirmative action changed the status quo? Data suggest that it has opened doors but maintained ceilings. According to Sterba (2003), native-born White males account for about 41% of the U.S. population, yet they constitute 97% of senior management in the top 1,000 corporations identified by *Fortune* magazine. In education, White males dominate leadership roles, representing 97% of K–12 school district superintendents and 80% of all tenured professor positions in higher education. White males still earn more income and control more wealth than people of color, and Kivel (2002) said that of 3,000 discrimination complaints filed over a 3-year period, only 100 alleged reverse discrimination and only six of the cases were successful. As Leman (1997) has written, the rationale for affirmative action is still legitimate today:

> Every child born in America doesn't have access to good schools . . . [some] live in the toughest family circumstances. To argue that by late adolescence [racial minorities] have run a fair competitive race and that if they're behind whites in educational standards they deserve to be permanently barred from the professional and managerial classes is absurd. (p. 53)

In addition, advocates for affirmative action argue that these programs have benefited some White males because of the strict scrutiny required in hiring and promotion today. In the past, decisions often were based on "who you knew," which favored White male applicants who had relationships with current employees or employers (Swain, Greene, & Wotipka, 2001). For these reasons, affirmative action advocates insist that reverse discrimination is a myth, and they reject color-blind strategies to achieve equality, arguing that such strategies tend to promote exclusion when Americans ought to be promoting inclusion of diverse people into the mainstream of society.

Preference over Merit Stigmatizes Women and Minorities

Although this criticism appears to address issues of merit on college campuses as well as in the workplace, the focus tends to be on admissions procedures in higher education, especially by highly selective, prestigious universities. As Hurtado (2001) has concluded: "The most contentious conflicts within the diversity debate have primarily been manifest in challenges to policies that consider race as a factor in college and university admissions" (p. 188).

Many affirmative action opponents insist that the only fair way for colleges and universities to make admissions decisions is on merit as measured by scores on standardized tests such as the Scholastic Aptitude Test (SAT). Although it is widely known that studies report that minorities and women tend to receive lower scores than White males on such tests, Sterba (2003) asserted that not as well known are the studies that report the lack of correlation between high scores on these tests and high grades in college or to predict successful careers. This lack of correlation also has been reported at the graduate level. A study of Law School Admission Test (LSAT) scores at the University of Pennsylvania law school concluded that these scores had no correlation with the grades of first-year law students and also did not correlate with conventional measures of success for law school graduates, such as income or self-satisfaction reports (Sterba, 2003).

Concerning the determination of merit, Laird (2005) has argued that "merit isn't reducible to a number . . . it isn't a grade-point average or an SAT score but rather everything that a person has achieved measured against every set of challenges and opportunities that person has faced" (pp. 21–22). Sterba (2003) reported that the best predictor of good grades in college was the quality of the curriculum at the high school in which a student received good grades. Claude Steele has argued that using SAT scores to admit students to college is analogous to using the ability to make free throws to select players for a college basketball team. Accepting only those who can make 10 out of 10 free throws will result in selecting some good players, but some of the greatest players in the history of basketball—from Wilt Chamberlain to Shaquille O'Neal—were notoriously poor free throw shooters (Sterba, 2003).

As for affirmative action stigmatizing women and students of color, there is some evidence for this argument. In one study, 60% of Black students believed that their academic abilities were doubted by their White peers, and 60% felt that their White professors doubted them as well. Yet less than one third of these students said they sometimes experienced self-doubt, and most of them strongly endorsed the use of affirmative action to provide opportunities for women and minorities (Crosby, Ferdman, & Wingate, 2000). Such findings have caused affirmative action advocates to argue that being stigmatized should be viewed as a problem for White students engaged in such stereotyping. Opponents cite studies reporting that only 40% of Black college students graduate in comparison to 59% of White students, but as Rudenstine (2001) has argued, this difference is a result of multiple factors, mostly economic, and not an outcome of students being stigmatized or their lack of ability.

It is fair to assume that stigmatization would be even more intense at the most selective colleges where merit and ability get far more emphasis, yet 75% of Black students graduate from such colleges—an even higher number than those graduating from less selective colleges (Rudenstine, 2001). Kellough (2006) cited the 1998 Bowen and Bok study reporting enrollment increases for minorities and women in private and public universities with no evidence that these students were not qualified for admission, and he noted that "they competed effectively with their white counterparts and graduated at comparable rates" (p. 139).

Crosby, Ferdman, and Wingate (2000) described a 1998 study that surveyed more than 350 college undergraduates who were students of color. A large majority of African American, Latino, and Native American students said they believed that most people on their campus assumed that they were admitted only because of affirmative action, and many of them believed that their White professors and peers doubted their academic abilities based on racial and ethnic stereotypes. Yet these students overwhelmingly supported affirmative action, believing that their admission to these colleges and universities offered them an opportunity to demonstrate their academic abilities and refute those stereotypes. One final point—a little-known consequence of admissions procedures implemented because of affirmative action is that they have benefited non-minorities. Sterba (2003) cited a study reporting that 20% of non-minorities admitted to selective schools would have been rejected using traditional admissions procedures.

Despite such results, critics have continued to argue that affirmative action programs force universities and colleges to lower their standards. However, if their issue is really lower standards, then the critics should focus their attention on children of financially advantaged families who are alumni of the prestigious institutions—legacy students. According to Sterba (2003), a Harvard study found that legacy students were significantly less qualified than the average student who was selected through affirmative action admissions procedures. Studies have reported that students admitted to college based on racial preferences constituted only 5–10% of all students, but those admitted as legacy students represented approximately 25% of all students (Sterba, 2003). It also could be argued that legacy students illustrate racial preferences since the vast majority of them are White.

In addition to denying that affirmative action lowers standards, some advocates have insisted that it enhances education for all students. Hurtado (2001) described theory and research concerning cognitive gains from interactions with diverse individuals, yet she admits that merely bringing diverse students to a campus does not guarantee interactions that achieve those outcomes: "Placing students of diverse backgrounds in a classroom is a necessary but insufficient condition for learning" (p. 189). This point was reinforced by a study of undergraduate African American students attending predominantly White institutions; 40% of them said White students often or always refrained from interacting with them outside of the classroom (Schofield, 2001). Hurtado (2001) reported some positive outcomes occurring when diverse students participated in learning activities as part of a group, including the development of cross-racial friendships. Hurtado also described instructional strategies utilizing diversity that resulted in cognitive gains not just in student knowledge but in higher order thinking skills.

Opponents have argued that affirmative action also has stigmatized women and minorities in the workplace, causing their co-workers to doubt their abilities and to view them as less competent than their White male peers. Yet Crosby, Ferdman, and Wingate (2000) report that a 1998 study of

800 women of color in American corporations concluded that most of these women regarded affirmative action "as a set of practices which enhances and does not displace, the true reward of merit" (p. 135). There is also evidence that employers do not routinely stigmatize employees who are hired because of affirmative action. Beauchamp (1997) discussed two studies that surveyed about 500 corporations and found almost 75% of corporate leaders were supportive of affirmative action programs, believing that hiring more women and people of color improved productivity. As for how women and minorities feel about affirmative action, the studies report that they overwhelmingly support it (Swain, Greene, & Wotipka, 2001). Yet, their support raises the question—has affirmative action actually made a significant difference in corporate hiring and promotion for women and people of color?

Kellough (2006) reviewed research on the effectiveness of affirmative action programs. In the early 1970s, studies reported significant improvement in the employment of women and Black men, but a 1976 study reported that affirmative action motivated White men to improve their skills for advancement, which contributed to an increasing wage gap between White male and Black male employees. Studies from the 1980s continued to document gains in employment for women and minority males, although a study of national employment data from 1961 to 1983 reported that White women had been the major beneficiaries of affirmative action programs, followed by minority women (Kellough, 2006).

Yet studies of specific fields of employment, such as the construction industry, or specific metropolitan areas have reported employment gains for people of color as well as women. Reskin (2000) described a study conducted on the impact of affirmative action in four urban areas—Atlanta, Boston, Detroit, and Los Angeles. The study found that employers with affirmative action procedures hired 10% more women and 20% more African Americans than employers not using such procedures. As for hiring qualified workers, the same study reported that there was no difference in the performance evaluations of employees hired with or without affirmative action plans. Reskin (2000) also cited studies reporting an increase of women in managerial positions due to affirmative action promotion procedures. In 2000 and 2005, Holzer and Neumark conducted affirmative action studies, and both studies concluded that affirmative action programs were responsible for women and minorities making significant employment gains (Kellough, 2006).

The effectiveness of affirmative action perhaps is best documented in the growth of the Black middle class in the United States. Rubio (2001) argued that there was virtually no Black middle class when affirmative action was first implemented, but in the following 40 years the Black middle class expanded to include almost half of all African American families. Economic problems and job discrimination persist, but there have been major gains in employment over a wide range of occupations, especially jobs that require postsecondary preparation. Given these data, should we conclude that affirmative action has achieved its goal of creating a more just society in its promotion of equal opportunity for minorities and women? Katznelson (2005) argued that problems remain, but after reviewing the historical evidence, he offered this assessment:

> Affirmative action has done more to advance fair treatment across racial lines than any other recent public policy. If affirmative action did not exist, the United States would be a vastly more segregated country. (p. 148)

AFFIRMATIVE ACTION TODAY

Kellough (2006) has argued that affirmative action was necessary because it was critical for a nation as diverse as the United States to utilize the talents of all its people, not only for reasons of social justice but on a practical basis, recognizing that consumers are becoming increasingly diverse, especially in the global economy. In 2003, the Supreme Court's decision in *Grutter v. Bollinger* affirmed that race could be used as a factor in college admissions because racial diversity enhanced the education of all students. Recognizing their obligation to prepare students to function effectively in our diverse national and global societies, colleges and universities have made the recruitment of diverse students a major goal, and most students appear to be aware of the value of that diversity. Palmer (2001) cited a study reporting that 90% of college students agreed that the racial diversity on their campus enhanced their learning experiences at least moderately, if not in a clearly positive way.

Colleges are not the only institutions promoting the value of diversity. Clayton and Crosby (2000) described how corporations have changed their perspective on affirmative action from one of offering opportunity to minorities and women to recognizing that eliminating discrimination in hiring and promotion practices serves corporate interests in two major ways: (1) employers do not overlook talented people, and (2) women and minority employees are not prevented from working up to their potential. Beauchamp (1997) compared affirmative action with eliminating the color barrier in professional baseball. Just as that decision made it possible to discover the talents of Jackie Robinson and many others, corporations are now discovering talents of women and people of color who historically had been prevented from proving their abilities in the competitive corporate setting.

In 1986, the National Association of Manufacturers declared that affirmative action programs represented good business policy and practice: "[They] allowed the industry to benefit from new ideas, opinions, and perspectives generated by workforce diversity" (Kelly & Dobbin, 2001, p. 98). Beginning in the 1970s, major employers increasingly have filed amicus briefs supporting affirmative action programs in various lawsuits, especially for critical cases brought before the U.S. Supreme Court. As the 20th century was ending, a survey of 128 corporations with the largest net incomes reported that 95% of the CEOs interviewed said they planned to continue using affirmative action plans to ensure fairness for women and minorities in decisions to hire and promote employees (Reskin, 2000). Corporate leaders have reported that because of affirmative action, their workplace diversity was much more likely to produce "diversity of ideas, different perspectives on strategic planning, and improved, more open personnel policies" (Beauchamp, 1997, p. 222).

Winbush and McLemore (2003) report that there is "ample research" supporting the benefits of diverse employees at the workplace, but it also has been reported that work groups with diverse members can have problems that must be resolved to gain the benefits of their diversity. Kellough (2006) described studies reporting initial difficulty in intergroup communication among diverse employees, impeding group cohesion and reducing group effectiveness, but as members of a diverse group became more familiar and more comfortable with one another, they surpassed homogeneous groups in their ability to deal effectively with complex challenges. A 1993 study created 36 work groups of which 17 were homogeneous and the other 19 consisted of diverse individuals. These groups were given a series of problem-solving tasks over 4 months. The 17 homogeneous groups initially earned higher scores based on performance, but by the end of the 4 months, the groups with diverse members received the highest scores based on developing a range of perspectives and using alternative strategies to solve complex problems (Kellough, 2006). Such outcomes have motivated business leaders to place more emphasis on the value of diversity for their organizations than on affirmative action.

R. Roosevelt Thomas, Jr., coined the term *diversity management* and argued that this approach should replace affirmative action because "sooner or later, . . . affirmative action will die a natural death" (1990, p. 107). Although he recognized that affirmative action was responsible for significant achievements, Thomas believed that it was destined to become outdated and that corporations eventually would employ a more forward-looking approach. He established the American Institute for Managing Diversity in 1983 (Thomas, 1992), and in 1991 the first National Diversity Conference was held to inaugurate an annual event involving the presentation and promotion of concepts for managing diversity (Kelly & Dobbin, 2001). Thomas and Ely (1996) argued that managing diversity was essential not simply to improve organizational efficiency but also to increase profits. They argued that benefits derived from a diverse workforce included its potential to enhance organizational flexibility and creativity, and to strengthen the ability to respond and adjust to market changes.

By the end of the 1990s, the corporate sector had largely accepted diversity management as an important aspect of human resource management. In part, this was a response to a 1987 report by the Hudson Institute predicting that White women, immigrants, and people of color would represent 85% of the growth in America's workforce by 2000 and that this trend would continue in the 21st century (Brazzel, 2003). Employers understood that they had no choice about having diverse employees—the challenge was to determine how to manage diverse employees to achieve maximum productivity and profit. This would require organizational change because, as Cross (2000) noted, "U.S. companies, created by and in the image of white men, were completely unprepared to welcome or even tolerate the new workers" (p. 54). With Fortune 500 companies taking the initiative, other business leaders also embraced diversity management, and Kellough (2006) observed their use of pluralistic rhetoric to emphasize "that differences should be valued, and that organizations should be managed in a way that allows people from different backgrounds to succeed" (p. 68). The Clinton administration encouraged this development. A 1993 study reported that no federal agencies or subagencies had implemented any diversity management programs, but a 1999 survey reported diversity management programs in 88% of these federal organizations (Kellough, 2006).

Some of the early diversity initiatives were ineffective. Cross (2000) described "ethnic dinners" that not only avoided raising crucial issues but did not "attempt to change the power dynamics in the organization" (p. 90). As more diversity management programs were implemented, some of them included affirmative action programs, but most human resource professionals did not view these two areas as synonymous. This was because diversity management was not limited to issues of race or gender but was inclusive of a mix of diverse people based on factors such as national origin, disability, age, sexual orientation, background, and education (Kellough, 2006). Diversity management included the development of diversity recruitment strategies and diversity training programs so corporations could benefit from diversity not only in the workforce but among their consumers. Diversity training often emphasized working collaboratively with others, learning conflict resolution strategies, and creating a positive work environment for all employees (Kelly & Dobbin, 2001).

In 1999, executives from nearly 500 U.S. corporations publicly expressed their commitment to diversity by signing a document called "Diversity in the Workplace: A Statement of Principle," but a commitment to hire diverse employees was no longer adequate. As the workforce in the 21st century continued to change, diversity management continued to evolve and began to incorporate concepts of social justice. Brazzel (2003) has written: "Diversity and social justice are two sides of the same coin. They can be viewed separately and they cannot be separated" (p. 53).

A few corporations had already established a commitment to social justice. In the early 1990s, people in top management positions at Levi Strauss and Company designed a decision-making guide to ensure that their commitment to valuing and rewarding diversity was perceived as credible. The company would not engage in a business relationship with other companies (e.g., suppliers) that violated Levi Strauss's ethical commitment with regard to diversity (Hopkins, 1997). One influence on Levi Strauss was its ongoing competition with corporations in the European Union that also were implementing policies and practices related to diversity based on a pluralistic perspective. Similar global pressures have caused other corporations to become more involved in social justice issues.

In the 1960s, a new Nike Corporation wanted to experiment with the concept of marketing shoes but not manufacturing them. Nike designed the shoes, but then purchased the final product from independent contractors in Asian or Southeast Asian countries where wages were low. This innovative approach was so profitable that it soon became the norm for American corporations, but by the 1990s media stories highlighted the inhumane labor conditions at many of Nike's overseas factories. Nike executives insisted that they only purchased the shoes, and that it was not their responsibility to tell the Asian or Southeast Asian factory owners how to run their businesses. As the media continued reporting on disturbing allegations such as child labor abuses, Nike's stock value dropped. To counter these news reports, Nike executives implemented programs to ensure better monitoring of labor conditions for local workers at factories making its products. As reported by Frank (2008), Nike now pre-screens factories before signing contracts with a supplier, and it has become a role model for other corporations because of its careful monitoring of work site conditions for ethical treatment of employees.

The Coca Cola Corporation's emphasis on the need to value diversity in its workforce was due not merely to increasing diversity among U.S. consumers. According to Schoeff (2008), Coca Cola markets in more than 200 countries and 80% of its revenue comes from outside the United States. To reflect the diversity of its consumers, Coca Cola has been emphasizing diversity at its Atlanta headquarters, which has a staff representing 65 different nationalities. But that was not enough. Coca Cola informed its outside law firms that it wanted to be represented only by those firms that have demonstrated a commitment to diversity.

Schoeff (2008) described similar efforts by General Motors (GM) and DuPont. GM no longer hires law firms that do not demonstrate a commitment to diversity, and in an annual report GM noted that of all the lawyers in its outside law firms, 16.1% were minorities and 28.6% were women. Since 1992, DuPont has required outside law firms to document their diversity in an annual survey. Although DuPont used to work with hundreds of law firms, it now works with only about 40 firms. In addition to reinforcing their commitment to diversity, the company's officials argue that they spend millions of dollars on legal counsel and that the addition of diversity to their legal representation has produced more creative thinking and better legal outcomes. To further encourage law firms to become more diverse, 126 corporate executives signed a 2004 document entitled "A Call to Action: Diversity in the Legal Profession" (Schoeff, 2008).

The commitment to social justice is a recent development in diversity management, and it is not universally accepted among corporations. Many corporate executives feel that the commitment to hiring and promoting diverse employees and creating a positive work environment is adequate. Although most organizations seem to have become more comfortable with diversity issues, Brazzel (2003) has concluded that many of them maintain "an ambivalence about whether to fully address both diversity and the elimination of oppression" (p. 86). Yet social justice issues continue to be a point of emphasis in diversity management literature, and with the diversity of employees inevitably increasing in the future, addressing social justice issues may become a more significant factor in measuring a corporation's commitment to diversity.

CHAPTER 5

The Struggle for Identity
What Does It Mean to Be an American?

My identity locates me in social space and orients me to the world I live in so that I can have effective commerce with my environment. Without a clear identity, I have no direction, no goal, no purpose, and no sense that I am an integrated person.

—Donald Taylor, 2002, pp. 49–50

A friend once told me a story illustrating the wit of scholar and activist Vine Deloria, Jr. As a Lakota Indian and an expert on Lakota history and culture, Deloria was called to be a witness for the defense at the trial of several Lakota men accused of committing violence against federal agents on a Lakota reservation. After Deloria was sworn in, the prosecuting attorney began the examination by attempting to rattle the witness. This strategy consisted of respectfully asking Deloria what he would prefer to be called, followed by a list of possible names pronounced with increasing sarcasm, including Indian, American Indian, Amerindian, Native American, First American, indigenous person, and several more. At the conclusion of this list, the prosecutor repeated his initial request by asking Deloria which of these names (or some other) he would prefer to be called. Deloria replied, "Indian is fine with me; most of us are just happy Columbus wasn't looking for Turkey." Most people in the courtroom laughed, and the prosecutor abandoned this strategy.

Several years later, I had the pleasure of dining with Vine Deloria during a diversity conference. I asked him if that story was accurate, and he admitted that "something like that" had occurred. He also went on to say that he didn't pay much attention to the labels that other people gave to Indians: "What's more important is what we think about ourselves." Deloria was talking about identity, and especially about the importance of Indian people having a collective identity grounded in their culture. He knew that it was no easy task for an American Indian today to develop a collective identity; he had described how non-Indians contributed to the problems for young

Indians in creating their sense of identity: "Experts paint us as they would like us to be. Often we paint ourselves as we wish we were or as we might have been" (Deloria, 1969, p. 9).

Deloria's concern illustrated his understanding that personal identity does not develop in isolation, but in social interactions that are not likely to be restricted to those within one's own group. For members of subordinate groups in a diverse society, the attitudes and actions of dominant group members will have an effect, and it will not be an affirming one if the person accepts even a portion of the negative images of his or her group being perpetuated by the dominant group. Freire (1970) described the dilemma for individuals who succumb to such images:

> They are at one and the same time themselves and the oppressor whose consciousness they have internalized. The conflict lies in the choice of being wholly themselves or being divided . . . between human solidarity or alienation, between following prescriptions or having choices, between being spectators or actors. (pp. 32–33)

THE IMPORTANCE OF A COLLECTIVE IDENTITY

Deloria probably would have agreed with psychologist Donald Taylor that the best way for American Indian youth to avoid internalizing racist ideas about their group would be to embrace a collective identity offered by American Indian cultures. Influenced by his work with indigenous people in Canada, Taylor (2002) came to the conclusion that "a person's collective identity is the most important and psychologically primary component to the self-concept" (p. 40). Cross-cultural scholars also have acknowledged the important psychological role of a collective identity: "Collective identities structure the way in which people organize their ideas, evaluate experiences concerning the community and situate themselves as individuals in their relationship to others" (Eder, Giesen, Schmidtke, & Tambini, 2002, p. 148). Taylor (2002) said a collective identity provided a "template" on which personal identity could be formed, but he did not restrict the basis for a collective identity to ethnicity.

If a collective identity based on ethnicity is not available to someone, he or she can claim a collective identity based on some other social group defined by gender, sexual orientation, disability, and so on. Using a clearly defined collective identity as a foundation, individuals can successfully create a personal identity. Having a collective identity influences not only one's sense of personal identity or self-concept, but also one's sense of self-esteem because a collective esteem is an inevitable part of a collective identity.

On the other hand, Taylor (2002) argues that individuals who are unable to achieve a clearly defined collective identity fail to receive the "blueprint" on which they can construct their personal identity. This produces lower self-esteem and a reduced sense of competence; it also results in "a profound lack of self-identification and comprehension" (p. 89). Scholars agree that self-esteem is essential in order for adolescents to develop into psychologically healthy adults (Guindon, 2010). Taylor (2002) has described a healthy adult as one who is "prepared to engage in meaningful and purposive interaction with his or her physical and social environment" (p. 87). This person is prepared not only to function in the existing society, but to deal with the changes that may occur in that society.

Ethnicity provides individuals with a collective identity because ethnicity is grounded in a specific group's history and culture. When was the concept of an ethnic group first formed? Although the term *ethnic* has roots in ancient Greek culture, it has achieved its current meaning only in modern times. According to Eriksen (2002), *ethnic* was derived from the Greek "ethnos," which evolved from the earlier "ethnikos"; both terms referred to people who were regarded as "heathen or pagan" (p. 4). This meaning was maintained until World War II when "ethnics" was used as a polite form of address for Jews, Italians, Irish, and others deemed inferior to Anglo Saxons. David Riesman was the first academic to use the term, in 1953, as a more objective label for people from diverse cultural backgrounds, but it wasn't until the 1960s that ethnic groups and ethnicity became a primary preoccupation among scholars in social and cultural anthropology (Eriksen, 2002). *Ethnic* finally made its first appearance in the Oxford English Dictionary in 1972, and the increasing interest in ethnicity is clearly documented by the extensive research on ethnic groups that has been conducted, especially in the 1980s and 1990s. Eriksen (2002) reported that these studies tended to focus on how ethnicity shaped an individual's sense of identity or on how ethnicity was used to gain political power.

Fenton (1999) has asserted that at the present time "all commentators on the concept of ethnic group agree that it refers to the social elaboration of collective identities whereby individuals see themselves as one among others like themselves" (p. 6). This suggests that a diverse society is a necessary context for ethnicity so that an ethnic group can identify obvious similarities among its members and obvious differences from those who do not belong to the group. The most important similarities for ethnic groups tend to pertain to ancestry, culture, and language.

Since the 1960s, the issue of identity has been integral to diverse social justice movements in the United States. Mayo (2000) noted that these movements have spread to other nations and represent a global effort to promote positive collective identities and also to contest "the negative identities which have been associated with the prejudices of racist, sexist, homophobic, ageist and ableist societies" (p. 3). With regard to such prejudices, one of the ongoing areas of public confusion concerns the lack of a clear distinction between ethnicity and race.

ETHNICITY AND RACE

The terms *ethnicity* and *race* often were used synonymously in public discourse, but since the 1930s scholars increasingly have identified race as a social construct based on perceptions of physical differences, whereas ethnicity refers to cultural heritage and a collective identity that a group offers its members. The fundamental flaw of all racial classification systems is not that they designate differences between groups of people, but, as Fenton (1999) concluded, that they inevitably lead to racism by becoming "a system of social classification designating peoples as being of inherently unequal worth" (p. 219). Michael Banton has proposed that ethnicity is concerned primarily with "the identification of 'us,'" but race is "more oriented to the categorization of 'them'" (Eriksen, 2002, p. 6).

Scholars widely recognize also the extent to which the concept of race has been used historically to justify injustice, and this has contributed to the preference of scholars since the 1970s to engage in research and analysis on ethnicity. Ethnicity usually is regarded as referring to a group from a specific region of a country or having ancestors who voluntarily emigrated from a particular nation. As Mayo (2000) explained: "The terms 'ethnicity' and 'ethnic groups' have been used to identify difference . . . without recourse to such inherently flawed terminology as that of 'race'" (p. 64). Fenton (1999) argued:

> The term race is associated with mistaken science. . . . It is typically seen as malign and racial ideologies have been associated with compulsion and oppression. By contrast, ethnic can be taken as an analytic term in social science, is often seen as the voluntary identification of peoples and as (at least potentially) benign. (p. 69)

In addition, the study of race does not readily allow a focus on the racial group itself, but inevitably requires a study of racism, since any examination of a racial group cannot avoid addressing negative attitudes of the dominant group that have led to exclusion and oppression. Ethnicity, on the other hand, tends to focus on the nature of the group and individuals included in the group. In one of the earliest studies of ethnicity, Glazer and Moynihan (1963) rejected the melting pot concept, arguing that for many individuals immigrating to the United States, adapting to a new homeland did not require the eradication of their ethnic differences but led to an increased interest in their cultural heritage. The historic presence of ethnic enclaves in urban areas documented the desire to preserve ethnicity. Even after two or three generations, many descendants of immigrants have persisted in identifying themselves as members of their ethnic group.

Although race and ethnicity are not synonymous, it is problematic to exclude African Americans from a discussion of ethnicity and restrict them only to discussions of race. African Americans could be excluded from discussions of ethnicity because (1) their ancestors were primarily involuntary immigrants from West Africa and (2) African Americans are not likely to know the specific ethnic group (e.g., Mandinka, Fulani, Ibo, Hausa, Coromantes, etc.) from which they are descended (Fenton, 1999). African slaves who spoke the same language typically were separated to prevent them from forming relationships that might lead to resistance or revolt. As Fenton (1999) noted: "The effect of enslavement was to erase most traces of ethnic identity and culture within a generation or so" (p. 42).

The development of the term *African American* was in part an effort to reclaim a diminished African identity. Many scholars were motivated to engage in research that identified and described remnants of African cultures in the language and behavior of African Americans. In this way, Black "ethnicity" was created as a response to the historic and persistent reality of White supremacy in American society (Dalton, 2008). As Fenton (1999) has written, "The terms African and black have been embraced, black as an expression of unity and pride, African as an expression of peoplehood" (p. 68). Because scholars have tended to view ethnicity as a form of collective identity by groups of people claiming some kind of common descent, many of them have included African Americans in research on ethnicity, ethnic groups, and ethnic identity.

ETHNIC IDENTITY

Although ethnic groups have existed historically within geographical areas, immigrants have been the focus of much research on ethnicity and ethnic identity. Appleton (1983) described the once-dominant view among American political scientists that maintaining a cultural identity was limited largely to immigrant families where group cohesiveness and group identity served as a strategy to achieve economic stability for the group. This was seen as a temporary strategy; it was assumed that immigrants who maintained their native culture eventually would experience conflict stemming from differences between their native culture and their adopted one. As immigrants began to adopt American culture and behave in accordance with American norms, this adaptive strategy ultimately would lead to their successful assimilation. Once members of the group assimilated, their self-identification was supposed to transform from an ethnic identity to a national identity as they began to view themselves as Americans.

In reality, many immigrants continued to identify with their native culture, causing some scholars and social activists such as John Dewey and Jane Addams to develop an appreciation for the strengths embedded in the cultures of ethnic groups (Daniels, 2002). They challenged traditional assumptions about assimilation, arguing that allowing members of diverse ethnic groups to maintain their cultures would benefit the larger society. The persistence of ethnic identification required a reconsideration of traditional assumptions. Eventually, scholars acknowledged that ethnic identity fulfilled a positive purpose because it addressed basic human needs. Appleton (1983) believed that an ethnic identity could provide "a greater sense of purpose and of being" as well as helping individuals to "make sense out of the day-to-day affairs of ordinary life and provide an enduring continuity" (p. 45).

According to Royce (1982), a major factor explaining the appeal and persistence of ethnic identity in opposition to a national identity is that nationalism, as we understand it today, is of relatively recent origin. Empires have existed for much of human history, but nations began to emerge primarily in the 19th century. Once these nations had formed, dominant groups within them established what was to be considered the national identity and they challenged members of subordinate groups to relinquish group loyalty and their group identity by viewing themselves primarily as citizens of the nation. Although some ethnic identities disappeared over time, many people have continued to define themselves according to their ethnicity. Royce (1982) described Edward Spicer's model that explained how a persistent identity system could successfully promote ethnic identity by demonstrating flexibility in facing new challenges and by being "responsive to and reflective of the larger social context" (p. 50).

According to Mary Pipher, knowing one's ethnic heritage is essential in forming a personal identity: "If you don't know your history, if you don't know about your family . . . you're a little particle of flotsam out floating in this giant sea" (Hackney, 1997, p. 104). For many people of color, their ethnic community provides them with a basis for forming a personal identity because it is the community that nurtures their emotional development and their social and political awareness in ways that do not occur in mainstream society (Hing, 1997). For that reason, ethnic identity should be understood as not only looking backward at one's cultural heritage, but looking to the future as well. Royce (1982) has made a similar point about the pride that accompanies ethnic identity, asserting that ethnic pride is not simply about heritage, but "is the savor and remembrance of the past. More important, it is the promise of the future" (p. 232).

According to De Vos (2006), ethnic identity is primarily about acknowledging one's origins (the past), but it also means being a member of a cultural group with legitimate claims on one's loyalty (the present) and a sense of pride and continuity passed on to one's children (the future). The development of an ethnic identity means knowing "who we are" based on similarities of attitudes and behaviors with other members of our group, rather than defining ourselves by our differences from others. Rotheram and Phinney (1987) acknowledged that ethnicity was rooted in ancestry, but they argued that ethnicity was primarily a cultural phenomenon that shaped patterns of thinking, feeling, and behaving among ethnic individuals. To belong to an ethnic group requires individuals to accept and model cultural aspects of the group as reflected in values, customs, language usage, and rules for social interaction. Ethnic identity should be understood as "the individual's acquisition of group patterns" (Rotheram & Phinney, 1987, p. 13).

Baumann (1999) agreed that ethnicity is cultural and rejected the proposition that one's ethnic identity has a biological or genetic basis: "Ethnicity is not an identity given by nature, but an identification created through socialization" (p. 21). He further argued that to think of ethnic identity as largely genetic ultimately results in the kind of racism that tainted the eugenics movement. In cross-cultural studies, scholars have tended to agree that ethnic identities cannot be claimed simply as a birthright or arbitrarily assigned; they are socially constructed by means of a process that is never fully completed but represents an ongoing evolution (Eder, Giesen, Schmidtke, & Tambini, 2002; Rosenthal, 1987).

Baumann (1999) compared ethnic identity to wine making. The basic ingredients—an individual's ethnic affiliations—are provided by nature, but nature alone does not produce wine. Like the fermentation process, ethnic affiliations need to connect to political and economic interests before they can emerge in the form of an ethnic identity that provides a basis for behavior in daily life. Just as wines age to attain distinctive flavors, the development of ethnic identities is dependent on the social climate in which they develop. Baumann (1999) described the end result of this process: "Ethnic identities can be stressed or unstressed, enjoyed or resented, imposed or even denied, all depending on situations and context" (p. 64).

The consensus appears to be that ethnic identity may originate as a function of birth and ancestry, but that it is ultimately a selected identity that must be achieved. Some scholars question this concept by arguing that for individuals to identify with the ethnic group of their parents does not represent a genuine choice, but Royce (1982) insists that it is still a choice: "Birth and a lengthy period of socialization into an ethnic heritage provides a person with a minimal competency in the identity . . . [but] individuals must affirm and reaffirm their identity in order for it to remain a salient feature of their personalities" (p. 185). Giddens argued that individuals aren't likely to be satisfied by claiming "an identity that is simply handed down, inherited, or built as a traditional status. A person's identity has to be discovered, constructed, actively sustained" (Mayo, 2000, p. 43). As Eder and colleagues (2002) have written, an ethnic identity is "fundamentally concerned with meaning" and is not merely "an instrument to arrive at some goal" (p. 19). Instead, the ethnic identity is the goal, satisfying basic human needs for belonging, solidarity, and trust.

Since ethnicity is defined by culture, the process of forming an ethnic identity must be understood as a dynamic process because cultures are not static. People learn about their culture in dialogue with one another; therefore, culture will always be modified over time. As the culture changes, so do the ethnic or national identities of people who are shaped by the culture. In the past, immigrants were most likely to identify themselves by using the name of their village and possibly their religion; a 19th-century Middle Eastern immigrant to the United States might have said he was a Chaldean Christian from Telkaif rather than an Iraqi (Royce, 1982). Today, immigrants may still make such identifications, but they are more likely to view themselves in nationalistic terms as Iraqis, claiming that as their ethnic group. An ethnic identity also will evolve over time, and as the Iraqi immigrant is influenced by the national culture he or she will likely become an "Iraqi American."

The evolution of ethnic identity inevitably will result in generational differences. Young people who identify as Chinese American today are not likely to view themselves in the same way as young people who identified themselves as Chinese American in the 1970s or in the 1930s. Although there probably will be some areas of overlap, there will be significant differences. What remains the same is that the strength of an individual's sense of ethnic identity will be a measure of the strength of that person's connection to his or her group. As Brubaker (2006) noted, a strong sense of ethnic identity is usually grounded in a vision of group similarity, and of "a clear boundary between inside and outside" (p. 37).

According to David Taylor (2002), the degree to which one's ethnic identity dominates one's personal identity is difficult to assess, but members of an ethnic group are more likely to share elements of a clearly defined ethnic identity when they have a shared history (oral or written), reside in proximity to one another, and create their own institutions. Yet having an ethnic identity does not imply that each person in a group is exactly the same. What it does mean is that differences between individuals don't matter to other members of the group. According to Appleton (1983), an ethnic group must offer its members "a source of identity and belonging not easily provided by other social factions of society" (p. 49), but groups do not tend to require complete conformity from their members. Although ethnic identity usually is regarded as an affirmation of self, it also can be the source of negative attitudes and behaviors toward others. De Vos and Romanucci-Ross (1995) concluded: "As in all forms of belonging, [ethnic identity] can be used to express one's humanness or to deny the humanness of others" (p. 359). This attitude can lead to ethnic conflicts unless group members promote a sense of reciprocal respect between ethnic groups.

Because the collective group shapes and affirms one's individual sense of identity, that identity is sustained by the group's continuity. An individual's sense of personal survival is shaken by the perception that his or her group may be faced with the threat of extinction. That potential extinction refers not only to literal genocide but to cultural genocide such as that faced by many indigenous people in the United States and around the world. De Vos (2006) has argued: "In its deepest psychological level, ethnicity is a sense of affiliative survival. If one's group survives, one is assured of survival, even if not personally" (p. 12).

The power of ethnicity and ethnic identity is documented by their persistence not only in democratic, capitalistic societies of the West, but also in repressive societies. This has become especially apparent following the decline and collapse of the United Soviet Socialist Republic as ethnic groups have drawn increased attention in emerging Eastern European nations (Fenton, 1999). Mayo (2000) argued that ethnic identity should be recognized as a global phenomenon—of all the members of the United Nations, only about 10% represent countries having no ethnic diversity. Around the world people are being challenged to recognize not only the diversity of groups, but also the diversity of ethnic identities within groups to ensure that they do not engage in stereotyping members of ethnic groups.

BUILDING A PERSONAL IDENTITY BASED ON ETHNIC IDENTITY

The roots of identity are nurtured in childhood, but the process of determining one's identity takes place largely during adolescence. Many parents of color encourage their children to develop an ethnic identity as a strategy for helping them to become more resilient as they encounter prejudice and discrimination. As Tatum (1997) noted, the parents "want their children to achieve an internalized sense of personal security" (p. 74). Tatum also argued that schools should support these parents by reinforcing the development of an ethnic identity, yet many teachers do not feel competent to do this. Tatum (1997) identified the main reason for their dilemma:

> When I talk to educators about the need to provide adolescents with identity-affirming experiences and information about their own cultural groups, they sometimes flounder because this information has not been part of their own education. (p. 74)

Although parental membership in an ethnic group is important, Rosenthal (1987) insists that it is especially important that the ethnic community provide "a subculture in which cultural values are legitimated" (p. 161). This goal is facilitated when a group establishes its own churches, schools, clubs, and organizations promoting social interactions among group members. When adolescents begin developing a sense of ethnic identity, it is because they perceive positive benefits from being regarded as a member of the group. This is especially important for the adolescent children of immigrants as they develop their sense of personal identity.

Some immigrant families have opted to assimilate by identifying completely with the dominant culture. As described by Suarez-Orozco and Suarez-Orozco (1995), some Latino families refused to speak Spanish at home, and as their children learned the values and practices of the dominant culture, they did not develop an ethnic identity based on their parents' native culture. Some Latino adolescents from immigrant families have attempted to combine the two cultures to create a blended identity, including the use of a blended language called "Spanglish." Still others have tried to create an ethnic identity that is bicultural, with the ability to operate competently in both cultures and with fluency in both English and Spanish languages. No strategy has guaranteed that members of the dominant society will respond positively to the individual Latino or that he or she will be accepted; therefore, many second-generation Latinos reject the dominant society and its institutions (including schools) that they perceive as rejecting them, and they seek refuge with their peers. This refuge may be an informal group of friends or a formal gang organization (Suarez-Orozco & Suarez-Orozco, 1995).

The strategies of Latino adolescents illustrate the point made by De Vos and Romanucci-Ross (1995) that ethnic identity is involved not only with one's sense of self, but with how that self is projected to others: "Ethnic identity, like any form of identity, is not only a question of knowing who one is subjectively, but of how one is seen from the outside" (p. 366). How one is perceived is one of the factors ensuring that ethnicity and ethnic identity are not static from one generation to the next, and do not remain the same for one person throughout his or her life. As Fenton (1999) noted, ethnic identities "are constructed in ways which can and do change" (p. 235). What does not change is the need to use the collective identity provided by the ethnic group as the basis for the adolescent to develop a personal identity.

Other members of an ethnic group usually have been the foundation upon which an individual builds his or her personal identity; the developmental process requires adolescents to decide what values and attitudes they want to integrate into their personality, and to select certain behaviors to which they are willing to conform. As noted previously, individuals do not have to conform to every aspect of their ethnic group, but every individual will conform to some aspects of the group in order to claim an ethnic identity. If there is insufficient conformity, individuals who are functioning effectively in mainstream society will be accused of rejecting their ethnic identity in order to be accepted by those outside the group. This reaction is illustrated by the widespread descriptions of a person of color as sharing only the skin color of the group, but being "White on the inside," as expressed in traditional metaphors: an Oreo (for African Americans), an Apple (for American Indians), a Coconut (for Latinos), and a Banana or Twinkie (for Asian Americans).

These accusations also attack an individual's self-esteem because a consequence of rejecting a collective identity is to lose the collective esteem that comes with it. David Taylor (2002) has argued that for any individual, the development of a personal identity requires engaging in a process of answering the question: "Who am I?" At the same time, he or she must develop self-esteem based on the acquisition of sufficient evidence to support a positive response to the question: "Am I worthy?" (p. 35). Embracing a collective identity provides a basis for developing both personal identity and self-esteem.

Another positive outcome for the adolescent who develops an ethnic identity is having sufficient confidence in his or her abilities to provide a sense of competence. As De Vos and Romanucci-Ross (1995) have noted, the strength of the sense of competence depends upon the group's beliefs: "It is thus psychologically easier for members of certain groups to move up to expectations of group competence if there is a collective confidence shared by the group" (p. 371). This sense of competence enhances self-esteem, but it also strengthens the person's ability to set goals and achieve them. Any individual must believe that he or she has the ability to achieve a goal before he or she will attempt it. The person's perception of his or her competence is more critical than the person's actual abilities. As David Taylor (2002) has asserted: "The issue is not whether the person can *actually* achieve the goal but rather the extent to which they *believe* they can achieve it" (p. 112, emphasis in original).

One of the curiosities of ethnicity in the United States is the persistence of ethnic identity despite the reduction of perceived differences between ethnic groups. In a study of ethnicity that involved people from diverse ethnic groups, individuals claiming an ethnic identity were asked to describe what made their group culturally distinct. Most people responded with the same descriptors: "A family closeness, caring for the elderly, a sense of loyalty and communal values" (Fenton, 1999, p. 228). What their answers suggested was that American ethnic groups may be rejecting the historic emphasis on individuality within the American culture in favor of an orientation found in many cultures that emphasizes family and community.

In some cases, racial identification may be of more significance than ethnic identity. A longitudinal study of adolescents from blue-collar urban families living in a racially and ethnically diverse neighborhood found that ethnicity and culture were not major factors in identity formation for these adolescents. Despite the mix of ethnic groups in the neighborhood, these adolescents did not view the neighborhood as having a significant amount of cultural diversity. On the other hand, the adolescents were very aware of the racial diversity of their neighborhood. They did not view this as a problem; instead they viewed it as "a distinguishing feature of their community . . . this was seen as positive, and [the adolescents] talked openly and eagerly about it" (Sleeter, 1996, p. 169).

Based on studies of identity development, it would seem that anyone's individual identity is an outcome of multiple influences, of which ethnicity is only one. Ethnicity could be a major influence or only a minor one or somewhere in-between. As Fenton (1999) has stated: "No one is a full-time ethnic, . . . [acting] in the same way in all settings" (p. 95). The many forces shaping identity include religion, geographical location (not only regions such as the South or Midwest, but rural, urban, or suburban), abilities (being talented enough to participate in activities such as music or sports), occupation or profession, and others. In addition, when Latinos of Mexican descent call themselves "Mexican Americans," the second half of the term, for those of various ethnic groups that choose to use it, has implications for identity. Many Americans of color have reported that when they travel out of the country, the people they meet often regard them as an American first and only secondarily as a member of a racial or ethnic group, even in the countries where the American tourists' ancestors originated.

Despite the seeming solidarity of ethnic groups, the various forces that shape personal identity inevitably produce complexity within a group. Not only can there be a generation gap as youth find more satisfaction being around their peers than even family members of a previous generation, but differences of gender, sexual orientation, status, and wealth, along with other factors, will likely influence the relationships between group members. Such differences usually are expressed only within the group, but may be expressed publicly if a woman of color declares herself a feminist, or if a man of color comes out of the closet. As Stuart Hall has written:

> All of us are composed of multiple social identities . . . we are all complexly constructed through different categories, of different antagonisms, and these may have the effect of locating us socially in multiple positions of marginality and subordination, but which do not operate on us in exactly the same way. (in Baumann, 1999, p. 145)

Nieto and Bode (2008) use the term *hybridity* to discuss the fusion of diverse cultures in developing individual identities, asserting that individuals form their identity from diverse influences that not only include race and ethnicity, but encompass "gender, sexual orientation, geographic locations and professional affiliation" (pp. 173–174). Although David Taylor (2002) agreed that many self-identifications influence personal identity, he insisted that ethnicity is a cultural identity from a collective group and therefore takes priority over other influences: "My professional role identity may provide me with a blueprint in terms of job-related activities, but my cultural identity provides me with a blueprint for everything" (p. 44).

One of the first manifestations of multiple identities was reflected in the efforts of some individuals to become bicultural, to learn how to function in the mainstream culture while maintaining the skills to interact effectively within their ethnic group. Children from ethnic families have been challenged explicitly or implicitly to develop bicultural competence so that they can be economically and socially successful in mainstream society without losing their ability to interact within their ethnic group. Some people have claimed a bicultural identity simply as a function of birth, without having attained any significant bicultural (or bilingual) competence. Hackney (1997) quotes an Arab American describing what becoming bicultural meant to him: "You preserve your identity, but under the overarching American umbrella. We want to preserve our culture but still be part of the whole" (p. 111).

Because many people have demonstrated their competence at becoming bicultural, some diversity advocates have promoted the development of "multicultural" competence involving the ability to "acquire the norms, attitudes and behaviors of their own and another, perhaps several other, ethnic groups" (Rotheram & Phinney, 1987, p. 24). Some have questioned the ability of one person to acquire sufficient knowledge and values to represent more than one group authentically, but the need to represent all of the groups may not be the purpose in claiming them. Individuals who affirm multiple identities may simply be naming the groups with whom they have a connection and with whom they identify because each of these groups has had some influence on the development of their personal identity. The complexity of these issues for personal identity has caused some to question whether it is even possible to speak of an "American identity."

THE BASIS FOR AN AMERICAN IDENTITY IN A GLOBAL CONTEXT

It is one of the ironies of our contemporary era that as transportation and global communication have been radically transformed to create what we call a "global village," many diverse communities have responded by reaffirming their cultural distinctiveness from other groups. David Taylor (2002) believes that this was a consequence of the proliferation of information about global cultures, because it threatened the sense of collective identities of many groups. In cases where nationality and culture are identical or integrated, the individual is not as likely to experience an identity conflict, but most nations are multicultural and at least parts of one's ethnic identity are likely to be in conflict with a national identity. Increased emphasis on national identity in our global village has caused people in many nations to engage in a conscious embrace of the collective identity of their ethnic group to sustain what Taylor (2002) has called their cultural "blueprint for life."

In the United States, assertions of ethnic identity frequently have been political. Because racial and ethnic groups historically have encountered prejudices and discriminatory behavior, they have had to denounce this oppression and demand equitable treatment. Some scholars have described the persistence of these groups as necessary for their survival, but activities labeled "identity politics" also have been criticized as an effort to gain resources at the expense of others. Yet Mayo (2000) observed that people in ethnic groups and social justice movements who promoted a positive collective identity for their members understood that they could not avoid addressing social problems. The demand for cultural recognition from the dominant society was necessary for an ethnic or social group to introduce accumulated evidence of historical discrimination against their group, and to lobby for resources to fund positive actions and to provide opportunities intended to redress the past oppression. The latter part of their response often involved engaging in research and then disseminating information to affirm the group's history or heritage and its collective dignity (De Vos, 2006).

In the United States, many members of the dominant society have been critical of "identity politics" as being antithetical to our national identity, but advocates insist that such actions merely reflect an American tradition of legitimate efforts by groups in our diverse society to achieve collective and individual goals (Fuchs, 1990). Other critics have argued that this resource competition has pitted racial and ethnic groups against one another, undermining efforts to promote collaborative activities among oppressed groups against common sources of exploitation and discrimination.

Another criticism of identity politics is that it has forced people claiming multiple identities to prioritize them and identify primarily with one group in order to participate in that group's political activities. Advocates acknowledge these issues, but they argue that intergroup collaborative efforts are already in place and they are increasing. Further, they view the trend toward claiming multiple identities as part of the solution to reducing divisiveness among groups. As more people acknowledge the influence of multiple identities on the formation of one's personal identity, the possibilities for nurturing more intergroup understanding will be enhanced and collaborative actions will likely increase.

Ultimately, there is a national identity for Americans, but like ethnic identity it is not a static phenomenon. Human beings are influenced by their national culture, but in the United States members of the culturally dominant group often have emphasized their group as the defining aspect of that identity. Tatum (1997) described how White Americans do not recognize the influence of being White on their identity and simply claim to be "normal," often expressed as being "just an American." Despite our nation's increasing diversity, such sentiments are still expressed. Shortly after Republican Scott Brown won his surprising victory in 2009 for the Massachusetts Senate seat formerly held by Ted Kennedy, some pundits suggested that his victory might have expressed, in part, the voters' desire to elect someone who looked the way we expect politicians to look (i.e., middle-aged White male). Peggy Noonan agreed, saying that Brown appeared to be "a regular guy" who "looks like an American" (Extra!, 2010, p. 3).

All people in the United States must move beyond such limited perceptions of what it means to be an American. The historic image of an American as a White male must give way to multiple images that better represent the diversity in our society. Scholars no longer assume White people are the norm but study Whiteness as the perspective of a dominant group in a multicultural America, investigating how this group uses its power and privilege to influence our society. Despite the reality of multiple identities and the recognition of diversity among Americans, Fuchs (1990) and others argue that there is a common set of core values that unifies us as a people and draws us close together. Hing (1997) described those core values as "respect for laws, the democratic political and economic system, equal opportunity and human rights" (p. 4). Hing also emphasized that having a core concept for "an American" does not require the end of ethnic communities or ethnic identities. Instead he regards ethnic identity or the claim of multiple identities as essential: "Indeed, diversity must be the basis for an 'American' identity" (p. 4).

CHAPTER 6

Multicultural Education in K–12 Schools

Preparing Children and Youth to Function Effectively in a Diverse, Democratic Society

Compulsory school attendance laws and the great expenditures for education both demonstrate our recognition of the importance of education to our democratic society. . . . It is the very foundation of good citizenship.

—Brown v. Board of Education, 1954

Although many people associate the term *multicultural education* with the 1960s and the Civil Rights Movement, the roots of this educational reform program extend far deeper. Some scholars identify these roots in the work of early ethnic studies researchers such as Charles C. Wesley, W. E. B. Du Bois, and Carter G. Woodson, who advocated in 1933 that school curricula incorporate the history and culture of African Americans in his book *The Mis-Education of the Negro*. Yet, nearly a decade before the publication of that book, a White woman named Rachel Davis DuBois was already incorporating multicultural information into her high school curriculum.

THE ORIGINS OF MULTICULTURAL EDUCATION

In 1915, Rachel Davis graduated from Bucknell University, married Nathan DuBois, and got a teaching job at Glassboro, New Jersey. Being a Quaker and a committed pacifist, Davis DuBois left her teaching position, and with her husband's financial support engaged in peace activities and attended several international conferences on women's rights that also addressed issues of peace and social justice. These activities inspired her to return to teaching, but with a new focus on respect for diversity (C. A. M. Banks, 2005).

In 1924, Davis DuBois began teaching at Woodbury High School in New Jersey in classrooms that included a diverse student population. Because of the continuing emphasis on Americanization, teachers tended to present American history and culture without reference to or respect for the diverse cultural heritages of students from immigrant families. Many families tried to preserve their cultural heritage in their homes or through community activities if they lived in ethnic neighborhoods. Some communities had ethnic organizations and printed ethnic newspapers, and in some cases their cultural heritage was affirmed in their church or labor union (Reich, 2002).

Dissatisfied with traditional curricula, Davis DuBois was constantly searching for better ways to educate ethnically diverse students. Rejecting the Americanization approach urged in popular educational pamphlets and influenced by the writings of W. E. B. Du Bois, she gathered racial and ethnic information to infuse into her curriculum, and she also developed innovative teaching strategies (D. L. Lewis, 2000). She was influenced by John Dewey, who had argued in 1916 that an American was a "hyphenated character," and that public schools should take this factor into account by teaching "each factor to respect every other, and . . . to enlighten all as to the great contributions of every strain of our composite make-up" (Reich, 2002, p. 15).

By 1926, Davis DuBois had created a unique approach that she called "the Woodbury Plan"—a multicultural curriculum incorporating aspects of immigrant cultures such as music, dress, and cuisine, as well as information on the history of racial and ethnic communities in America. In 1930, she retired from her high school position to focus on further development of her curriculum and to promote what was called interracial or intercultural education (Pak, 2006). Although urban schools were especially diverse, most urban teachers used traditional teaching strategies and believed they should Americanize immigrant children by eliminating all traces of their ethnic heritage. Helped by the growing influence of Progressive education, advocates like Davis DuBois encouraged educators to respect student ethnicities. In the Woodbury Plan, students were asked to write about their ethnic heritage and about their experiences as part of an immigrant family (Pak, 2006). Davis DuBois worked with schools in New Jersey, New York City, and Boston to implement the Woodbury Plan (D. L. Lewis, 2000).

In her work with schools, Davis DuBois was adamant that teachers had to go beyond simply promoting tolerance to promoting pluralistic attitudes. In her curriculum she described the contributions of people like Lue Gim Gong, a Chinese American who received awards for his work in developing a new type of orange more resistant to frost. Criticized for focusing on individual ethnic achievements and the heritages of ethnic immigrants, Davis DuBois argued that her approach provided a more realistic and accurate description of how all groups had participated in the development of American society. Her materials addressed such subjects as American history and literature, music and art, economics, and science. She called her method of infusing multicultural knowledge into the curriculum an "incidental approach" because this information was "woven incidentally into our classroom work without harming either the College Board or Regents Exam" (Pak, 2006, p. 8).

The relationship between Davis DuBois and the Progressive Education Association was not incidental. She shared John Dewey's vision that diverse students who came together in schools should learn not only subject matter but how to live in a diverse, democratic society. In 1934, Davis DuBois and other educators established a Service Bureau for Human Relations as a branch of the Progressive Education Association. After she helped coin the term *intercultural education*, the name was changed to the Service Bureau for Intercultural Education (SBIE) and Davis DuBois was named its first director (Pak, 2006). The SBIE provided educational materials based on American ethnic diversity, disseminated journal articles and reading lists, and provided instructional models for secondary and college educators. Beyond providing information about ethnic diversity and ethnic contributions, SBIE materials often confronted racism; they addressed racial segregation and discrimination in the United States and debunked racial and ethnic stereotypes (C. A. M. Banks, 2005; Pak, 2006).

Teacher education programs as well as elementary and secondary schools across the United States contacted the SBIE to request copies of its curricular materials. The history curriculum identified the first national holiday in America (until it was replaced by the Fourth of July), which commemorated the death of the first martyrs of the American Revolution—the four who died during the Boston Massacre, including Crispus Attucks, a Black man. The science curriculum identified Dr. Daniel Hale Williams, an African American surgeon responsible for the first successful operation on the human heart. These materials not only informed students about ethnic groups, but explored issues of what it meant to be an American and a citizen of a democratic society (Pak, 2006).

In 1938, Davis DuBois contacted the CBS radio network about sponsoring a series of radio programs on ethnic diversity. Although NBC had already rejected her proposal, she persuaded CBS to sponsor *"Americans* All"–a series of radio dramatizations that ran for 26 weeks based on the experiences of American ethnic groups. Not only was Davis DuBois a tireless promoter of intercultural education, but her "innovative presentations of racial and ethnic instructional materials were to make her a major, recognized precursor of multiculturalism" (D. L. Lewis, 2000, p. 270). Despite her success, Davis DuBois had critics, even within the ranks of other educational reformers, and the opposition intensified during the 1940s. C. A. M. Banks (2005) explained what happened to Davis DuBois and other educators who shared her vision: "Intercultural educators who embraced cultural pluralism ultimately found themselves on the margins of a movement that they helped to create" (p. 22).

America's involvement in World War II caused a resurgence of patri otism and a growing desire among educators to teach about similarities be- tween Americans, not differences. Some school administrators made public statements that drawing attention to racial differences among students would "do more harm than good" (Pak, 2006, p. 12). After the war, the Progressive Education Association became a victim of the McCarthy era as it was ac- cused of promoting un-American ideas and having communist sympathies; Davis DuBois was required to testify before Senator McCarthy's committee. Pak (2006) described the conservative National Council for American Edu- cation disseminating pamphlets with the titles "The Commies are Active in the Schools" and "The Commies Go after Your Kids" (p. 19). By 1954, the SBIE had ceased to exist, soon to be followed by the Progressive Education Association, but some of those who had been involved with these groups would support efforts to desegregate schools, and activists such as Davis DuBois participated in the Civil Rights movement. They would find allies among those who advocated multiculturalism and pluralism, and from these efforts an educational reform movement emerged that reflected the vision Rachel Davis DuBois had promoted more than 40 years earlier.

According to J. A. Banks (2006), the Civil Rights Movement sparked an affirmation of ethnic identity in the 1960s that challenged traditional expecta- tions regarding assimilation in the United States and became a global phe- nomenon when indigenous and ethnic groups in Western nations reclaimed their unique identities, described their marginalization, and demanded that societal institutions address their issues and needs. In the 1960s, ethnic stud- ies in the United States was a growing field as more people of color rejected the traditional assimilation model of conformity and asserted their pride in their ethnic identity. Ethnic studies courses led to an interest in multiethnic education in which information on America's diverse ethnic groups was in- fused into social studies and English curricula. People of color challenged a status quo that required conformity as a prerequisite for social and eco- nomic success. They asserted their right to be different and demanded that the United States embrace pluralism as a more appropriate strategy for a nation so culturally diverse. Such arguments were persuasive to some educa- tional leaders, and in 1972 the American Association of Colleges for Teacher Education approved an official statement, "No One Model American," that rejected the traditional emphasis on conformity and advocated a pluralistic perception of Americans (Pai & Adler, 1997).

Before long, concerns for inequities beyond race and ethnicity created pressure on advocates for multiethnic education to address issues related to poverty, gender, disabilities, religion, and regional groups. Although race and ethnicity still played a major role, the movement expanded to include additional cultural groups, and it was called multicultural education (J. A. Banks, 1994). Advocates emphasized not simply the ethics of being more inclusive but academic concerns. They argued that the monocultural content of American classrooms was a significant factor in the disparity between the educational achievements of White students and students of color that had been reported for decades. These advocates insisted that if teachers included multicultural information that affirmed ethnic identities of culturally diverse students in their curricula, the academic achievements of students would significantly increase (Baker, 1994).

In its evolution as an educational reform movement, multicultural education has had many influences. In the 1970s, addressing the needs of students with disabilities attracted passionate advocates, supportive educators, and staunch opponents, but the commitment to students with special needs reflected the ideals and principles of multicultural education. With increasing immigration of non-English speakers, multicultural education advocates promoted bilingual education, an approach that reinforced their commitment to affirming differences and promoting multiple perspectives. As demands for educational reform have gained strength worldwide, multicultural education has become a global movement, with indigenous and ethnic groups challenging schools in many Western nations to include information about their cultures and histories.

In 1976, the National Council for the Accreditation of Teacher Education acknowledged the growing presence of diverse students in America's schools by including multicultural education in its accreditation standards. Multicultural content was added to curriculum guidelines for all but one of the 17 identified national subject areas (Banks et al., 2005). Despite these achievements, multicultural education got the attention primarily of theorists and educational organizations until the 1980s, when increasing numbers of schools started to implement its ideas and strategies. Sleeter (1996) has described why this occurred:

> As classrooms across the U.S. became more culturally diverse and teachers increasingly began asking for help and as many turned to the growing literature

base in multicultural education, more and more Euro-American teachers who had never been involved in social movements took ownership in multicultural education. (p. 229)

It is not surprising that a backlash to multicultural education would occur in the 1980s. Before the end of the decade, 37 states attempted to pass "English only" laws and the Reagan administration drastically reduced funding for bilingual education. In 1987, Alan Bloom's bestselling book *The Closing of the American Mind* argued that multicultural education contradicted American culture by emphasizing cultural diversity and pluralism instead of individualism. Scholars such as Schlesinger (1991) weighed in on the debate by accusing multicultural education of promoting a national fragmentation. Pai and Adler (1997) insisted that much of the criticism in the popular press was based on inaccurate and distorted views of multicultural education.

Despite the criticism, multicultural education continued to attract advocates, and in 1991 a National Association for Multicultural Education was established. By the early 1990s, 40 of the 50 states were requiring instruction in some aspect of multicultural education as part of their teacher preparation programs (Banks et al., 2005). The success of the movement increased the ranks of critics, primarily conservatives who had ignored multicultural education's reform efforts as long as they were restricted to educational conferences and a few urban schools. According to Sleeter (1996), what alarmed the critics now was the inclusion of multicultural education at major universities and its incorporation into curricula and pedagogy even at predominantly White K–12 schools, but their criticisms were largely unpersuasive. Multicultural education continued to promote curricular and pedagogical reforms to enhance the academic achievement and social development of all students, and the ongoing diversity and demographic predictions for more diversity in the future provided a compelling rationale for educators to persist in exploring multicultural education as the best way to serve the needs of their diverse students.

THE IMPLICATIONS OF DEMOGRAPHIC DATA

Reich (2002) argued that America's schools, especially urban schools, have always contained students from diverse populations: "Multiculturalism is in fact a new word applied to an old issue" (p. 16). Yet Reich overlooked the challenge for contemporary educators to determine how to teach about America and its fundamental values to these diverse students. Racial and ethnic differences are a major factor, but not the only one. Over the past 3 decades, economic changes have resulted in an increased number of students coming from low-income families, with more than 20% of all K–12 students living in poverty (Children's Defense Fund, 2008). The growing presence of openly lesbian, gay, bisexual, and transgender students in K–12 schools is the result of a decline in the average age for people "coming out"–14 for males and 17 for females (Gay, Lesbian and Straight Education Network, 2008).

The challenge to educators is greater than ever because the diversity is greater than ever–including increased racial and ethnic diversity. Banks and colleagues (2005) report that students of color attending American schools constituted only 22% of all students in 1972, but today they make up nearly 40%. In addition, students of color now constitute the majority of students in the District of Columbia and in the states of Arizona, California, Hawaii, Louisiana, Mississippi, New Mexico, and Texas (Gollnick & Chinn, 2009). Based on their observations at a California elementary school, Darling-Hammond and Garcia-Lopez (2002) provided an illustration of this diversity:

> In a typical classroom in the heart of the Silicon Valley, a teacher can find herself facing a room of students less than half of whom were born in this country. In addition to historical minority groups such as African Americans, Mexican Americans, and Chinese Americans, there are likely to be students from places like Zambia, South Africa, Russia, Bosnia, Brazil, Cambodia, Vietnam, Samoa, and the Philippines. Diversities in learning styles, interests, developed abilities, sexual orientations, and socioeconomic status are also evident for teachers who have developed eyes to see the many facets of each of their students' lives and identities. (p. 10)

This California school represents an optimistic view of the future; a pessimistic view emerges from descriptions of segregated schools in urban areas (Kozol, 2005). Students of color are now the majority of students in 23 of the 25 largest school districts in the United States (Villegas & Lucas, 2002). According to Hancock (2006), White students constitute less than 11% of all students in six of the ten largest urban districts in the United States (Los Angeles, Chicago, Houston, Detroit, Dallas, Miami, and Memphis). By contrast, many suburban and rural schools have overwhelmingly White student populations, with few students of color. To support an optimistic view of the future, American schools need to be organized so that they consist of an array of diverse students. If America's children and youth continue to attend segregated schools, Americans will have to resolve educational challenges and social justice issues inevitably arising within a nation that is characterized by persistent racial apartheid in its neighborhoods and schools.

The U.S. Census Bureau predicts that people of color will constitute half of the population of the United States by 2050 (J. A. Banks, 2006), but this demographic change will happen even faster in the schools. Some project that students of color will constitute almost half of students by 2020 (Gollnick & Chinn, 2009); others report more cautiously that it will be 2035 when students of color become the majority (Banks et al., 2005). By 2050, demographic projections for all K–12 students predict a White/non-White ratio of 44%/56%, with 30% being Latinos, 16% African Americans, 9% Asian Americans, and 1% American Indians (Villegas & Lucas, 2002).

Given these numbers, multicultural educators express concern about the lack of diversity among teachers. As the 21st century began, teachers of color constituted only 9% of the 3 million K–12 public school teachers (Irvine, 2003). Teacher education programs report an ongoing pattern of 80%–93% of their students being White—a pattern that shows no sign of changing in the future (J. A. Banks, 2006). This has significant implications for teacher education and multicultural education. Determining the most effective way to teach diverse students will be a major focus for teachers in the 21st century. As Howard (1999) wrote: "Diversity is not a choice, but our responses to it certainly are" (p. 2).

MULTICULTURAL EDUCATION TO AFFIRM DIVERSITY

Although the debate about how to respond to racial and ethnic diversity in American public schools has a long history, in recent years the debate has changed. According to Reich (2002), the focus is no longer on whether schools should recognize the diverse racial and ethnic identities of students, but on the extent to which this diversity should be recognized and affirmed in school curricula. His argument is not that schools no longer marginalize students based on race, ethnicity, or other factors, but that schools are no longer overtly oppressive. Reich (2002) insists that oppressive behavior in schools today would violate stated policies in most public and private schools. What has stayed the same in the debate about diversity is the concern about fostering an American identity and about how to promote citizenship in a diverse, democratic society.

Pai and Adler (1997) noted that advocates for pluralism believe that multicultural education is appropriate for a democratic society because "participatory democracy is fundamentally pluralistic . . . it entails the acceptance of the intrinsic worth of all human beings and their unique individuality" (p.

104). Yet opponents of multicultural education often characterize it as another manifestation of the demand for group rights and contend that an emphasis on groups may foster separatist attitudes and behaviors. In response, Darling-Hammond (2002) asserted: "Far from encouraging separatism, acknowledgment of diverse experiences creates new associations that helps us ultimately to build the common ground in which a more inclusive and powerful learning community can rest" (p. 3).

Yet critics of multicultural education say this approach fosters group conflicts by being anti-White and anti-male, and that multicultural education also encourages negative attitudes toward the United States (Gorski, 2006). Some advocates have responded by insisting that teaching about diverse groups and diverse perspectives in American society attempts to provide students with a more inclusive and more accurate portrayal of an American society that has always been diverse. The purpose of teaching multiple perspectives is to develop an understanding of diverse perspectives that can lead to an understanding of what motivates the behavior of others. It also should encourage students to examine their own beliefs and attitudes. Multicultural educators insist that when schools provide the perspective of a dominant group only, they are not promoting patriotism but are engaging in propaganda—"If mine is the only way of life I know, how can I judge that it is in fact a worthy and valuable way of life?" (Reich, 2002, p. 133).

In describing the ideological thinking behind the resistance to multicultural education, Vavrus (2010) identified six ideological assumptions:

- Racism is a historical artifact that is only manifested through aberrant individual behaviors, rather than a regular experience for many children and youth of color.
- Schools and classrooms are sites of fairness, not of institutional racism.
- Eurocentric curricula offer superior academic experiences.
- Academic achievement is independent of lived histories, even for those who experience forms of subordination through racism, classism, and sexism.
- Students of color and poor whites come to schools with knowledge deficits and lack the competence to succeed academically.
- The source of student academic failure rests with the family and community, not the learning environment of the school and a teacher's disposition toward social justice. (p. 26)

These ideological assumptions are held by some teachers and by individuals outside of schools who want to maintain the status quo of educational practice. Villegas and Lucas (2002) have explained why maintaining the status quo in schools is unacceptable: "Built into the fabric of schools are curricular, pedagogical, and evaluative practices that intentionally or unintentionally privilege the affluent, white, and male segment of society" (p. 30). Pluralists have called traditional education undemocratic because of this unequal opportunity it has provided to students based on socioeconomic status, ethnicity, and other factors.

Many scholars have addressed the aims, goals, and purposes of multicultural education, and an analysis of their work suggests five major student outcomes:

1. All students should be encouraged to affirm themselves as unique individuals and they should accept and respect the differences shaping individual identities of other students. J. A. Banks (1999) has written: "The claim that multicultural education is only for ethnic groups of color and the disenfranchised is one of the most pernicious and damaging misconceptions with which the movement has had to cope" (p. 5).

2. Students should learn about their group from the school curriculum and about the diverse groups in American society to have a basis of appreciation and respect for cultural diversity. Pai and Adler (1997) have described the value of this outcome for students and adults: "Appreciating different cultures, which should be viewed as pools of collective experiences, knowledge, wisdom, and the vision of other people, can make our own lives richer" (p. 122).

3. Students should engage in intergroup dialogues that promote cross-cultural communication skills and reduce biases and prejudices. Gorski (2006) has written that multicultural education must "institutionalize inclusivity, to engage a broader set of worldviews that, woven together, provide all of us with a deeper understanding of the world and ourselves" (p. 69).

4. Students should learn to be critical thinkers able to analyze historical and contemporary issues in order to make intelligent decisions about problems and conflicts. Appleton (1983) addressed the need for historical analysis: "Multicultural education must deal with the social and historical realities of American society and help students gain a better understanding of the causes of oppression

and inequality and the ways in which these social problems might be eliminated" (p. 216).

5. Students should engage in activities that address social justice issues and should be encouraged to develop and implement strategies to respond to such issues in their school and their community. J. A. Banks (2006) described the relationship between diversity and social justice: "Diversity . . . provides schools, colleges and universities with an opportunity to educate students in an environment that reflects the reality of the nation and the world and to teach students from diverse groups how to get along and how to make decisions and take actions in the public interest" (p. 144).

Given these student outcomes, advocates for multicultural education have insisted that if a diverse society is to thrive, citizens must respect and value diversity. Reich (2002) has argued that respect for diversity depends upon learning about diversity: "I may tolerate people without the least bit of knowledge about them; I may not, however, respect them" (p. 136). Multicultural education goes beyond tolerance by teaching about the need for mutual respect between people belonging to diverse groups. In addressing this issue, Nieto (2002) asks a critical question: "If all we expect of students is tolerance, can we ever hope that they will reach the point where they understand, respect, and affirm differences?" (p. 257).

Teaching to promote mutual respect does not mean that only positive information about diverse groups should be presented. Human history is a record of persistent flaws in human thought and behavior, and no group is exempt from this reality. Nieto (2002) has rejected what she called a "sunny-side-up diversity" that celebrates diversity as an abstract concept and "attempts to paper over important differences" (p. 111). Multicultural education engages in a critical examination of power and structural inequities, and explores conflicts between and within groups. By presenting human flaws and group conflicts as well as the achievements of diverse groups, Reich (2002) believes that multicultural education teaches "why [students] should respect views that they may consider to be false" (p. 136).

The theory behind multicultural education may sound persuasive, but has it been effective in practice? The main difficulty with assessing programs claiming to illustrate multicultural education is the different goals established by different schools. Nieto and Bode (2008) have described four types of programs whose goals vary widely: (1) *tolerance* simply emphasizes getting along with people who are different and denies the significance of differences; (2) *acceptance* acknowledges that differences are important to people but does not affirm diversity; (3) *respect* views differences in a positive light and promotes learning about diversity; and (4) *affirmation, solidarity, and critique* entail a commitment to social justice issues beyond the classroom, rejecting a romanticized view of culture and promoting the idea that culture is dynamic, changing over time. In his review of multicultural education programs regarded as effective in promoting intergroup relations, Stephan (2004) supported Nieto's advocacy for the fourth type of program in his description of common themes, among them:

> Differences are to be prized, not disparaged; people from different groups treat each other with respect, not disdain; social justice is a lived reality, not just an ideal; and co-existence means more than merely tolerating the presence of other groups. (p. 266)

Although multicultural education is a reform that can be initiated at the classroom level, Banks and colleagues (2005) emphasized that for educators to be successful in addressing the problems of the traditional approach, it is more effective if multicultural education is implemented as a school-wide reform:

> Without an explicit agenda . . . to look for ways to recognize and support all students, to offer all individuals and groups a rich and meaningful curriculum, and to build positive relationships across students, many schools inadvertently (and sometimes knowingly) distribute opportunities for learning and success inequitably. (p. 254)

This situation exists in many schools today, but those supporting the status quo say that multicultural education will lead to social conflict and a loss of national unity. Advocates counter that intergroup conflict already exists in the United States, but their reform movement addresses the need to abide by a set of national norms and still value cultural diversity. Reich (2002) has put it this way: "The challenge of any educational theory . . . is to navigate successfully between protecting the *pluribus* while also promoting an *unum*" (p. 116).

IMPLEMENTING MULTICULTURAL EDUCATION

J. A. Banks (2006) believes that multicultural education should "*American-ize* America" by assisting students in gaining the knowledge and skills to appreciate the ideals expressed in the founding documents of this nation (p. 146, emphasis in original). Perhaps the biggest threat to multicultural education is what some have called the trivialization of this reform effort. Gorski (2006) described the experience of a team of consultants who had been invited to an urban high school. They met with students and heard many complaints about racism at the school; they later met with administrative staff. They asked about the school's vision for multicultural education, and the principal said: "We must celebrate the joys of diversity. We must find ways to share our cultures–our food, our dress, our art. We pride ourselves on celebrating diversity" (pp. 62–63). It is easy to say the right words, but it takes commitment and effort to achieve the goals of multicultural education. Gorski (2006) argued that schools will fail if "in place of equity and social justice, we offer festivals, sensitivity training, and cultural tourism, often resulting in little more than a deeper entrenchment of stereotypes and assumptions" (p. 71).

Multicultural Curricula

Sleeter (1996) has criticized schools that trivialize multicultural education in focusing exclusively on cultural differences as represented by "folksongs and folktales, food fairs, holiday celebrations and information about famous people" (p. 145). The "information" Sleeter refers to often includes superficial facts about famous people that typically avoid their controversial words or actions. Kozol (2011) described how historical figures who were engaged in social change, such as Helen Keller and Martin Luther King, Jr., are portrayed in textbooks in a way that: "drain[s] the person of nine tenths of his real passion, guts and fervor" (p. 320). English classes teach "The Miracle Worker" showing the young Helen Keller learning how to speak, but her radical speeches as an adult fighting for social justice are not addressed. Textbooks focus on King's "I Have a Dream" speech while ignoring his radical advocacy for poor people and his anti-war activities.

In her review of studies analyzing curricular content, Gay (2010) explained why textbooks must be included in any discussion of curricular reform. Although technology makes alternative information more accessible, textbooks retain their dominant position, accounting for 70%–95% of the assigned curriculum content. Textbooks have been revised in recent years to include more multicultural information, but most experts still regard them as inadequate. Gay (2010) concluded: "Most textbooks used in schools are controlled by the dominant group (European Americans) and confirm its status, culture, and contributions" (p. 129). Sefa Dei (2006) agrees, arguing that individual teachers who want to teach a multicultural curriculum must not rely on textbooks but rather infuse multicultural content in their classrooms because in textbooks "Eurocentric knowledge masquerades as universal knowledge" (p. 30). Akbar (2011) provided some examples to illustrate Sefa Dei's assertion:

- Despite its thousands of years of precedent history, America is defined as originating at the moment White people appeared on these shores a little over 1,500 years ago. America is suddenly "discovered" with the entrance of the White man.
- The logical methods known as science and mathematics are presented as *their* (White) creative genius.
- Architecture, art, philosophy, religion, or any other arena of human endeavor begins at the White privileged benchmark.
- Healing practices of non-whites (are described) as magic . . . and superstition until White scientists decipher the codes and define these same herbs and methods as medicinal and scientifically legitimate.
- Civilization begins with (White people) and the only information worth knowing is information about or from them. (pp. 43–44)

Teaching such a curriculum sends a message to all students—a message that may seem engaging and affirming to White students but irrelevant and even punitive to students of color. Sefa Dei (2006) maintains: "Either education does something *for* you or *to* you" (p. 30, emphasis in original). An education does something *to* racial and ethnic students when it describes the genius of Thomas Jefferson but not the genius of W. E. B. Du Bois, when it describes the efforts of Jane Addams to improve the lives of immigrants but doesn't describe similar efforts by Cesar Chavez, when it includes literature written by award-winning White authors such as William Faulkner and Ernest Hemingway but does not include award-winning ethnic writers such as Maxine Hong Kingston, Sandra Cisneros, Leslie Marmon Silko, and Toni Morrison. J. A. Banks (2006) cited research reporting improved academic achievement among students of color when the knowledge and the culture of their ethnic groups was included in the curriculum. This is how a curriculum can do something *for* students.

Another way that supplemental materials can do something *for* students of color is by providing a more realistic portrayal of ethnic minorities to offset the pervasiveness of stereotypical images on television. These visual images are a powerful source of information for both children and adults. Gay (2010) described the stereotypes on television, including Black men often presented as violent and socially irresponsible, and Black women often portrayed as having "an attitude"—meaning that they are angry and domineering. Native Americans most often are portrayed as historical figures, and if contemporary Native Americans appear, the focus tends to be on social problems such as poverty or alcoholism. Asian Americans usually reflect a version of the model minority stereotype, yet also are portrayed as perpetual outsiders unable to assimilate. The perpetual outsider image is used for Latinos as well, and urban Latinos often are presented as violent gang members.

Certain subjects such as art, music, literature, history, and other social sciences can incorporate readily available content addressing historic and current stereotypes, but some teachers argue that a subject such as science includes objective information that is universal—an atom is an atom regardless of a student's race, ethnicity, gender, or income. Yet, Villegas and Lucas (2002) described a science lesson on weather created by a multicultural educator. The teacher began by explaining how elders in early African cultures accurately predicted the weather: "careful observations of natural signs, such as the behavior of birds, cloud formations, and the color of the sky" (p. 104). The teacher had the students engage in research on how other cultures predicted the weather and asked them to interview elders in their own communities to discover whether they made weather predictions based on their bodily aches and pains or other signs. The Internet has many websites providing lesson plans and resources for a multicultural approach to science and math, and there are also print resources (Cirillo, Bruna, & Herbel-Eisenmann, 2010; Dean, 2008–2009; Gutstein & Peterson, 2005; Melear, 1995).

A multicultural curriculum requires students to recognize the diverse groups that constitute the United States and to include students of all colors, faiths, and other human differences in their concept of an American. For decades multicultural educators have argued that because it is more inclusive, a multicultural curriculum is more accurate than the traditional curriculum. At an undergraduate workshop on multicultural education, a professor offered that rationale for infusing multicultural content into school classrooms. When asked if there were any comments or questions, an African American student said: "It's about tellin' the truth, you know? We need to tell the truth."

Multicultural Pedagogy

Banks and colleagues (2005) report that concepts and principles of multicultural education have tended to be incorporated into most teaching preparation programs, but there are still those who resist this approach. In 2004, the state of Washington adopted a new system for the evaluation of preservice teachers that incorporated multicultural education principles. Prior to its final adoption, conservative state legislators and business leaders successfully lobbied to delete language about students developing an understanding of White privilege and the inadequacies of a color-blind approach in classrooms (Vavrus, 2010). Resistance also comes from inside teacher preparation programs, as when students demand assurances that the strategies associated with multicultural education will be effective. Although no educational approach can make such guarantees, some students justify being unwilling to use multicultural education strategies when they become teachers without such assurances (Gay & Jackson, 2006).

From their review of research, Villegas and Lucas (2002) report that many White, middle-class teachers regard student diversity as a problem to be overcome rather than an asset. With such negative attitudes toward diversity, teachers may have low expectations for some students—especially students of color or students from low-income families. They also may blame the parents for a child's lack of motivation or poor academic skills rather than attribute such academic problems to the inequalities students have encountered in school or society. In a study of teachers from 26 urban elementary schools, Irvine (2003) asked the teachers to explain academic failure among three groups of students—African Americans, Latinos, and Vietnamese. The teachers tended to view lack of parental support as one of the major factors for all three groups, and as the primary factor for African Americans. For Latino and Vietnamese students, teachers identified the main factor as a consequence of students' difficulties with the English language, and they identified having a negative self-concept as a factor in the academic failure of African American and Vietnamese students. The teachers rejected all options suggesting that the school environment or teachers themselves could have contributed to students' academic problems.

Many educators say that what's most important is to treat students equally, and they are committed to that concept. Yet when educators say they treat students equally, most often they mean treating students "the same," as if all students had the same strengths and needs. Cymrot (2002) provided examples of the absurdity of this approach:

> "Equality" meant testing a Laotian-born young poet, a devourer of novels, and placing her in a remedial English class. Equality is the word of the day when schools plan parent–teacher conferences during a single weekday with no alternative scheduling, blind to the mysterious trend that those who show up are the young, suburban, stay-at-home moms. Equality is the paint-by-the-numbers discipline procedure that is so "fair" and "equitable" that the fact that

the detention halls are populated almost solely by the young Black boys in a multiracial school is not questioned. (pp. 15–16)

Whether stemming from a fear of rejection or simply a fear of differences, studies have found that people generally are attracted to others who seem most like themselves (Aronson, 2008). Teachers must acknowledge this attraction, and they must make every effort in their classrooms to ensure that it is not affecting their relationships with their diverse students, or the students' relationships with one another. Even if racial or ethnic diversity is not present, Cymrot (2002) described other kinds of diversity: "They are a spectrum of students with different learning styles. They are the readers and the nonreaders. They are the young scholars and the young athletes. . . . They are students with full bellies who are dropped off at school as their parents head to work, and the students who come to school each day hungry and malnourished" (p. 14). Students are aware of this diversity, and it may be one reason why they avoid interacting with certain other students. J. Steele (2002) described the challenge facing the multicultural teacher: "Because the attraction toward similarity is so strong, teachers often fight an uphill battle to persuade students to acknowledge and appreciate diversity" (p. 18).

Some teachers want to emphasize similarities among students and downplay differences; they may or may not advocate being "color-blind," but they want to avoid talking about race as if doing so would promote racism. By contrast, multicultural educators insist that failing to confront racist information and attitudes harbored among students allows their racism to persist. As Sefa Dei (2006) has asserted: "Those who speak about race do not create a problem that is nonexistent. . . . Refusing to speak [about] race does not enable any resistance to the negative interpretation of racial differences" (p. 36). In exploring racial issues, teachers must not merely focus on racial differences but discuss the concept of multiple identities so that students can understand how meaningless it is to focus on a single factor like race as a way to understand another person and interpret his or her actions.

In schools with diverse student populations, Reich (2002) argued that teachers should facilitate cross-cultural dialogues. Having students engage in such discussions in the context of mutual respect should provide a deeper understanding of other perspectives and of their own culture and identity, perhaps compelling enough at times to change their perspective with regard to self-perceptions or perceptions of others. Based on the experiences of her children at a diverse high school where race and other multicultural issues were routinely discussed, Kugler (2002) concluded that schools with diverse students could provide the best education for White students as well as students of color because of the exposure to diverse perspectives, which motivated students to reflect more deeply and thoughtfully on their own beliefs.

All teachers bring their own culture into the classroom, but multicultural educators must be committed to learning about the diverse cultures their students represent and to working with students to create classrooms that accommodate cultural differences. Multicultural educators challenge teachers not to view culturally diverse students as having cultural "deficits," but to regard cultural differences as assets for teachers to strengthen and build upon (Pai & Adler, 1997). Nieto and Bode (2008) believe that learning about diverse cultures should produce a transformation: "Becoming a multicultural teacher . . . means becoming a multicultural person" (p. 424). This transformation will require teachers to confront their own prejudices and biases, and learn how to interpret and understand reality from perspectives other than their own.

Teachers can honor diverse cultures and families in diverse communities by respecting the knowledge embedded in those communities and building on that knowledge. This is what Hancock (2006) called "cultural literacy," and he argued that teacher preparation programs must address the cultural illiteracy of their students if future teachers are to be successful in classrooms with diverse students. Especially in urban schools, students are more likely to respond positively to teachers who build on their existing knowledge "rather than try to force students to fit into the middle-class, Eurocentric ideology of school curriculum practices" (Hancock, 2006, p. 105). When teachers implement multicultural education, Reich (2002) believes the goal should not be "to teach students who they already are . . . rather the goal is to enable children to decide who they want to become and to be able to participate as informed citizens in a democratic and diverse state" (p. 140).

The teacher's role in multicultural education is to assist students in making connections between what they have already learned and what they are learning. Villegas and Lucas (2002) explain how teachers can play that role:

> This involves drawing on students' strengths, challenging their misconceptions, embedding new ideas in problem-solving activities that are relevant and meaningful . . . explaining new concepts with illustrations or examples taken from [students'] everyday lives, and providing opportunities for them to display what they know about the topic. (p. 79)

To play this role effectively, teachers should talk with school paraprofessionals who live in the community, visit community centers and agencies, and talk to community leaders and to people who work in the community. The goal is to gain enough knowledge so that the teacher understands what students are saying about their everyday lives.

Multicultural teachers not only learn about diversity, but address inequities between diverse groups in society. Derman-Sparks (2004) has argued: "It is impossible to teach about diversity without paying attention to the systemic power dynamics in the United States, which assign privilege and lack of privilege based on race, gender, class, physical ability and sexual orientation" (p. 20). Being aware of existing inequalities in society is the first step for multicultural educators in addressing the inequalities in their classrooms, especially in schools with racially and ethnically diverse students. Yet for students to gain the potential advantages of attending a school with a diverse population, the history of desegregation demonstrates that the presence of diverse students is not enough.

In reviewing studies of desegregated schools, Cooper and Slavin (2004) concluded: "Simply placing students in an ethnically and racially varied environment, however, does not ensure that all students will interact across racial lines or that they will view diversity as a constructive quality of their scholastic environment" (p. 56). Although desegregation may bring students together, integration requires an educational setting that actively promotes positive relationships among diverse students. Athletic teams provided some of the first examples of the difference between desegregation and integration. Studies reported that when compared with other students, those involved in sports were more likely to have racially diverse friends and to view diversity as a positive factor at their school (Cooper & Slavin, 2004).

Part of this success in sports was that students were actively engaged in activities with a meaningful purpose. Many multicultural educators have promoted the use of active learning strategies such as those suggested by Appleton (1983): "role playing, simulation games, nondirective styles of leading discussions, having students lead discussions, breaking the class down into small discussion groups, or having students pursue individual or group projects and having them report back to the class on their findings" (p. 213). One of the most highly regarded and well-researched teaching strategies is cooperative learning. Studies evaluating cooperative learning have reported that students developed positive attitudes toward racial diversity, and they also reported a positive effect on student academic achievement and other social measures (Gay, 2010). Based on their review of cooperative learning studies, Cooper and Slavin (2004) concluded: "Students who participate in cooperative learning activities tend to have higher academic test scores, higher self-esteem, a greater number of positive social skills, and fewer negative stereotypes of individuals based on their race or ethnic group" (p. 70).

As our schools become more diverse, it will be even more necessary for teachers to learn about the diverse cultures of their students. Being knowledgeable about the assets in a student's background, as well as difficulties a student may encounter, should help teachers develop a positive attitude toward students from culturally diverse families, making it easier to incorporate aspects of the students' cultures into the classroom. Gay (2010) has described programs incorporating cultural content into the English curriculum at a K–8 school and a 6–12 school. Both schools reported positive effects on academic achievement measured by increased vocabulary and improved reading comprehension and writing skills, and also on student attitudes toward completing reading and writing assignments. The 6–12 school also reported increased scores on standardized tests.

In recent years, some multicultural educators have advocated *culturally responsive teaching* as the most effective strategy for a classroom of diverse students. Gay (2010) defined culturally responsive teaching as: "using the cultural knowledge, prior experiences, frames of reference, and performance styles of ethnically diverse students to make learning encounters more relevant to and effective for them" (p. 31). Culturally responsive teaching does not merely affirm each student's ethnic identity and cultural heritage, but fosters a respect among students for other cultures and ethnic identities. Unlike a traditional competitive classroom, culturally responsive teaching emphasizes academic achievement as a collaborative effort: "Students are held accountable for one another's learning as well as their own" (Gay, 2010, pp. 32–33).

Villegas and Lucas (2002) identified goals of culturally responsive teaching:

a. that all students develop advanced literacy and numeracy skills and facility with technology so they can gain access to rapidly changing information;

b. that they acquire critical thinking skills, including the ability to analyze and interpret complex information, understand social problems, and envision potential solutions to those problems;

c. that they learn to respect and understand multiple perspectives and, at the same time, to evaluate the merit of different positions; and

d. that they become skilled at working collaboratively, making collective decisions, and communicating effectively in cross-cultural settings. (p. 1)

Villegas and Lucas (2002) also described an important task of culturally responsive teachers: "to promote a classroom atmosphere that is conducive to conversation, both between students and teacher and among students themselves. To engage in conversations, students need to feel safe to ask questions, argue, and share views" (p. 94).

Implementing culturally responsive teaching could have a positive impact both academically and socially for students who have not been successful in traditional schools. Gay (2010) believes the underachievement of many marginalized students is a result of "not being taught in school as they learn in their cultural communities. . . . Filtering teaching through the cultural lens of Native, Latino, African, and Asian American students can lead to much greater school success. These students deserve nothing less" (p. 214). Reviewing several studies describing the implementation of culturally based instructional strategies in schools with diverse student populations, Banks and colleagues (2005) concluded that effective implementation of cultural strategies tended to produce the following four outcomes: individual differences are accepted, students feel supported by the teacher and other students, each student's strengths are emphasized, and students are encouraged to pursue diverse perspectives and share them with other students.

Some educators reject taking the culturally responsive teaching approach because it seems overwhelming, but Gay (2010) argued that it should not be viewed as difficult: "Teaching does not have to replicate the cultural features and procedures of different ethnic groups in their entirety. But it should *begin* with [teachers] being informed by and reflective of them" (p. 214, emphasis in original). Multicultural educators who advocate that teachers understand the learning styles of ethnic students also have noted that it is inaccurate to assume that all children in an ethnic group learn the same way. Ladson-Billings (2006) acknowledged the potential for stereotyping if teacher responses to students are based on a static view of culture.

Gay (2010) also has emphasized the diversity within groups: "No ethnic group is culturally or intellectually monolithic" (p. 18). Yet she still contends that learning styles may reflect cultural patterns that influence the way that many children in a particular ethnic group learn. The teacher may enhance student learning by making the teaching and learning process more congruent with cultural patterns. Ladson-Billings (2006) argued that teachers must develop cultural competence to help students "recognize and honor their own cultural beliefs and practices while acquiring access to the wider culture" (p. 36). Although it is important that teachers learn as much as possible about the diverse cultures of their students, the focus of culturally responsive teaching is not on what teachers learn but on how they use what they learn to improve student learning.

Finally, culturally responsive teaching requires teachers to use diverse forms of assessment of student learning, recognizing that no single form of assessment is adequate to measure overall student learning. In addition to traditional testing, assessments could include a finished paper or project, an oral presentation, or a portfolio of academic work created over a period of time (Villegas & Lucas, 2002). Although culturally responsive teaching is a fairly recent development, studies evaluating the effectiveness of this approach have reported positive results. Yet, as Gay (2010) admitted: "The body of evidence about these classroom practices is still relatively small" (p. 236). More experimentation and research eventually will determine whether culturally responsive teaching represents an effective way to teach students in a diverse classroom.

English Language Learners

English language learners (ELL) have a unique set of needs that are different from those of mainstream students, and ELL students are becoming an increasingly significant segment of K–12 student diversity in the United States. In just a decade (1985–1995), the number of ELL students doubled from 1.5 million to 3.2 million (Banks et al., 2005). According to Gort (2005), 25% of students in the United States attending K–12 schools live with a family speaking a language other than English. Goldenberg (2008) reported that there are now 5 million ELL students in American schools, and 80% of them are Spanish speaking. With such increasing numbers of ELL students, language diversity now is routinely included in discussions of diversity in American schools.

Since students in ELL programs are most likely to be students of color, from immigrant families, and often living in low-income homes, multicultural education is especially important for programs preparing ELL teachers. Multicultural educators reject the view that language diversity is a problem; instead, they recognize its academic potential. Since one goal of multicultural education is to identify the strengths that culturally diverse students bring to school and to build on them, ELL teachers need to recognize and build on the language skills of ELL students.

Multicultural educators recommend that ELL teachers learn about historical events involving language discrimination and analyze these events with their students. By discussing such issues, students can develop a context for a better understanding of this ongoing discrimination. For example, there are several linguistic myths in the United States, such as the belief that there has been a decrease in the use of English, and that students living in a home where a language other than English is spoken have more difficulty becoming fluent speakers and writers of English. Gay (2010) debunked both myths and provided evidence that students from homes where another language or a dialect of English is spoken are just as likely as English-speaking students to read, speak, and write Standard English fluently. Nieto and Bode (2008) reported that of K–12 students who speak a language other than English, over 75% are fluent in English and only 7% speak no English at all.

Research studies have concluded that students who come to school speaking a language other than English require 5 to 7 years to become fluent in English (Nieto, 2002). Beginning in the 1990s, most studies comparing alternative approaches to teaching ELL students found that bilingual education was the most effective (Salas, 2006). Despite this research, bilingual education is still a controversial issue. In 1998, California voters passed Proposition 227, virtually terminating bilingual education programs despite the publication of several studies prior to the vote that documented their effectiveness. In one study, students who had completed a bilingual education program tended to have higher scores on tests of reading, math, language, and spelling than their peers who were native English speakers (Nieto, 2002).

English-only programs typically involve a total immersion approach where only English is spoken in the classroom. Although Goldenberg (2008) reports that approximately 60% of ELL learners are receiving some form of English-only instruction, advocates for this approach can produce no credible studies to support it—offering instead only anecdotal evidence. Gort (2005) reviewed several linguistic studies and reported: "A growing body of research points to the educational, social, and psychological benefits associated with educating bilingual learners in their native language as they develop skills in English" (p. 25). Nieto (2002) concurred, citing international studies that were virtually unanimous in concluding: "Children from language minority backgrounds benefit from bilingual programs when their native language plays a major role in their instruction" (p. 61).

Multicultural educators have challenged all teachers to regard bilingual or multilingual students as a resource rather than focusing on their deficiencies in English. Noted linguist Skutnabb-Kangas (2000) has observed that nations throughout the world perceive monolingualism as a deficiency, and she criticized the United States for being almost alone among nations in discouraging its youth from becoming multilingual or even bilingual. Kymlicka (1995) described paradoxical American perceptions of a native English speaker who learns a foreign language as well educated and having a higher social and economic status, whereas immigrants who maintain fluency in their native language while learning English often are portrayed as poorly educated, economically disadvantaged, and even unpatriotic. Gay (2010) charged opponents of bilingualism and bilingual education with being inconsistent, if not hypocritical, because they still support foreign language requirements in high schools or colleges.

In 2006, the National Literacy Panel published its review of research on programs educating ELL students, and in that same year the Center for Research on Education, Diversity and Excellence published its review of these programs. Literacy expert Claude Goldenberg of Stanford University engaged in a meta-analysis of these two major reviews of literacy studies to determine what conclusions could be reached. Although test results showed that ELL students tended to have low scores, they took tests that were written in English so it was not possible to know whether the low scores reflected poor content knowledge or simply the limitations of the students' proficiency in English. More important, Goldenberg (2008) reported that both reviews of literacy studies were in agreement about how to teach ELL students effectively: "Teaching students to read in their first language promotes higher levels of reading achievement in English" (p. 14).

This conclusion was consistent with four previous meta-analyses of research on ELL students, and Goldenberg (2008) addressed the significance of that: "No other area in educational research with which I am familiar can claim five independent meta-analyses based on experimental studies, much less five that converge on the same finding" (p. 15). Goldenberg's analysis of both research reviews also concluded that ELL students in bilingual education programs tended to develop literacy skills that achieved fluency in speaking two languages (i.e., bilingual) and also fluency in reading and writing in both languages (i.e., biliterate).

Despite such impressive results, few of the 5 million ELL students in K–12 public schools today in the United States are likely to be enrolled in bilingual education programs. In 2002, Congress failed to renew the federal Bilingual Education Act, and federal policies continue to emphasize English-only programs for ELL students. Since multicultural education is a reform based on ethical as well as educational principles, it is critical that its advocates join with ELL teachers to confront this injustice and promote the increased implementation of bilingual education programs. The fundamental commitment of advocates for multicultural education is the improvement of academic achievement for all students. It is based on a belief that "no child left behind" should not be an empty promise but a realistic goal achieved by teachers working collaboratively with students and parents to implement the best practices as supported by research.

FUTURE CONCERNS

Since its inception in the 1960s, multicultural education has made significant progress, but its advocates continue to encounter resistance, especially from a dominant White community that includes the vast majority of those enrolled in teacher education programs. That resistance reflects a historic discomfort with diversity despite the pluralism expressed in mission statements and public pronouncements from K–12 schools, colleges, and universities. This is part of a broader social issue—the ongoing racial segregation in our schools and communities. Franklin, Lee, and Orfield (2003) report that White students are the most segregated group because the schools they attend, on average, are 80% White. Sleeter and Bynoe (2006) observed: "White students who live in homogeneous communities, are educated in the traditional Western paradigms, and remain within an isolated geographic location may find it difficult to achieve their career aspirations and/or life goals because of cross-cultural incompetence" (p. 169).

In a multicultural society, it is essential for all people to have sufficient knowledge of diverse groups to interact competently with members of those groups. When that doesn't happen, the individual is not likely to function effectively in a diverse society. Pai and Adler (1997) reinforce Sleeter and Bynoe: "If a person operates rigidly in terms of a single culture . . . that person will be less effective in accomplishing his or her purposes," and there are societal consequences with regard to addressing social problems. The United States needs to have all parts of our diverse society involved if we are to make progress together. Too many White people do not yet grasp the point that Cymrot (2002) has made so eloquently: "Diversity is not just a word but a vast and vital conversation within which all of us are privileged to be taking part" (p. 17).

Sefa Dei (2006) criticized contemporary schools with a "gated-community mentality" regarding the education of diverse students. He has argued for a more inclusive approach: "In opening these proverbial gates, the circle of educational inclusion is widened to more voices, more meaningful participation, and the potential for societal gains" (p. 40). There is some evidence of these gates being opened. In describing teacher preparation programs, J. A. Banks (1999) observed that "more classroom teachers today have studied multicultural education concepts than at any previous point in our nation's history" (p. 9). Stephan and Vogt (2004) described examples of multicultural education programs implemented in K–12 schools and higher education classrooms that have been viewed as highly successful in maintaining or strengthening academic achievements while promoting intergroup relations.

It is likely that evidence supporting multicultural education will continue to grow. As Nieto and Bode (2008) insist: "Anything less than a program of comprehensive multicultural education will continue to short-change students in our schools" (p. 431).

Multicultural education advocates certainly will persist in building upon their current achievements, but one of the unresolved issues is the extent to which this reform should be involved with social change. Many advocates want to emphasize the individual by having high expectations for all students, fostering academic achievement, ensuring equality of opportunity for all students, and promoting the value of diversity. Other advocates have maintained that multicultural education must include a social justice component that cannot be satisfied merely by talking about social injustices, but that requires identifying such injustices in the community or in the school and taking action to address them. As Sleeter (1996) noted: "Multicultural education can best be understood as a form of resistance to oppression" (p. 9). This emphasis on oppression and social justice parallels proposals by diversity management theorists, and perhaps there may be opportunities for future collaboration between members of these professional groups.

Finally, as immigration makes diversity increasingly a global issue, American multicultural educators are finding useful ideas and strategies coming from educators in other nations. Multicultural curricula and strategies have been developed and implemented in such nations as New Zealand, Australia, Canada, and England. Perhaps, in a future not so far away, educators around the world will be working together toward the broader purpose that J. A. Banks (2006) described for future students: "We should educate students to be effective citizens of their cultural communities, the nation, and the world" (p. 145).

CHAPTER 7

Globalization, Diversity, and Pluralism

Finding the Common Ground

The challenge in this era of globalization—for countries and individuals—is to find a healthy balance between preserving a sense of identity, home and community and doing what it takes to survive within the globalization system.

—Thomas Friedman, 1999, p. 35

It took thousands of years for the human population to reach 1 billion people in 1800, but only 125 years to reach 2 billion and 35 years to add another billion. In 1974 we reached 4 billion and in another 14 years we were up to 5 billion. By 1999 the number was 6 billion and ten years later the total was approaching 7 billion (Münz & Reiterer, 2009). Approximately 58% of this global population lives in Asia, 12% in Europe, 10% in Sub-Saharan Africa, 9% Latin America, 6% in North Africa/the Mideast, 5% in the United States/ Canada, and .005% in Australia/New Zealand and Pacific nations (Larsen, 2002). The 7 billion people live in over 190 nation-states that include more than 6,000 ethnic groups (Müller, 2009). There are over 2,000 "nationalities" in the world, but only about 200 nation-states acknowledged under international law (Rifkin, 2004). The majority of people today are minorities living either in the country of their birth or having immigrated. About 1.4 billion people live in poverty, earning less than $1.25 a day (Appleby, 2010).

The 21st century will bring a new issue–global aging. In 1970, almost half of the world's population was over 22 years of age; by 2008, half of the world's population was over 28. By 2050, demographers predict that more than half of the world's population will be over 38. By 2020, the European Commission projects that the number of Europeans over 65 years of age will increase by 22% and the number aged 55 to 64 will increase by 20%; by 2050, the median age in Europe will be 52.3 years (Rifkin, 2004). In the United States, half of the residents are over 36 years old, but by 2050 half of Americans are expected to be over 40. With increasing longevity rates in all nations, the numbers of elderly are growing at a time of declining fertility rates in many nations. As Münz and Reiterer (2009) noted: "At a global level, rapid aging of the world population has never occurred before. Now it is becoming the most important feature of demographic change" (p. 235).

The geographic regions with large populations of young people include Africa, Asia, and South America (Münz & Reiterer, 2009). Globalization has facilitated immigration, allowing many young people to escape poverty. The recent migrations to Germany, France, Spain, Greece, and Italy were a response to population declines, such as the 500,000 Romanians who immigrated to Italy to fill a labor gap in that aging nation (Appleby, 2010). Japan and some European nations are discussing ways of attracting more immigrants with needed skills to make up for the low fertility rate. Experts have termed this "replacement migration" (Münz & Reiterer, 2009).

In addition to global aging and global poverty, climate change represents another issue that must be addressed. Opponents of globalization argue that it has exacerbated environmental problems such as greenhouse gases because of increased factory production and increased shipping of products around the world (Stiglitz, 2010). In response, the United Nations convened a climate change convention in 1997 to get the world's nations to agree on what steps they should take to reduce their greenhouse gas emissions, but hopes for a successful outcome for this convention were severely diminished when the United States, the world's major polluter, refused to sign the Kyoto Protocol. Even though the Clinton administration was receptive to signing, Republican opposition in the Senate could not be overcome. Since then, the United States has increased its pollution levels, and leading experts are predicting that in the near future the United States will be responsible for producing half of the global emissions (Stiglitz, 2010).

The election of President George W. Bush strengthened the resistance to signing the Kyoto Protocol, but its failure to endorse the Kyoto agreement was not the only example of the Bush administration's refusal to cooperate with its global partners. The administration violated international law when it engaged in a "pre-emptive strike" on Iraq and ignored the Geneva Convention by holding prisoners without bail or a trial at Guantanamo. Guided by neoconservative ideology, the Bush administration indicated its intent to use its moral and military superiority to promote American economic development and political interests unrestrained by international agreements, and to bring about a new world order by taking decisive action against dangerous "rogue states." It failed to achieve these objectives. As Müller (2009) observed: "With every move of the Bush Government disorder grew. In this period, the U.S. failed miserably as the leading power. This failure has . . .

cost the world a lot of time which could have been used for urgently needed global measures" (p. 193). Despite such setbacks, global issues need to be addressed through international cooperation if globalization is to success-fully sustain a growing and aging population, alleviate poverty, and address environmental problems worldwide. There is also concern over whether glo-balization will preserve or destroy cultural diversity.

THE ORIGIN OF GLOBALIZATION

Bhagwati (2004) has observed that although globalization operates on many levels, including culture, communication, and media, most often the term is used in reference to economic issues that have international implications. Held and McGrew (2002) define globalization as "the expanding scale, grow-ing magnitude, speeding up and deepening impacts of transcontinental flows and patterns of social interaction" (p. 1). They insist that the term does not im-ply an inevitable emergence of a harmonious world order or the integration of global activities representing a convergence of diverse nations and cultures. Marling (2006) described globalization simply as: "the increased economic integration and interdependence of nations, driven by liberalized trade and capital flows" (p. vii). The concept of globalization first began to attract aca-demic interest in the 1970s based on evidence that world nations were becom-ing more interdependent due to developments in transportation, commerce, and communication, but this was not the first time such global developments had occurred.

In the late 19th century, the first globalization era evolved because of inventions such as the steamship, railroad, telegraph, and later the telephone. In 1875, an economic crisis resulted from stock markets crashing around the world, one crash feeding off another, prompting the German entrepre-neur Baron Carl Meyer von Rothschild to comment: "The world is a city" (Kristoff, 2000, p. 35). As Friedman (1999) has described it, "This first era of globalization before World War I shrank the world from a size 'large' to a size 'medium'" (p. xiv). In some ways, globalization was a stronger force then than it is today. Kristoff (2000) quotes an economist commenting on the earlier globalization era: "We're still not back to where we were 100 years ago" (p. 35). One advantage for workers, as reflected in immigration data, was that they could travel around the world freely, without passports, in search of jobs. That era ended largely because of two world wars, the Russian revolution, and a global depression. Bhagwati (2004) believes that current globalization is an almost inevitable consequence of the new trade policies and technological innovations developed over a century ago that integrated the global economy.

In 1945, participants at the Bretton Woods Conference in Washington, D.C., conceived the idea of establishing a World Bank and the International Monetary Fund (IMF). These two organizations were supposed to provide financial resources for development, with the IMF focusing on government loans. In 1947, 27 nations formed the World Trade Organization (WTO), and since then another 126 nations have joined. The 153 WTO members constitute almost all of the nations on the planet. Since it was initiated, the IMF has expanded its role significantly, overseeing economic reform efforts in over 70 developing nations. Unseem (2000) has suggested that the IMF was playing "so instrumental a role in those countries' everyday affairs as to border on a shadow government" (p. 111). The World Bank, WTO, and IMF continue to play a key role in the evolving global economy.

In the 1990s, the new globalization began to take shape due to the fall of the Soviet Union, the rapid development of computer technology, and the increasing speed and scope of telecommunications with satellite TV and the Internet. As Friedman (1999) has written: "Thanks to the combination of computers and cheap telecommunications, people can now offer and trade services globally—from medical advice to software writing to data processing—that could never really be traded before" (p. xvi).

As globalization evolved, early criticism described it as a force that would diminish national sovereignty in favor of regional power. Yet, Held and McGrew (2002) pointed out that the number of nations has doubled since World War II, and Enriquez (2000) similarly observed that 75% of current nations did not exist in 1950. Such factors as religion and ethnicity or language and culture are compelling forces for further division, as illustrated by the controversy in Belgium over splitting into two nations—Flanders (with Dutch-speaking Flemish citizens) and Wallonia (with French-speaking Walloons). As Enriquez (2000) observed: "After centuries of ebb and flow, conflicts such as [these] . . . are sometimes best understood by looking at maps that are centuries old" (p. 25). This tendency toward more and smaller nations also is illustrated by amicable agreements in places such as the United Kingdom where the British Parliament granted Scotland the right to re-establish its parliament with specified powers and also made political and linguistic accommodations for Wales.

Held and McGrew (2002) agree with the critics who charge that globalization is challenging the historic territorial principle of nation-states, a principle that assumes "a direct correspondence between society, economy and polity within an exclusive and bounded national territory" (p. 7). Held and McGrew argue that the principle is still relevant, but globalization has required revision and reconfiguration in terms that go beyond territorial boundaries to reflect emerging regional boundaries; some changes, such as the European Union (EU), have been formally implemented. Benhabib (2002) observed: "The new global economy permits the growth of regional networks over and beyond the boundaries of nation-states, making it plausible for them to short-circuit traditional centralized decision making in banking, finance, communications, and transportation" (p. 17).

One of the major concerns of globalization critics is the degree to which corporations are replacing nation-states in producing and promoting the spread of globalization. As Navarro (2002) noted, of the 100 largest economic entities in the world, 47 are corporations, and each of these 47 corporations controls more wealth than 130 nations in the world. Anti-globalization scholars also criticize the WTO, the IMF, and the World Bank for assuming powers formerly reserved for national governments. Critics have accused globalization of having an adverse effect on many people at the local level, but especially workers of color and women workers in the manufacturing sector. Navarro (2002) argued: "An unregulated global economy forces workers, communities, and countries to compete with each other in an effort to attract corporate investment" (p. 185).

Many critics argue that too much corporate power resides in American corporations, and yet the United States is no longer the home of many multinational corporations. Although General Motors is a major corporation, its market is mainly in the United States, whereas other automobile manufacturers are truly global. Volkswagen sells more vehicles in China than all the American auto manufacturers combined, and more South Americans purchase Peugeot/Citroën cars than any American brand (Marling, 2006). Wal-Mart still ranks as the world's largest corporation, but three Chinese corporations are the second, third, and fifth largest corporations in the world. The world's largest bank and the four largest insurance companies are all located in Japan (Marling, 2006). The global picture has become more confusing because many foreign-owned corporations have purchased and manufacture products with familiar American names, such as Lifesavers candy, Alpo dog food, Rolling Rock beer, and *Car and Driver* magazine (Marling, 2006).

HOW GLOBALIZATION DEVELOPED

Americans may not have been thinking of globalization in 1991 when the United States and Canada signed a free trade agreement, but the term was widely used in the debate 3 years later as this agreement was expanded to become the North American Free Trade Agreement (NAFTA). Because NAFTA reduced or eliminated tariffs on goods traded among Canada, Mexico, and the United States, it significantly increased trade among the three countries. From 1993 to 2008, trade more than tripled as these countries engaged in $12.5 billion in trade every day. Canada and Mexico are now the two largest markets for U.S. exports (Murphy, 2010).

NAFTA's critics were correct in predicting a decline in U.S. manufacturing jobs, but according to Murphy (2010), this decline began in 1979, 15 years before NAFTA became law. Since then, industrial production increased by 57%, and the 3 million manufacturing jobs that were lost, were not exported to other countries but tended to result from increased productivity due to technology and innovation, and requiring fewer workers (Murphy, 2010). Lee (2010) blamed NAFTA for the wages of American workers decreasing or staying the same since it was implemented, increasing the income inequality in the United States. In addition, Lee noted that since NAFTA was enacted, the U.S. trade deficit increased from $75 billion in 1993 to $720 billion in 2005.

The mixed reaction to NAFTA in the United States has been reflected in the international response to globalization. Critics have insisted that a major failure of the emerging global economy has been its inability to address social justice issues such as poverty and economic inequality. Yet Müller (2009) argued that globalization opponents have not acknowledged the economic gains made by many nations—poverty has been reduced and there have been improvements in many societies, including more stability in government, with some nations doing better than others.

In the EU, the Scandinavian countries have been more successful than France or Italy; in Asia, India's success has been much greater than that of Pakistan or Bangladesh; and in Southeast Asia, Vietnam has been more successful than Cambodia or Myanmar (Müller, 2009). In addition, some nations have engaged in successful efforts to reduce inequality. For example, Taiwan's policies with regard to land reforms have been identified as a major factor not only in reducing income inequality but in enhancing overall economic growth. South Africa has redistributed its economic resources to improve health care for all children, resulting in fewer school dropouts and a higher literacy rate among its people (Heintz, 2002). As Müller (2009) observed: "Globalization does not have a fixed effect, but instead its consequences are moderated by the responses of government at various levels" (pp. 97–98).

In the late 1950s, China and India implemented various economic reforms that had no impact on their poverty for more than 2 decades. In the

1970s, both countries began to shift toward more open trade policies and more foreign investment. As reported in an Asian Development Bank study, from 1978 to 1998, China's poverty went from 28% to 9%, and about that same time, poverty in India decreased from 51% to 26% (Bhagwati, 2004). Despite such claims, globalization critics emphasize that almost half of the global population still lives in poverty; nearly 1 billion people live on less than a dollar a day, with another 2 billion living on 1 to 2 dollars a day (Münz & Reiterer, 2009). Health studies have provided clear evidence that malnutrition robs people of their strength, adversely affects their immune system, reduces their productivity, and causes developmental disorders in children and youth; therefore, having such an extraordinarily high rate of global poverty has enormous implications for the future.

Bhagwati (2004) cites a study of economic data gathered from almost 100 nations from 1970 to 1998 concluding that economic growth was consistently responsible for reducing poverty in each nation. According to Friedman (1999), developing countries made more economic progress in the last 3 decades of the 20th century than the entire industrialized world made during the previous century. Such outcomes support those economists who insist that trade contributes to economic growth and reduces poverty, but economic growth does not automatically benefit poor people. Bhagwati (2004) has observed that economic growth in the mainstream economy may not help those largely disconnected from that economy, as was the case for diverse impoverished populations ranging from tribal groups in rural India to residents of inner cities in the United States. Yet there is evidence that in many developing nations infant mortality rates and malnutrition have decreased significantly, while literacy rates have increased. Globalization advocates also note increased philanthropic efforts to address poverty and health issues. Yet, even those advocates may have to agree with Bill Gates, who, assessing those philanthropic efforts, told the 2008 World Economic Forum, "The world is getting better, but it's not getting better fast enough, and it's not getting better for everyone" (Olopade, 2010, p. 17).

Heintz (2002) described another poverty issue—the adverse effect of globalization on low-income individuals' access to credit. This deprives a significant portion of a nation's citizens from being able to pursue more education or other opportunities to enhance their economic status. Some globalization critics have argued that sustained inequality may promote reluctance among financially secure citizens to invest in programs to improve services for the poor, such as health care or education. Lack of adequate services could reduce growth by lowering productivity due to increased health problems and the inadequacies of a poorly educated workforce (Heintz, 2002).

Although the population is growing in many developing nations, this does not inevitably result in diminished economic growth. Amartya Sen, who won the 1998 Nobel Prize in Economics, has studied this issue and concluded that a better explanation was ineffective governance that did not address inadequate infrastructure and poorly functioning public institutions (Münz & Reiterer, 2009). Proponents have emphasized that in the past 30 years globalization has allowed 300 million poor people to escape poverty in China, India, South Korea, and Taiwan. Illustrating the prosperity that globalization has brought to India, it is currently Asia's fourth largest automobile market, and more than one in three Indians are purchasing a car for the first time (Appleby, 2010).

Production has been globalized today. Although Thailand's economy has always been dominated by rice production, in just 15 years it was transformed into the world's second largest manufacturer of pickup trucks and fourth largest manufacturer of motorcycles (Friedman, 1999). With rising salaries and more disposable income, more people are investing in the stock market, causing further economic development. As Friedman (1999) noted: "Already 30 million Chinese own stock . . . [and] lots of underground newspapers and magazines have sprung up, because investors are demanding real economic news" (p. 155). Friedman believes the need for accurate information about the economy will drive the development of a free press in China to expose economic corruption in business and politics.

One of the poorest regions of the world is Africa, and many globalization opponents insist that increasing poverty in Africa represents a failure of the global economy, but Müller (2009) argued that "Africa is not a hopeless case" (p. 21). Some Africans have overcome major problems and formed relatively stable governments in nations such as Botswana, Mali, Senegal, and Benin. With economic support, what these nations have done could be replicated in other African nations, leading to significant numbers of people escaping poverty as in China and India. Proponents insist that globalization has the potential to address poverty issues and ethnic conflicts. After acknowledging that some criticisms of globalization were legitimate, Wright (2000) concluded: "Don't get me wrong. Globalization is great. On balance, it makes the world's people less poor. . . . And it fosters fine-grained economic interdependence that makes war among nations less thinkable" (p. 104).

The major criticism of globalization is its failure to alleviate income inequality. Münz and Reiterer (2009) have argued that the richest 20% of the global population use 85% of its energy resources and commodities. Müller (2009) has described inequality not only between individuals but between social groups and nations. Often, small economic changes have done more than large ones to help the poor, especially women, as illustrated by the mi-cro-credit programs lending minimal sums of money to poor people for in-vestments that have improved their economic situation (Kristoff & WuDunn, 2009). No matter what efforts are implemented to make the global economy more effective, social justice issues must be acknowledged and actions need to be initiated to address inequalities. If global measures do not adequately address these problems, "disadvantaged parties will regard such measures as illegitimate" (Müller, 2009, p. 14).

For globalization to be successful, the fears of the anti-globalists will have to be addressed. Bhagwati (2004) has asserted that globalization proponents must debunk a widespread assumption: "If capitalism has prospered and economic globalization has increased while some social ill has worsened, then the first two phenomena must have caused the third" (p. 29). Global-ization proponents admit that even though globalization can be a positive progressive force to improve conditions for nations around the world, it also may contribute to inequities and social injustices. Bhagwati (2004) agrees: "Globalization must be managed so that its fundamentally benign effects are ensured and reinforced" (p. 35).

Although early economic theorists such as Adam Smith believed that inequalities would necessarily be produced by economic growth, recent re-search challenges this belief. According to two studies first reported in the 1990s, those nations with less inequality tended to experience more eco-nomic growth. Heintz (2002) cited a report contrasting Argentina and Japan. From 1960 to 2000, Argentina had a higher per capita income but more eco-nomic inequality than Japan. During that time, the Japanese economy con-sistently experienced more economic growth than Argentina. Heintz (2002) argued: "Such patterns of growth support the argument that less inequality contributes to relative [economic] success" (p. 347).

According to Appleby (2010), for critics and advocates of globalization, "the full meaning of globalization in the twenty-first century hit home with the first worldwide recession" (p. 400). The American economic crisis spilled far beyond the nation's borders, affecting countries that had been extraordi-narily successful under globalization, such as China, Germany, and Japan. Iceland nearly went bankrupt, and this had adverse economic consequences for those who had invested in Iceland's high-interest bonds (Appleby, 2010). Critics and proponents agreed that the global economy needs safeguards to anticipate and prepare for problems. For example, Schwenninger (2010) described how American corporations significantly increased their profits by exploiting China's inadequate environmental standards and low wages, but that also contributed to wages and family income stagnating in the United

States, producing increased income inequality. From 2001 to 2008, 4 million U.S. manufacturing jobs were lost. Schwenninger (2010) was advocating not the elimination of globalization, but more economic oversight: "Globalization is not necessarily bad if properly regulated" (p. 96).

Rifkin (2004) argued that globalization is changing the adversarial capitalist marketplace, rewarding participants who pursue a network model of cooperative commerce. In a network relationship, suppliers do not try to maximize their interests at the expense of buyers, but focus on enhancing benefits for all parties engaged in an economic activity. With a network model, autonomous firms must relinquish some of their autonomy to receive the benefits from sharing resources and risks. The foundation for such networks is not competition but cooperation based on reciprocity and trust. Rifkin (2004) described such a cooperative relationship as one where the parties are required to "share knowledge, make their operations transparent, and allow their partners to know a lot more about how they conduct business" (p. 187). By sharing their expertise within a network partnership, corporations also stimulate more creativity and innovation.

Friedman (1999) compared globalization to a sprinter having to run race after race without resting. Rifkin (2004) agreed, arguing that therefore the network model was better suited to globalization because it provided a team of runners. A single firm operating alone cannot keep up the pace and eventually will lose to a competitor using the network model. As Rifkin (2004) concluded: "Only by pooling resources and sharing risks and revenue streams in network-based relationships can firms survive" (p. 191). Another advantage of network relationships is that they promote democratic principles.

GLOBALIZATION AND DEMOCRACY

According to critics of globalization, trade agreements such as NAFTA and the General Agreement on Tariffs and Trade (GATT) have given corporations increased power, allowing them to demand that nations take certain actions and enact particular policies. Despite the growth of democracy among the world's nations, corporate executives are not democratically elected and yet they can require democratic governments to do what the corporation requires. Parenti (2010) observed that all of GATT's 500 pages of regulations concern government actions, not corporate actions. If democratic nations do not agree to corporate demands, the appointed leaders of the WTO can fine them or impose trade sanctions to coerce them into compliance. This is why Parenti (2010) has argued: "Free trade is not fair trade; it benefits strong nations at the expense of weak ones, and rich interests at the expense of the rest of us" (p. 39).

Mandelson (2010) disputed the claim that government power has been diminished: "States and effective governance are what makes globalization possible: they preserve open markets, enforce rules and responsibilities, and manage the risks for individuals and society" (p. 107). Mandelson did accept the need for improved oversight and regulations for the global economy to function effectively. Friedman (1999) acknowledged that globalization reduced political power, describing it as a trade-off where the economic benefits from increased trade reduced the options that nations had to a narrower range with regard to implementing political or economic policies. Held and McGrew (2002) have argued that despite limitations, most nations "fiercely protect their sovereignty—their entitlement to rule" (p. 14).

Proponents insist that globalization promotes democracy because with the prosperity it brings, comes an expanding middle class that will advocate for the larger voice in governance offered by a democracy. Although conservatives often espouse anti-globalization arguments, even arch conservative Tom DeLay supported inviting China to be part of the WTO, arguing that growing numbers of entrepreneurs in China "are now the instruments of reform. . . . This middle class will eventually demand broad acceptance of democratic values" (Bhagwati, 2004, p. 94). Presidents Bill Clinton and George W. Bush also have expressed this view. Although much of China's economic progress is in cities, Harvard anthropologist James Watson has observed that even for Chinese people living in villages, the quality of their lives has improved compared with what it was 30 years ago. Watson also argued that China is becoming a more open society: "Partly because of the demands of ordinary people . . . globalism is the major force for democracy in China" (Zwingle, 2000, p. 154).

Friedman (1999) affirmed Watson's observation, arguing that globalization should produce more-democratic societies, for three significant reasons—flexibility, legitimacy, and sustainability. He cited the 1997 economic downturn in Asia when nations with the most effective democratic governments, such as Taiwan and Singapore, were least affected, while the countries with ineffective democratic governments suffered more; the nation hurt the most was Indonesia, where the government was both authoritarian and corrupt. Democracy scholar Larry Diamond has explained why nations without democratic governments will not benefit as much from participating in the global economy:

> You cannot sustain good software with an authoritarian regime that is not itself accountable, does not permit the free flow of information, does not permit an

independent judiciary to pursue corruption, and does not permit free elections so that the political management can be changed. (Friedman, 1999, p. 159)

Diamond's argument may explain why so many emerging nations have embraced democracy after the collapse of the Soviet Union and other dictatorial governments. Griswold (2010) reported that today almost two thirds of the world's governments are democracies, and, based on his examination of cross-country data, concluded: "Governments that grant their citizens a large measure of freedom to engage in international commerce find it dauntingly difficult to deprive them of political and civil liberties" (p. 31).

Another globalization issue involves how nations have defined citizenship. Since the demise of the Soviet Union, Europe is no longer one of the major sources of immigrants, but one of their main destinations. Because European nations in the past have not encouraged or even allowed immigrants to seek citizenship, over half of immigrants in Europe are not naturalized citizens (Münz & Reiterer, 2009). This increased immigration has included "irregular immigrants," called "undocumented workers" in the United States, often hired for jobs in the service industry, such as domestic workers, caregivers, and nannies. In response to about 3.5 million irregular immigrants entering European nations from 1995 to 2008, the EU established amnesty programs to provide them with work and residence permits; several nations, such as Austria, Denmark, and Germany, now have mandatory language courses and courses on how to integrate into mainstream society (Münz & Reiterer, 2009).

The global immigration that took place in the last 2 decades of the 20th century was the largest migration since the beginning of that century (Rutz, 2002). Although recent immigrants have continued the historic pattern of migrating from less developed to more developed nations, Benhabib (2002) has observed that current immigrants no longer feel obligated to sever their connection with their native land. In response, many nations today are affirming some aspects of cultural pluralism to deal with these culturally diverse populations. For example, an increasing number of nations permit immigrants to have dual citizenship, allowing them to vote and even run for political office in their native land (Rifkin, 2004). J. A. Banks (2006) says: "The ways in which people are moving back and forth across national borders today challenge the notion of educating citizens to function in one nation-state" (p. 153).

Benhabib (2002) noted that the concept of "flexible citizenship" has become the norm in countries throughout Southeast Asia and Latin America, and 90% of American immigrants come from countries that allow dual citizenship. As Rifkin (2004) noted: "The old idea of tying citizenship to nationality appears almost quaint" (p. 274). In response to the acceptance of dual citizenship and other efforts by many nations to honor cultural diversity, some indigenous populations have demanded recognition for their culture and related legal issues.

GLOBALIZATION AND CULTURAL DIVERSITY

Many critics of globalization argue that it is creating a homogenized world culture based largely on a Western model, especially an American model. In 1972, the first European McDonald's was established in France, and despite French complaints, in just 30 years France became McDonalds' third largest market in Europe (Bhagwati, 2004). During those 30 years McDonald's established over 20,000 stores in 119 nations other than the United States. Somewhere in the world, a new McDonald's is opening its doors every 17 hours (Watson, 2000). According to Bhagwati (2004), China has so enthusiastically welcomed McDonald's that a recent study reported that nearly half of all Chinese children believed McDonald's originated in China. The success of such American exports as fast food, music videos, clothing, video games, soap operas, and more has provided ample evidence to critics who complain that the United States is engaging in cultural imperialism on a global scale (Watson, 2000).

Former Indian Prime Minister I. K. Gujral stated the case for preserving diverse cultures: "[India's] traditions are a thousand years old. You cannot just let them go like that. The world will be much richer if the colorations and diversities are sustained and encouraged with different cultures" (Friedman, 1999, p. 234). When he was the WTO director-general, Renato Ruggiero recognized this problem: "Managing a world of converging economies, peoples and civilizations, each preserving its own identity and culture, represents the great challenge and the great promise of our age" (Rutz, 2002, p. 70). Friedman (1999) acknowledged that the United States has been an aggressive participant in the global economy: "Globalization has a distinctly American face: It wears Mickey Mouse ears, it eats Big Macs, it drinks Coke or Pepsi and it does its computing on an IBM or Apple laptop, using Windows 98, with an Intel Pentium II processor and a network link from Cisco Systems" (p. 309).

Addressing this criticism of globalization, Marling (2006) described getting off a train in a Japanese city and seeing familiar signs for McDonald's, KFC, Burger King, and Mister Donut as two Japanese boys walked by wearing Oakland Athletics baseball caps. Such experiences have caused many people to describe globalization as the Americanization of world cultures. Yet Marling goes on to observe that of the 200 signs in the area near the train station, 70 were for restaurants specializing in local cuisine such as sushi, dumplings, and noodles, and only five restaurants were American. He also noticed that most signs were written in Japanese, with a few in English and Korean, and one sign was written in Tagalog. When he entered Burger King he found that the hamburgers were flavored with teriyaki, wasabi, or shichimi, and he also found that Mister Donut was more likely to serve its customers miso and rice pudding instead of donuts (Marling, 2006).

What Marling observed is part of what Friedman (1999) means in arguing that diverse nations need to create some "cultural filters" that are strong enough to withstand the pressure for cultural homogenization. Some strategies that Friedman suggested to strengthen local cultures included passing zoning laws, creating protected areas, and having educational programs that emphasize the unique attributes of a nation—its geography, history, and cultural heritage. Another way to preserve a nation's cultural heritage is to promote tourism. Tourists do not travel to a country to encounter the same franchises they have at home but to sample new foods, new sights, and a different culture.

Although globalization advocates largely believe that cultural and individual diversity are likely to persist, they also believe that nations will have to adopt a global political perspective in decision making and policies, even at the local level. As Held and McGrew (2002) have argued, the nation-state can no longer "deliver many sought-after public goods and values without regional and global collaboration" (p. 31). That reality is why nations are being challenged to resist homogenization. As Israeli political theorist Yaron Ezrahi described this dilemma: "Either globalization homogenizes us only on the surface, and local cultural roots remain, or it homogenizes us to our very roots and it becomes environmentally, culturally and politically lethal" (Friedman, 1999, p. 245).

Friedman (1999) argued that for developing nations in particular, preserving their culture is not an impractical luxury, but a necessary strategy in order to be successful in the global economy: "You cannot build an emerging society . . . if you are simultaneously destroying the cultural foundations that cement your society and give it the self-confidence and cohesion to interact properly with the world" (p. 243). Globalization proponents argue that it is easier today for nations and immigrants to maintain their cultural identity. As Rifkin (2004) observed, cultures are becoming transnational: "Cultures exist in multiple domains, both virtual and real. . . . Cultural diasporas provide a vehicle that allows people to retain their sense of identity while negotiating their way in an increasingly globalized world" (p. 262). Television highlights unique aspects of a culture, and satellite TV broadcasts programs from the native countries of many immigrants, in some cases for 24 hours a day. The Internet provides access to cultural websites, allowing immigrants to remain closely connected to their native land, while email and cell phones enhance the ability of immigrants to maintain relationships with family and friends back home.

Because global relationships are being maintained, some globalization critics acknowledge that nation-states have resisted cultural homogenization (Held & McGrew, 2002). National identity continues to be a significant factor in shaping individual identities. Although faster and easier global communication provides more interaction between people from diverse cultures, it also serves to highlight and reinforce cultural differences. Although television programs are a major export for the United States, many nations provide local versions. Spanish language soap operas are far more popular in Latin America than the American imports, and reality programming inspired *Big Brother Africa* as well as several European versions of *Survivor, American Idol,* and roommate programs, all featuring local participants (Marling, 2006). Shanghai television producers borrowed ideas from the American children's show *Sesame Street,* but asked Chinese educators to redesign it so that the programs would teach Chinese values and traditions. One producer described the result: "We borrowed an American box . . . and put Chinese content into it" (Zwingle, 2000, p. 155).

Enriquez (2000) described another way globalization has nurtured culture—by offering small nations an opportunity to be independent from larger, neighboring nations, or to re-establish their independence from a dominant nation. As an example, European separatist groups such as the Basques supported the inclusion of Spain into the EU. Basques used to carry Spanish passports and could look for work only in Spain, but now they carry EU passports and can work in any EU nation. If the Basques decide to separate from Spain, it would not require new currency, new customs laws, or loss of privileges concerning trade, travel, or employment. As Enriquez (2000) has written: "Country disintegration is enabled by integration on a supranational level" (p. 26). Other cultural groups such as the Scots and the Catalonians in Spain also regard the EU as a source of greater freedom. As Rifkin (2004) explained, local subcultures "can often bypass nation-state constraints and establish political, commercial, and social ties at the EU level, affording them a greater degree of independence and autonomy than they have known under nation-state rule" (p. 242).

Another criticism of globalization is that it obliterates cultural differences because it inevitably will result in a global government and unified culture, and the culture will likely reflect Western ideas and values. As evidence, the critics refer to the dominance of the English language in the global marketplace. While Marling (2006) acknowledged the history of colonialism that imposed English on many people, especially in African nations and India, he noted that France, Spain, and other colonial powers did the same. Many former colonies have reverted to the national language today, such as India (Hindi), Pakistan (Urdu), and central Africa (Swahili). Although English has become the common language in fields such as business, science, and diplomacy, it still does not rank as the most commonly spoken world language. In 2000, native speakers of English represented less than 8% of the world's population, while there were almost twice as many native Mandarin Chinese speakers, the language spoken by most people today. As for increasing usage, three of the fastest growing languages are Arabic, Hindi, and Spanish (Marling, 2006).

Despite these arguments, linguists view globalization as partly responsible for a likely reduction of diversity in the world's 6,000 languages. As reported by the *New York Times* (2000), by the end of the 21st century, half of these languages will become extinct, with only 5% of languages designated as "safe" because they have the backing of a nation and are spoken by at least a million people; according to a Yale linguist, the languages of indigenous people are especially vulnerable: "There are hundreds of languages that are down to a few elderly people and are for the most part beyond hope of revival" (p. 143). An Alaska University linguist explained why this loss is viewed as a cultural disaster: "The human race evolved with a diversity of languages, which formed a rich pool of varied ideas and world views, but the pool is shrinking fast" (*New York Times*, 2000, p. 144).

Bhagwati (2004) has countered that as globalization activity has increased over the past 3 decades, there has been a revival of indigenous languages, a resurgence of interest in ethnicity, and an increasing number of advocates for multiculturalism and cultural pluralism. He noted that the United Nations Educational, Scientific and Cultural Organization (UNESCO) sponsored a study reporting that the share of cultural products (e.g., film, music, literature, and media) exported by developing nations had increased from a 12% to a 30% share from 1978 to 1998. Because it contains 100 nationalities and 87 different languages and distinct dialects, the EU has acknowledged the importance of preserving languages and has disseminated funds for education and research addressing language preservation (Rutz, 2002). Marling (2006) has argued that globalization has enhanced the survival of ethnic, religious, and language diversity because globalization "has promoted adaptation instead of imposition" (p. 205).

Another concern is how globalization will affect global conflicts. It is well known that there have been historic conflicts around the world between groups such as Hindus and Muslims, Spanish and Moroccans, French and Algerians, and civil wars between ethnic groups in Angola, Nigeria, and Rwanda. Even though antagonisms remain between some ethnic and religious groups throughout the world, a potentially positive outcome from globalization is a decrease in prejudice, bigotry, and negative behavior toward diverse cultural groups. Marling (2006) quoted theorist Wolfgang Iser: "In a rapidly shrinking world, many different cultures have come into close contact with one another, calling for a mutual understanding in terms not only of one's own culture but also of those encountered" (p. 198). At times antagonism cuts across cultural borders, as illustrated by negative responses toward Gypsies, also known as the Roma, who are scattered across Europe. Yet these negative responses prompted an EU investigation that resulted in a series of recommendations to EU nations.

Although it promotes maintaining cultural diversity, the EU also is raising a critical question—Is it possible for people to have multiple identities, such as being a Muslim of Turkish descent, a German, a European, and a citizen of the world at the same time? Rifkin (2004) believes it is not only possible but necessary, arguing that the future success of the EU will depend upon its ability "to make cultural identity, universal human rights, and European governance a seamless rather than a contradictory relationship" (p. 244). Globalization faces the same challenge, and one of the major obstacles to promoting cultural pluralism was revealed in a survey cited by the *World Culture Report, 2000.* Over 50% of European citizens surveyed reported negative perceptions of immigrants, including that they engaged in criminal behavior and that many were unemployed and therefore unnecessary. Further, in the 23 nations with the most immigrants, 65 to 75% of citizens expressed a desire for policies that would limit future immigration (Rutz, 2002).

Despite the diversity and divisiveness, there are areas of fundamental agreement that nations and religions share. According to cross-cultural studies and reports from the World Ethics project directed by Hans Küng, among diverse cultures there is agreement on the need to ease the suffering of the poor, a sense of stewardship over the environment, and a rejection of nuclear war and terrorism (Müller, 2009). Although solutions may differ, these moral and economic issues are viewed as problems that challenge every society. Marling (2006) has argued that claims for homogenization of world cultures have been based on viewing globalization in terms of the growth and spread of various multinational corporations rather than on how these businesses and their practices have been received. Despite their size and influence, many multinational corporations have adapted their practices to accommodate local cultures and communities. Rather than a force for homogeneity between world cultures, John Tomlinson has argued that it is more accurate to view globalization as the spread of modernity (Marling, 2006).

In response to increasing globalization, UNESCO appointed a committee in 1995 to gather information and identify the issues that national policies and programs should address to preserve cultural diversity and promote pluralism. In 2000, the committee produced three reports: *World Culture Report, 2000; World Heritage Sites;* and *Culture, Trade, and Globalization* (Rutz, 2002). The accommodations described in these reports called for a partnership among nations, corporations, international agencies, nongovernmental organizations, research institutions, and communities to promote acceptance of cultural diversity and cultural pluralism. These reports called on UNESCO to provide leadership for collaborative efforts between nations and organizations. Nancy Fraser, a contributor to the reports, urged nations with increasing cultural diversity to implement policies that provided for a redistribution of resources. Another contributor, Anthony Giddens, insisted that a democratic government was the best framework to promote cultural pluralism and achieve a more just distribution of resources (Rutz, 2002).

Since it would appear that the global economy is an ongoing reality, many scholars have echoed Fraser and Giddens by insisting that nations have an opportunity to shape globalization in how they address cultural diversity and social justice issues, and maintaining that part of the solution will come from how they educate their youth. As J. A. Banks (2006) has written: "A major problem facing nation-states throughout the world is how to recognize and legitimize differences and yet construct an overarching national identity that incorporates the voices, experiences, and hopes of the diverse groups that compose it" (p. 152). Education alone will not be enough, but it will be an important part of a variety of activities that nations will need to engage in to ensure that globalization affirms diversity, promotes democratic governance, and fosters collaborative global relationships to resolve problems peacefully in the years to come.

Epilogue

America is only America because the country is black, white, tan, beige, yellow, red, pink, and all shades not accounted for. What would happen if the bigots got their wish is that we would be stuck in a country unrecognizable to ourselves.
—Roger Rosenblatt (quoted in Hing, 1997, p. 223)

As this academic exploration comes to an end, it does not bring with it a sense of closure. There is still so much to read and reflect upon. In past discussions with colleagues, we readily acknowledged the difficulty of keeping abreast of our own field given the volume of research from the past and present that is available today. A sense of inadequacy becomes even sharper in exploring a variety of fields, as was necessary in writing this book. It is still possible to encounter a colleague and discuss the latest theory, but this outcome is increasingly less likely. Today, as Taylor (2002) has written, "No two of my colleagues are familiar with the same journals, theories, names or controversies. Specialties within disciplines have become increasingly narrow" (p. 95). Interdisciplinary scholarship contributes to the idiosyncrasy of what individual scholars are reading and thinking about.

Despite this frustration, there is also an excitement that we know so much more than we once did, and are likely to know so much more in the future. This plethora of information is like a complex jigsaw puzzle, and any one scholar will do well to complete one corner of it, or a section hanging in the middle, waiting for someone else to connect his or her section with other pieces coming down from the top of the puzzle or the side. This book represents an effort to complete a portion of the puzzle, and the meaning of that portion to some degree is reflected in Rosenblatt's quotation above.

Rosenblatt does not mean to imply that controversies over diversity are settled, or that those who advocate cultural pluralism have been declared the winner of the diversity debate. What he does say is that pluralism has made such strides in the United States and around the world that it is going to continue to be a factor in the perceptions and responses of a significant number of people in the future. Some pluralist advocates believe we are seeing the start of a backlash against diversity in the United States that may empower the most extreme factions against diversity, but Rosenblatt has a response to this fear as well. If such extremists were successful in imposing the image of a White person as the only legitimate symbol for being an American, Rosenblatt believes that "the rest of us would have to get out of here and go off in search of a new world, where differences make strength" (Hing, 1997, p. 223).

That new world is already out there, and it is being shaped by the forces of globalization. Although it is imperfect, it is a world that increasingly recognizes diversity as an asset. Yet it is not likely that the world will witness an American diaspora in search of a society that values differences. The 1980s were just beginning when Appleton (1983) asserted: "The United States appears to be on the verge of embracing cultural pluralism as a social ideal" (p. 1). He provided evidence in support of his assertion, including legislation responding to demands from "minorities" on federal and state levels, funding for pluralistic programs and projects in support of diversity provided by federal, state, and private sources, and the increasing recognition of diversity in content taught at K–12 schools, colleges, and universities, especially in teacher education programs.

During the 3 decades since Appleton made this claim, the evidence has increased. The debate no longer seems to be one of promoting pluralism or not; for most Americans, especially those in leadership positions, the increasing diversity not only within the United States but throughout the world has decided the debate. In the context of public awareness of American and global diversity, the debate today concerns how to best promote pluralism in ways that avoid negative consequences while benefitting from the potential of diversity to contribute to the well-being of individuals and to the good of the nation. The debate is now between what Appleton (1983) called "the competing ideological expressions of cultural pluralism (p. 149).

The diversity debates that will take place in the future are more likely to be a contest to determine how to respond to diversity most appropriately, how to take advantage of the strengths diversity offers, and how to benefit the most from the diversity that already exists and is being born. This will be not only an American debate, but a global one. The nations on the winning side of that debate will win much more than a trophy; they will be widely recognized and respected as world leaders and role models.

As the recent wars in Afghanistan and Iraq have demonstrated, being an acknowledged superpower and using our superior military might is not the most effective way to resolve global issues. The nations of the world probably will rely increasingly on the power of diplomatic and moral voices to address issues within and between nations. With its incredible diversity, America has the potential to be an especially compelling voice in the future. If that hope is realized, it will be because our people and our leaders have affirmed the value of human differences and demonstrated that commitment through our policies and practices. The colors within this hope paint a vision of an America that has achieved a unity far beyond the most ambitious dreams of the founders who dared to attempt this unique experiment to create a diverse, democratic society.

References

Adams, D. W. (1995). *Education for extinction: American Indians and the boarding school experience, 1875–1928.* Lawrence: University Press of Kansas.

Akbar, N. (2011). Privilege in black and white. In K. L. Koppelman (Ed.), *Perspectives on human differences: Selected readings on American diversity* (pp. 43–49). Boston: Pearson/Allyn & Bacon.

Appleby, J. (2010). *The relentless revolution.* New York: Norton.

Appleton, N. (1983). *Cultural pluralism in education: Theoretical foundations.* New York: Longman.

Aronson, E. (2008). *The social animal* (10th ed.). New York: Worth.

Baker, G. C. (1994). *Planning and organizing for multicultural instruction.* Reading, MA: Addison Wesley.

Banks, C. A. M. (2005). *Improving multicultural education: Lessons from the intergroup education movement.* New York: Teachers College Press.

Banks, J. A. (1994). *Multiethnic education: Theory and practice* (3rd ed.). Boston: Allyn & Bacon.

Banks, J. A. (1999). *An introduction to multicultural education* (2nd ed.). Boston: Allyn & Bacon.

Banks, J. A. (2006). Democracy, diversity, and social justice: Educating citizens for the public interest in a global age. In G. Ladson-Billings & W. F. Tate (Eds.), *Education research in the public interest: Social justice, action, and policy* (pp. 141–157). New York: Teachers College Press.

Banks, J. A., Cochran-Smith, M., Moll, L., Richert, A., Zeichner, K., LePage, P., Darling-Hammond, L., & Duffy, H. (2005). Teaching diverse learners. In L. Darling-Hammond & J. Bransford (Eds.), *Preparing teachers for a changing world: What teachers should learn and be able to do* (pp. 232–274). San Francisco: Jossey-Bass.

Baron, D. (2000). English in a multicultural America. In K. E. Rosenblum & T. C. Travis (Eds.), *The meaning of difference: American constructions of race, sex and gender, social class, and sexual orientation* (pp. 445–451). Boston: McGraw-Hill.

Baumann, G. (1999). *The multicultural riddle: Rethinking national, ethnic, and religious identities.* New York: Routledge.

Beauchamp, T. L. (1997). Goals and quotas in hiring and promotion. In F. J. Beckwith & T. E. Jones (Eds.), *Affirmative action: Social justice or reverse discrimination?* (pp. 214–226). Amherst, NY: Prometheus Books.

Benhabib, S. (2002). *The claims of culture: Equality and diversity in the global era.* Princeton, NJ: Princeton University Press.

Benokraitis, N. V., & Feagin, J. R. (1978). *Affirmative action and equal opportunity: Action, inaction, reaction.* Boulder, CO: Westview Press.

Berlin, I. (1991). *The crooked timber of humanity: Chapters in the history of ideas* (H. Hardy, Ed.). New York: Knopf.

Berns, W. (1998). Constitutionalism and multiculturalism. In A. Melzer, J. Weinberger, & H. R. Zinman (Eds.), *Multiculturalism and American democracy* (pp. 91–111). Lawrence: University Press of Kansas.

Bevir, M. (2007). Post-foundationalism and social democracy. In E. D. Ermath (Ed.), *Rewriting democracy: Cultural politics in postmodernity* (pp. 45–63). Burlington, VT: Ashgate.

Bhagwati, J. (2004). *In defense of globalization.* New York: Oxford University Press.

Bobo, L. D. (2001). Race, interests, and beliefs about affirmative action: Unanswered questions and new directions. In J. D. Skrentny (Ed.), *Color lines: Affirmative action, immigration, and civil rights options for America* (pp. 191–213). Chicago: University of Chicago Press.

Bohannan, L. (1966, August–September). Shakespeare in the bush. *Natural History*, pp. 18–23.

Boxill, B. (1998). Majoritarian democracy and cultural minorities. In A. Melzer, J. Weinberger, & H. R. Zinman (Eds.), *Multiculturalism and American democracy* (pp. 112–119). Lawrence: University Press of Kansas.

Brazzel, M. (2003). Historical and theoretical roots of diversity management. In D. L. Plummer (Ed.), *Handbook of diversity management: Beyond awareness to competency based learning* (pp. 51–94). Lanham, MD: University Press of America.

Brubaker, R. (2006). *Ethnicity without groups.* Cambridge, MA: Harvard University Press.

Caney, S. (2002). Equal treatment, exceptions, and cultural diversity. In P. Kelly (Ed.), *Multiculturalism reconsidered* (pp. 81–101). Cambridge, UK: Polity Press.

Ceaser, J. (1998). Multiculturalism and American liberal democracy. In A. Melzer, J. Weinberger, & H. R. Zinman (Eds.), *Multiculturalism and American democracy* (pp. 139–156). Lawrence: University Press of Kansas.

Chernow, R. (2004). *Alexander Hamilton.* New York: Penguin.

Chesterton, G. K. (1942). *Charles Dickens: The last of the great men.* New York: Press of the Readers Club. (Original work published 1906)

Children's Defense Fund. (2008). *Annual report 2007.* Retrieved May 9, 2009, from www.childrendefensefund.org

Chua, A. (2007). *Day of Empire: How hyperpowers rise to global dominance—and why they fall.* New York: Doubleday.

Cirillo, M., Bruna, K. R., & Herbel-Eisenmann, B. (2010, January–March). Acquisition of mathematical language: Suggestions and activities for English language learners. *Multicultural Perspectives, 12*(1), 34–41.

Clayton, S. D., & Crosby, F. J. (2000). Justice, gender, and affirmative action. In F. J. Crosby & C. VanDeVeer (Eds.), *Sex, race, and merit: Debating affirmative action in education and employment* (pp. 81–88). Ann Arbor: University of Michigan Press.

Clinton, B. (2004). *My life.* New York: Knopf.

Cohen, C. (2003). Section one: Why race preference is wrong and bad. In C. Cohen & J. P. Sterba (Eds.), *Affirmative action and racial preference: A debate* (pp. 3–188; pp. 279–304). New York: Oxford University Press.

Cooper, R., & Slavin, R. E. (2004). Cooperative learning: An instructional strategy to improve intergroup relations. In W. G. Stephan & W. P. Vogt (Eds.), *Education programs for improving intergroup relations: Theory, research, and practice* (pp. 55–70). New York: Teachers College Press.

Crane, S. (1967). A man saw a ball of gold in the sky. In E. Bradley, R. C. Beatty, & E. H. Long (Eds.), *The American tradition in literature* (3rd ed., p. 943). New York: Norton.

Crawford, J. (2000). *At war with diversity: US language policy in an age of anxiety.* Clevedon, UK: Multilingual Matters.

Crèvecoeur, J. Hector St. John de. (1912). *Letters from an American farmer.* London: J. M. Denton & Sons.

Crosby, F. J., Ferdman, B. M., & Wingate, B. R. (2000). Addressing and redressing discrimination: Affirmative action in social psychological perspective. In F. J. Crosby & C. VanDeVeer (Eds.), *Sex, race, and merit: Debating affirmative action in education and employment* (pp. 114–124). Ann Arbor: University of Michigan Press.

Cross, E. Y. (2000). *Managing diversity–The courage to lead.* Westport, CT: Quorum.

Cymrot, T. Z. (2002). What is diversity? In L. Darling-Hammond, J. French, & S. P. Garcia-Lopez (Eds.), *Learning to teach for social justice* (pp. 13–17). New York: Teachers College Press.

Dahl, R. A. (1982). *Dilemmas of pluralist democracy: Autonomy vs. control.* New Haven, CT: Yale University Press.

Dalton, H. (2008). Failing to see. In P. Rothenberg (Ed.) *White privilege: Essential readings on the other side of racism* (3rd ed.). New York, NY: Worth.

Daniels, R. (2002). *Coming to America: A history of immigration and ethnicity in American life.* New York: Perennial.

Darling-Hammond, L. (2002). Learning to teach for social justice. In L. Darling-Hammond, J. French, & S. P. Garcia-Lopez (Eds.), *Learning to teach for social justice* (pp. 1–7). New York: Teachers College Press.

Darling-Hammond, L., & Garcia-Lopez, S. P. (2002). Part I: What is diversity? In L. Darling-Hammond, J. French, & S. P. Garcia-Lopez (Eds.), *Learning to teach for social justice* (pp. 9–12). New York: Teachers College Press.

Dean, J. (2008–2009, Winter). The square root of a fair share. *Rethinking Schools, 23*(2), 46–51.

Deloria, V., Jr. (1969). *Custer died for your sins: An Indian manifesto.* New York: Avon Books.

Derman-Sparks, L. (2004). Culturally relevant anti-bias education with young children. In W. G. Stephan & W. P. Vogt (Eds.), *Education programs for improving intergroup relations: Theory, research, and practice* (pp. 19–36). New York: Teachers College Press.

De Vos, G. A. (2006). Ethnic pluralism: Conflict and accommodation. In G. A. De Vos & L. Romanucci-Ross (Eds.), *Ethnic identity: Creation, conflict, and accommodation* (pp. 15–47). Walnut Creek, CA: Altamira Press.

De Vos, G. A., & Romanucci-Ross, L. (1995). Ethnic identity: A psychocultural perspective. In G. A. De Vos & L. Romanucci-Ross (Eds.), *Ethnic identity: Creation, conflict, and accommodation* (pp. 349–379). Walnut Creek, CA: Altamira Press.

Du Bois, W. E. B. (2003). *The souls of Black folk.* New York: Modern Library. (Original work published 1903)

Dunne, J. (2003). Between state and civil society: European contexts for education. In K. McDonough & W. Feinberg (Eds.), *Education and citizenship in liberal-democratic societies: Teaching for cosmopolitan values and collective identities* (pp. 96–120). Oxford: Oxford University Press.

Durant, W., & Durant, A. (1961). *The age of reason begins.* New York: Simon & Schuster.

Eck, D. (2001). *A new religious America: How a "Christian country" has become the world's most religiously diverse nation.* New York: HarperCollins.

Eder, K., Giesen, B., Schmidtke, O., & Tambini, D. (2002). *Collective identities in action: A sociological approach to ethnicity.* Hampshire, UK: Ashgate.

Enriquez, J. (2000). Too many flags? In K. Sjursen (Ed.), *Globalization* (pp. 23–34). New York: H. W. Wilson.

Eriksen, T. H. (2002). *Ethnicity and nationalism* (2nd ed.). London: Pluto Press.

Extra! (2010, March). Soundbites. 23(3), p. 3.

Feagin, J. (1997). Old poison in new bottles: The deep roots of modern nativism. In J. F. Perea (Ed.), *Immigrants out! The new nativism and the anti-immigrant impulse in the United States* (pp. 13–43). New York: New York University Press.

Feagin, J., & Feagin, C. (2003). *Racial and ethnic relations* (7th ed.). Upper Saddle River, NJ: Prentice Hall.

Feagin, J., & Sikes, M. P. (1994). *Living with racism: The Black middle class experience.* Boston, MA: Beacon.

Fenton, S. (1999). *Ethnicity: Racism, class and culture.* New York: Rowman & Littlefield.

Fischer, C. S. (1999). Uncommon values, diversity and conflict in city life. In N. J. Smelser & J. C. Alexander (Eds.), *Diversity and its discontents: Cultural conflict and common ground in contemporary American society* (pp. 217–227). Princeton, NJ: Princeton University Press.

Frank, T. A. (2008, April). Confessions of a sweatshop inspector. *The Washington Monthly, 40*(4), 34–37.

Franklin, J. H., & Moss, A. A., Jr. (2000). *From slavery to freedom: A history of African Americans.* New York, NY: Alfred A. Knopf.

Franklin, E., Lee, C., & Orfield, G. (2003). *A multiracial society with segregated schools: Are we losing the dream? A descriptive report.* Cambridge, MA: Harvard Civil Rights Project.

Freire, P. (1970). *Pedagogy of the Oppressed.* New York, NY: The Seabury Press.

Fraser, J. W. (1999). *Between church and state: Religion and public education in a multicultural America.* New York: St. Martin's.

Freeman, S. (2002). Liberalism and the accommodation of group claims. In P. Kelly (Ed.), *Multiculturalism reconsidered* (pp. 18–30). Cambridge, UK: Polity Press.

Friedman, T. L. (1999). *The Lexus and the olive tree: Understanding globalization.* New York: Farrar, Straus & Giroux.

Fuchs, L. H. (1990). *The American kaleidoscope: Race, ethnicity, and the civic culture.* Hanover, NH: Wesleyan University Press.

Gaustad, E., & Schmidt, L. (2002). *The religious history of America: The heart of the American story from colonial times to today.* New York: HarperCollins.

Gay, G. (2010). *Culturally responsive teaching: Theory, research, and practice* (2nd ed.). New York: Teachers College Press.

Gay, G., & Jackson, C. (2006). Resisting resistance in multicultural teacher education. In V. O. Pang (Ed.), *Race, ethnicity, and education: Principles and practices of multicultural education* (pp. 201–222). Westport, CT: Praeger Perspectives.

Gay, Lesbian and Straight Education Network. (2008). *The 2007 national school climate survey.* Retrieved June 5, 2010, from http://www.glsen.org

Glazer, N., & Moynihan, D. A. (1963). *Beyond the melting-pot.* Cambridge, MA: Harvard University Press.

Goldenberg, C. (2008, Summer). Teaching English language learners. *American Educator, 32*(1), 8–23, 42–43.

Gollnick, D. M., & Chinn, P. C. (2009). *Multicultural education in a pluralistic society.* Upper Saddle River, NJ: Pearson/Merrill.

Gorski, P. (2006). The unintentional undermining of multicultural education: Educators at the equity crossroads. In J. Landsman & C. W. Lewis (Eds.), *White teachers/ diverse classrooms: A guide to building inclusive schools, promoting high expectations, and eliminating racism* (pp. 61–78). Sterling, VA: Stylus.

Gort, M. (2005). Bilingual education: Good for U.S.? In T. Osborn (Ed.), *Language and cultural diversity in U.S. schools: Democratic principles in action* (pp. 25–37) Westport, CT: Praeger.

Graham, K. (1996). Coping with the many-coloured dome: Pluralism and practical reason. In D. Archard (Ed.), *Philosophy and pluralism* (pp. 135–146). Cambridge, UK: Cambridge University Press.

Greeley, A. (2006). Introductory essay: "Why can't they be more like us?" In D. W. Engstrom & L. M. Piedra (Eds.), *Our diverse society: Race and ethnicity–Implications for 21st century American society* (pp. 3–8). Washington, DC: National Association of Social Workers Press.

Griswold, D. T. (2010). Globalization promotes democracy. In D. Haugen & R. Mach (Eds.), *Globalization* (pp. 24–36). Detroit, MI: Greenhaven Press.

Guindon, M. (2010. What is self-esteem? In M. Guindon (Ed.). *Self-esteem across the lifespan: Issues and interventions.* (pp. 3–24). New York, NY: Routledge.

Gutstein, E., & Peterson, B. (Eds.). (2005). *Rethinking mathematics: Teaching social justice by the numbers.* Milwaukee, WI: Rethinking Schools.

Hackney, S. (1997). *One America indivisible.* Washington, DC: National Endowment for the Humanities.

Hancock, S. D. (2006). White women's work: On the front lines of urban education. In J. Landsman & C. W. Lewis (Eds.), *White teachers/diverse classrooms: A guide to building inclusive schools, promoting high expectations, and eliminating racism* (pp. 93–109). Sterling, VA: Stylus.

Heintz, J. (2002). Income inequality. In V. Tomaselli (Ed.), *World at risk* (pp. 343–364). Washington, DC: CQ Press.

Held, D., & McGrew, A. (2002). *Globalization/anti-globalization.* Cambridge, UK: Polity Press.

Herberg, W. (1955). *Protestant–Catholic–Jew: An essay in American religious sociology.* Garden City, NY: Doubleday.

Hines, R. A. (2001). *Inclusion in middle schools* (Report No. EDO-PS-01-13). Champaign, IL: Children's Research Center, University of Illinois. (ERIC Document Reproduction Service No. 459000)

Hing, G. O. (1997). *To be an American: Cultural pluralism and the rhetoric of assimilation.* New York: New York University Press.

Hoover, J. (2003). A propaedeutic to the theorizing of cultural pluralism. In C. E. Toffolo (Ed.), *Emancipating cultural pluralism* (pp. 25–36). Albany: State University of New York Press.

Hopkins, W. E. (1997). *Ethical dimensions of diversity.* Thousand Oaks, CA: Sage.

Howard, G. R. (1999). *We can't teach what we don't know: White teachers, multiracial schools.* New York: Teachers College Press.

Hudson, W. S. (1973). *Religion in America: An historical account of the development of American religious life* (2nd ed.). New York: Scribner.

Hunter, J. D. (1991). *Culture wars: The struggle to define America.* New York: Basic Books.

Huntington, S. P. (2002). The clash of civilizations: In the world and the U.S. In R. Takaki (Ed). *Debating diversity: Clashing perspectives on race and ethnicity in America.* (3rd Ed.). (pp. 75-80). New York: Oxford University Press.

Hurtado, S. (2001). Linking diversity and educational purpose: How diversity affects the classroom environment and student development. In G. Orfield & M. Kurlaender (Eds.), *Diversity challenged: Evidence on the impact of affirmative action* (pp. 187–204). Cambridge, MA: Harvard Education Publishing Group.

Irvine, J. J. (2003). *Educating teachers for diversity: Seeing with a cultural eye.* New York: Teachers College Press.

Jefferson, T. (1786). *The Virginia act for establishing religious freedom.* Available at http://religiousfreedom.lib.virginia.edu/sacred/vaact.html

Josephy, A. M., Jr. (1994). *500 nations: An illustrated history of North American Indians.* New York: Knopf.

Kallen, H. M. (1956). *Cultural pluralism and the American idea: An essay in social philosophy.* Philadelphia: University of Pennsylvania Press.

Kallen, H. M. (1970). *Culture and democracy in the United States.* New York: Arno Press. (Original work published 1924)

Kane, R. (1994). *Through the moral maze: Searching for absolute values in a pluralistic world.* New York: Paragon House.

Katz, W. G., & Southerland, H. P. (1968). Religious pluralism and the Supreme Court. In R. N. Bellah & W. G. McLoughlin (Eds.), *Religion in America* (pp. 269–281). Boston: Beacon.

Katznelson, I. (2005). *When affirmative action was White: An untold history of racial inequality in twentieth-century America.* New York: Norton.

Kaufmann, E. P. (2004). *The rise and fall of Anglo-America.* Cambridge, MA: Harvard University Press.

Kavale, K. A., & Forness, S. R. (2005). History, rhetoric, and reality: Analysis of the inclusion debate. In J. M. Kauffman & D. P. Hallahan (Eds.), *The illusion of full inclusion: A comprehensive critique of a current special education bandwagon.* Austin, TX: Pro-ed.

Kellough, J. E. (2006). *Understanding affirmative action: Politics, discrimination, and the search for justice.* Washington, DC: Georgetown University Press.

Kelly, E., & Dobbin, F. (2001). How affirmative action became diversity management: Employer response to antidiscrimination law, 1961–1996. In J. D. Skrentny (Ed.), *Color lines: Affirmative action, immigration, and civil rights options for America* (pp. 87–117). Chicago: University of Chicago Press.

Kelso, W. A. (1978). *American democratic theory: Pluralism and its critics.* Westport, CT: Greenwood Press.

Kennedy, J. F. (1964). *A nation of immigrants.* New York: HarperPerennial.

Kivel, P. (2002). *Uprooting racism: How White people can work for racial justice.* Gabriola Island, British Columbia: New Society Publishers.

Kochhar, C. A., West, L. L., & Taymans, J. M. (2000). *Successful inclusion: Practical strategies for a shared responsibility.* Upper Saddle River, NJ: Prentice-Hall.

Koppelman, K. (2011). *Understanding human differences: Multicultural education for a diverse America.* Boston: Pearson/Allyn & Bacon.

Kosmin, B. A., & Lachman, S. P. (1993). *One nation under God: Religion in contemporary American society.* New York: Crown.

Kozol, J. (2005). *The shame of the nation: The restoration of apartheid schooling in America.* New York: Crown.

Kozol, J. (2011). Great men and women. In K. L. Koppelman (Ed.), *Perspectives on human differences: Selected readings on American diversity* (pp. 320–325). Boston: Pearson/Allyn & Bacon.

Kristoff, N. (2000). At this rate, we'll be global in another hundred years. In K. Sjursen (Ed.), *Globalization* (pp. 35–38). New York: H. W. Wilson.

Kristoff, N. D., & WuDunn, S. (2009). *Half the sky: Turning oppression into opportunity for women worldwide.* New York: Knopf.

Kugler, E. G. (2002). *Debunking the middle-class myth: Why diverse schools are good for all kids.* Lanham, MD: Scarecrow Press.

Kymlicka, W. (1995). *Multicultural citizenship: A liberal theory of minority rights.* Oxford, UK: Clarendon Press.

Ladson-Billings, G. (2006). "Yes, but how do we do it?" Practicing culturally relevant pedagogy. In J. Landsman & C. W. Lewis (Eds.), *White teachers/diverse classrooms: A guide to building inclusive schools, promoting high expectations, and eliminating racism* (pp. 29–42). Sterling, VA: Stylus.

Laird, B. (2005). *The case for affirmative action in university admissions.* Berkeley, CA: Bay Tree Publishing.

Larsen, U. (2002). Population. In V. Tomaselli (Ed.), *World at risk* (pp. 498–521). Washington, DC: CQ Press.

Lee, T. M. (2010). NAFTA harms America. In D. Haugen & R. Mach (Eds.), *Globalization* (pp. 194–203). Detroit, MI: Greenhaven Press.

Leiter, S., & Leiter, W. M. (2002). *Affirmative action in antidiscrimination law and policy.* Albany: State University of New York Press.

Leman, N. (1997). Taking affirmative action apart. In F. J. Beckwith & T. E. Jones (Eds.), *Affirmative action: Social justice or reverse discrimination?* (pp. 34–55). Amherst, NY: Prometheus Books.

Levy, A. (2009, November 16). The feminist revolution in retrospect. *The New Yorker,* pp. 78–80.

Lewis, D. L. (1993). *W. E. B. Du Bois: Biography of a race, 1868-1919.* New York, NY: Henry Holt.

Lewis, D. L. (2000). *W. E. B. Du Bois: The fight for equality and the American century– 1919-1963.* New York: Henry Holt.

Lewis, S. (1947). *Kingsblood royal.* New York: Random House.

Lind, M. (1995). *The next American nation: The new nationalism and the fourth American revolution.* New York: Free Press.

Lippy, C. H. (1994). *Being religious, American style: A history of popular religiosity in the United States*. Westport, CT: Praeger.

Lippy, C. H. (2006). Religious pluralism and the transformation of American culture. In D. W. Engstrom & L. M. Piedra (Eds.), *Our diverse society: Race and ethnicity—Implications for 21st century American society* (pp. 89–106). Washington, DC: National Association of Social Workers Press.

Littell, F. H. (1968). The churches and the body politic. In R. N. Bellah & W. G. McLoughlin (Eds.), *Religion in America* (pp. 24–44). Boston: Beacon.

Lynch, M. P. (1998). *Truth in context*. Cambridge, MA: MIT Press.

Mandelson, P. (2010). A better regulated globalization can limit the modern financial crisis. In D. Haugen & R. Mach (Eds.), *Globalization* (pp. 104–108). Detroit, MI: Greenhaven Press.

Marling, W. H. (2006). *How "American" is globalization?* Baltimore: The Johns Hopkins University Press.

Mayo, M. (2000). *Cultures, communities, identities: Cultural strategies for participation and empowerment*. Hampshire, UK: Palgrave.

Meacham, J. (2006). *American gospel: God, the founding fathers, and the making of a nation*. New York: Random House.

Melear, C. (1995, January). Multiculturalism in science education. *The American Biology Teacher, 57*(1), 21–26.

Melville, H. (1964). *Moby Dick*. New York: Bobbs-Merrill. (Original work published 1851)

Menand, L. (2001). *The metaphysical club*. New York: Farrar, Straus & Giroux.

Miller, G. T. (1976). *Religious liberty in America: History and prospects*. Philadelphia: Westminster.

Moghaddam, F. M. (2008). *Multiculturalism and intergroup relations: Psychological implications for democracy in a global context*. Washington, DC: American Psychological Association.

Müller, H. (2009). *Building a new world order: Sustainable policies for the future*. London: Haus.

Münz, R., & Reiterer, A. (2009). *Overcrowded world? Global populations and international migration*. London: Haus.

Murphy, S. (2010). Globalization is worsening the food crisis. In D. Haugen & R. Mach (Eds.), *Globalization* (pp. 172–178). Detroit, MI: Greenhaven Press.

Myers, G. (1960). *History of bigotry in the United States* (Rev. ed., G. Christman, Ed.). New York: Capricorn.

Myrdal, G. (1944). *An American dilemma: The Negro problem and modern democracy*. New York: Harper & Row.

Navarro, S. A. (2002). Las voces de esperanza/Voices of hope: La mujer obrera, transnationalism, and NAFTA-displaced women workers in the U.S.–Mexico borderlands. In C. Sadlowski-Smith (Ed.), *Globalization on the line: Culture, capital, and citizenship at U.S. borders* (pp. 183–200). New York: Palgrave.

New York Times. (2000). With world opening up, languages are losers. In K. Sjursen (Ed.), *Globalization* (pp. 143–145). New York: H. W. Wilson.

Nieto, S. (2002). *Language, culture, and teaching: Critical perspectives for a new century*. Mahweh, NJ: Erlbaum.

Nieto, S., & Bode, P. (2008). *Affirming diversity: The sociopolitical context of multicultural education*. Boston: Pearson.

Niezen, R. (2004). *A world beyond difference: Cultural identity in the age of globalization.* Oxford: Blackwell.

Nord, W. A. (1995). *Religion and American education: Rethinking a national dilemma.* Chapel Hill: University of North Carolina Press.

Norton, A. (1998). The virtues of multiculturalism. In A. Melzer, J. Weinberger, & H. R. Zinman (Eds.), *Multiculturalism and American democracy* (pp. 130–138). Lawrence: University Press of Kansas.

Olopade, D. (2010, October). Gatekeepers. *American Prospect, 21*(8), 12–17.

Osgood, R. L. (2005). *The history of inclusion in the United States.* Washington, DC: Gallaudet University Press.

Pai, Y., & Adler, S. (1997). *Cultural foundations of education* (2nd ed.). Upper Saddle River, NJ: Merrill Prentice Hall.

Pak, Y. (2006). Multiculturalism matters: Learning from our past. In V. O. Pang (Ed.), *Race, ethnicity, and education: Principles and practices of multicultural education* (pp. 3–22). Westport, CT: Praeger Perspectives.

Palmer, S. R. (2001). A policy framework for reconceptualizing the legal debate concerning affirmative action in higher education. In G. Orfield and M. Kurlaender (Eds.), *Diversity challenged: Evidence on the impact of affirmative action.* (pp. 49-80). Cambridge, MA: Harvard Education Publishing Group.

Parekh, B. (1996). Moral philosophy and its anti-plural bias. In D. Archard (Ed.), *Philosophy and pluralism* (pp. 117–134). Cambridge, UK: Cambridge University Press.

Parekh, B. (2002). Barry and the dangers of liberalism. In P. Kelly (Ed.), *Multiculturalism reconsidered* (pp. 133–150). Cambridge, UK: Polity Press.

Parenti, M. (2010). Globalization undermines democracy. In D. Haugen & R. Mach (Eds.), *Globalization* (pp. 37–49). Detroit, MI: Greenhaven Press.

Parini, J. (2008). *Promised land: Thirteen books that changed America.* New York: Doubleday.

Perea, J. F. (1997). The statue of liberty: Notes from behind the gilded door. In J. G. Perea (Ed.), *Immigrants out: The new nativism and the anti-immigrant impulse in the United States.* (pp. 44-58). New York, NY: New York University Press.

Reich, R. (2002). *Bridging liberalism and multiculturalism in American education.* Chicago: University of Chicago Press.

Reskin, B. F. (2000). The realities of affirmative action in employment. In F. J. Crosby & C. VanDeVeer (Eds.), *Sex, race, and merit: Debating affirmative action in education and employment* (pp. 103–113). Ann Arbor: University of Michigan Press.

Rifkin, J. (2004). *The European dream: How Europe's vision of the future is quietly eclipsing the American dream.* New York: Jeremy P. Tarcher/Penguin.

Roediger, D. R. (2005). *Working toward Whiteness: How America's immigrants became White.* New York, NY: Basic Books.

Rosenthal, D. A. (1987). Ethnic identity development in adolescents. In J. S. Phinney & M. J. Rotheram (Eds.), *Children's ethnic socialization: Pluralism and development* (pp. 156–179). Newbury Park, CA: Sage.

Rotheram, M. J., & Phinney, J. S. (1987). Introduction: Definitions and perspectives in the study of children's ethnic socialization. In J. S. Phinney & M. J. Rotheram (Eds.), *Children's ethnic socialization: Pluralism and development* (pp. 10–28). Newbury Park, CA: Sage.

Royce, A. P. (1982). *Ethnic identity: Strategies of diversity.* Bloomington: Indiana University Press.

Rubio, P. F. (2001). *A history of affirmative action: 1619–2000.* Jackson: University Press of Mississippi.

Rudenstine, N. L. (2001). Student diversity and higher learning. In G. Orfield & M. Kurlaender (Eds.), *Diversity challenged: Evidence on the impact of affirmative action* (pp. 31–48). Cambridge, MA: Harvard Education Publishing Group.

Rutz, H. J. (2002). Cultural preservation. In V. Tomaselli (Ed.), *World at risk* (pp. 68–88). Washington, DC: CQ Press.

Said, E. W. (2007). Citizenship, resistance and democracy. In E. D. Ermath (Ed.), *Rewriting democracy: Cultural politics in postmodernity* (pp. 24–33). Burlington, VT: Ashgate.

Salas, K. D. (2006). Defending bilingual education. *Rethinking Schools, 20*(3), 33–37.

Samuelson, R. J. (2002). The limits of immigration. In R. Takaki (Ed.) *Debating diversity: Clashing perspectives on race and ethnicity in America* (3rd ed.). (pp. 217–218). New York: Oxford University Press.

Sandefur, G. D., Martin, M. Eggerling-Boeck, J., Mannon, S. E., and Meier, A. M. (2000). In N. J. Smelser, W. J. Wilson, and F. Mitchell (Eds.), An overview of racial and ethnic demographic trends. In *America becoming: Racial trends and their consequences.* (p. 40-102). Washington, D.C.: National Academy Press.

Schlesinger, A., Jr. (1991). *The disuniting of America: Reflections on a multicultural society.* Knoxville, TN: Whittle Books.

Schlesinger, A., Jr. (1992, February 7). Speaking up: A look at noteworthy addresses in the southland. *Los Angeles Times,* p. B2.

Schoeff, M., Jr. (2008, July 14). Appeal for diversity. *Workforce Management,* pp. 31–36.

Schofield, J. W. (2001). Maximizing the benefits of student diversity: Lessons from school desegregation research. In G. Orfield & M. Kurlaender (Eds.), *Diversity challenged: Evidence on the impact of affirmative action* (pp. 99–110). Cambridge, MA: Harvard Education Publishing Group.

Schuck, P. H. (2003). *Diversity in America: Keeping government at a safe distance.* Cambridge, MA: Belknap Press of Harvard University Press.

Schwenninger, S. R. (2010). Mismanaged globalization is responsible for the modern financial crisis. In D. Haugen & R. Mach (Eds.), *Globalization* (pp. 94–103). Detroit, MI: Greenhaven Press.

Sefa Dei, G. J. (2006). "We cannot be color-blind": Race, antiracism, and the subversion of dominant thinking. In E. W. Ross (Ed.), *Racism and antiracism in education* (pp. 25–42). Westport, CT: Praeger.

Shaw, T. M. (2003). Introduction. In L. Cokorinos (Ed.), *The assault on diversity: An organized challenge to racial and gender justice* (pp. ix–xi). Lanham, MD: Rowman & Littlefield.

Shorris, E. (2001). *Latinos: A biography of the people.* New York: Norton.

Skillen, A. (1996). William James, "a certain blindness" and an uncertain pluralism. In D. Archard (Ed.), *Philosophy and pluralism* (pp. 33–45). Cambridge, UK: Cambridge University Press.

Skutnabb-Kangas, T. (2000). *Linguistic genocide in education—Or worldwide diversity and human rights?* Mahwah, NJ: Erlbaum.

Sleeter, C. (1996). *Multicultural education as social activism.* Albany: State University of New York Press.

Sleeter, C., & Bynoe, L. T. (2006). Antiracist education in majority White schools. In E. W. Ross (Ed.), *Racism and antiracism in education* (pp. 165–190). Westport, CT: Praeger.

Squires, J. (2002). Culture, equality and diversity. In P. Kelly (Ed.), *Multiculturalism reconsidered* (pp. 114–132). Cambridge, UK: Polity Press.

Steele, J. (2002). Acknowledging diversity in the classroom. In L. Darling-Hammond, J. French, & S. P. Garcia-Lopez (Eds.), *Learning to teach for social justice* (pp. 18–21). New York: Teachers College Press.

Steele, S. (1997). Affirmative action: The price of preference. In F. J. Beckwith & T. E. Jones (Eds.), *Affirmative action: Social justice or reverse discrimination?* (pp. 132–141). Amherst, NY: Prometheus Books.

Stephan, W. G. (2004). Conclusion: Understanding intergroup relations programs. In W. G. Stephan & W. P. Vogt (Eds.), *Education programs for improving intergroup relations: Theory, research, and practice* (pp. 266–279). New York: Teachers College Press.

Stephan, W. G., & Vogt, W. P. (Eds.). (2004). *Education programs for improving intergroup relations: Theory, research, and practice.* New York: Teachers College Press.

Sterba, J. P. (2003). Section two: Defending affirmative action, defending preferences. In C. Cohen & J. P. Sterba (Eds.), *Affirmative action and racial preference: A debate* (pp. 191–278; 305-349). New York: Oxford University Press.

Stiglitz, J. E. (2010). Globalization could help ease global warming. In D. Haugen & R. Mach (Eds.), *Globalization* (pp. 122–129). Detroit, MI: Greenhaven Press.

Strike, K. A. (2003). Pluralism, personal identity, and freedom of conscience. In K. McDonough & W. Feinberg (Eds.), *Education and citizenship in liberal-democratic societies: Teaching for cosmopolitan values and collective identities* (pp. 75–95). Oxford: Oxford University Press.

Suarez-Orozco, C., & Suarez-Orozco, M. (1995). Migration: Generational discontinuities and the making of Latino identities. In G. A. De Vos & L. Romanucci-Ross (Eds.), *Ethnic identity: Creation, conflict, and accommodation* (pp. 321–347). Walnut Creek, CA: Altamira Press.

Sugrue, T. J. (2001). Breaking through: The troubled origins of affirmative action in the workplace. In J. D. Skrentny (Ed.), *Color lines: Affirmative action, immigration, and civil rights options for America* (pp. 31–52). Chicago: University of Chicago Press.

Swain, C. M., Greene, K. R., & Wotipka, C. M. (2001). Understanding racial polarization on affirmative action: The view from focus groups. In J. D. Skrentny (Ed.), *Color lines: Affirmative action, immigration, and civil rights options for America* (pp. 214–237). Chicago: University of Chicago Press.

Takaki, R. (1993). *A different mirror: A history of multicultural America.* Boston: Little Brown.

Takaki, R. (2002). Reflections on racial patterns in America. In R. Takaki (Ed.), *Debating diversity: Clashing perspectives on race and ethnicity in America* (3rd ed., pp. 22–36). New York: Oxford University Press.

Tatum, B. D. (1997). *"Why are all the Black kids sitting together in the cafeteria?"* New York: Basic Books.

Taylor, B. R. (1991). *Affirmative action at work: Law, politics, and ethics.* Pittsburgh, PA: University of Pittsburgh Press.

Taylor, D. M. (2002). *The quest for identity: From minority groups to generation Xers.* Westport, CT: Praeger.

Thomas, D. A. and Ely, R. J. (1996, September–October). Making differences matter: A new paradigm for managing diversity. *Harvard Business Review,* pp. 79–90.

Thomas, R. R., Jr. (1990, March–April). From affirmative action to affirming diversity. *Harvard Business Review,* pp. 107–111.

Thomas, R. R., Jr. (1992). *Beyond race and gender: Unleashing the power of your total work force by managing diversity.* New York: Amacom.

Thornton, R. (2000). Trends among American Indians in the United States. In N. J. Smelser, W. J. Wilson, & F. Mitchell (Eds.), *America becoming: Racial trends and their consequences* (pp. 135–169). Washington, DC: National Academy Press.

Tocqueville, A. de. (2004). *Democracy in America.* New York: The Library of America.

Torres, M. A. (2006). Democracy and diversity: Expanding notions of citizenship. In D. W. Engstrom & L. M. Piedra (Eds.), *Our diverse society: Race and ethnicity— Implications for 21st century American society* (pp. 161–182). Washington, DC: National Association of Social Workers Press.

Unseem, J. (2000). There's something happening here. In K. Sjursen (Ed.), *Globalization* (pp. 109–116). New York: H. W. Wilson.

Vargish, T. (2007). Self-qualifying systems: Consensus and dissent in postmodernity. In E. D. Ermath (Ed.), *Rewriting democracy: Cultural politics in postmodernity* (pp. 118–133). Burlington, VT: Ashgate.

Vavrus, M. (2010). Critical multiculturalism and higher education: Resistance and possibilities within teacher education. In S. May & C. E. Sleeter (Eds.), *Critical multiculturalism: Theory and praxis* (pp. 19–31). New York: Routledge.

Vickers, J. (2002). No place for "race"? Why pluralist theory fails to explain the politics of "race" in "new societies." In S. Brooks (Ed.), *The challenge of cultural pluralism* (pp. 15–38). Westport, CT: Praeger.

Villanueva, I. (1997). The voices of Chicano families: Life stories, maintaining bilingualism and cultural awareness. In M. Seller & L. Weis (Eds.), *Beyond Black and White: New faces and voices in U.S. schools* (pp. 61–79). Albany: State University of New York Press.

Villegas, A. M., & Lucas, T. (2002). *Educating culturally responsive teachers: A coherent approach.* Albany: State University of New York Press.

Waldman, S. (2006). The framers and the faithful. *Washington Monthly, 38*(4), 33–38.

Waller, J. (2001). *Face to face: The changing state of racism across America.* Cambridge, MA: Perseus Books Group.

Watson, J. L. (2000). China's big mac attack. In K. Sjursen (Ed.), *Globalization* (pp. 52–65). New York: H. W. Wilson.

Whitman, W. (1983). *Leaves of grass.* New York: Bantam Books.

Winbush, V., & McLemore, J. (2003). Diversity and group dynamics. In D. L. Plummer (Ed.), *Handbook of diversity management: Beyond awareness to competency based learning* (pp. 203–222). Lanham, MD: University Press of America.

Wolfe, A. (2006). *Does American democracy still work?* New Haven, CT: Yale University Press.

Wright, R. (2000). Continental drift. In K. Sjursen (Ed.), *Globalization* (pp. 99–108). New York: H. W. Wilson.

Yeats, W. B. (2002). The second coming. In R. V. Finneran (Ed.), *The Yeats reader: A portable compendium of poetry, drama, and prose* (p. 80). New York: Scribner Poetry.

Young, M. C. (2003). Afterword: Interrogating the emancipation of cultural pluralism. In C. E. Toffolo (Ed.), *Emancipating cultural pluralism* (pp. 239–258). Albany: State University of New York Press.

Zangwill, I. (1915). *The melting pot.* New York, NY: Macmillan.

Zwingle, E. (2000). A world together. In K. Sjursen (Ed.), *Globalization* (pp. 146–164). New York: H. W. Wilson.

Index

About the Author

Kent Koppelman earned his Ph.D. in 1979 from Iowa State University and accepted a position at the University of Wisconsin–La Crosse. In 1988, Wisconsin's Department of Public Instruction selected him as "Teacher Educator of the Year." In addition to many conference presentations and journal publications, Dr. Koppelman wrote *Values in the Key of Life: Making Harmony in the Human Community* (2001). Pearson/Allyn & Bacon published his textbook, *Understanding Human Differences: Multicultural Education for a Diverse America* (2005, 2008, 2011). After Dr. Koppelman retired in 2007, Iowa State University presented him with the Lagomarcino Laureate Award for his career achievements. He has compiled and edited an anthology on diversity issues for Pearson/Allyn & Bacon entitled *Perspectives on Diversity: Selected Readings on Diversity in America* (2010). Dr. Koppelman and his wife Jan have been married for 40 years, and their daughter, Tess, is a broadcast journalist in Kansas City.